THE ANNOTATED WASTE LAND
WITH ELIOT'S CONTEMPORARY PROSE

EDITED, WITH ANNOTATIONS AND INTRODUCTION, BY
LAWRENCE RAINEY

The Annotated Waste Land with Eliot's Contemporary Prose

YALE UNIVERSITY PRESS   NEW HAVEN & LONDON

Set in Scala by Duke & Company, Devon, Pennsylvania

Printed in the United States of America.

Library of Congress Cataloging-in-Publication Data
Eliot, T. S. (Thomas Stearns), 1888–1965.
  The annotated *Waste Land,* with Eliot's contemporary prose / edited, with annotations and introduction, by Lawrence Rainey.
     p.   cm.
  Includes bibliographical references and index.
  ISBN 0-300-09743-3 (alk. paper)
  I. Rainey, Lawrence S. II. Title.
  PS3509.L43W3 2005
  821'.912—dc22
2004016626

A catalogue record for this book is available from the British Library.

The paper in this book meets the guidelines for permanence and durability of the Committee on Production Guidelines for Book Longevity of the Council on Library Resources.

10 9 8 7 6 5 4 3 2

CONTENTS

Illustrations follow page 74

THE ANNOTATED WASTE LAND
WITH ELIOT'S CONTEMPORARY PROSE

Introduction

Lawrence Rainey

WHEN DONALD HALL ARRIVED in London in September 1951, bearing an invitation to meet the most celebrated poet of his age, T. S. Eliot, he could only marvel at his strange good fortune. A young and aspiring American poet, he had earlier been an editor of Harvard University's celebrated literary magazine, the *Advocate*—as Eliot had once been—and more recently won a fellowship to Oxford—as Eliot had done, too, long ago, in 1914. Now he was going to meet the great man himself, the poet of his age, the man awarded the Nobel prize for literature in 1948. Hall was frankly terrified. His appointment was for three in the afternoon, but he turned up an hour early at the office of Eliot's employer, Faber and Faber, at 24 Russell Square, then decided to kill time by admiring the surrounding buildings. Finally, at three, he was duly escorted to Eliot's small office and greeted by Eliot himself, a person as diffident and distant as report had portrayed him. Their conversation went poorly. "I was so convinced of the monumentality of this moment—'I will be speaking of this, ages hence'—that I weighed every word as if my great-grandchildren were listening in, and I feared to let them down by speaking idiomatically, or by seeing the humor in anything." Eliot commented on some of Hall's poems, the hour passed swiftly, and by four it was time for Hall to leave. He leapt to his feet, sputtered ponderous thanks, and awaited Eliot's farewell:

Then Eliot appeared to search for the right phrase with which to send me off. He looked me in the eyes, and set off into a slow, meandering sentence. "Let me see," said T. S. Eliot, "forty years ago I went from Harvard to Oxford. Now you are going from Harvard to Oxford. What advice can I give you?" He paused delicately, shrewdly, while I waited with greed for the words which I would repeat for the rest of my life, the advice from elder to younger, setting me on the road of emulation. When he had ticked off the comedian's exact milliseconds of pause, he said, "Have you any long underwear?"

I told him that I had not, and paused to buy some on my dazzled walk back to the hotel. I suppose it was six months before I woke up enough to laugh.[1]

The reader who comes to Eliot's masterpiece for the first time faces much the same dilemma as Hall did. The poem is preceded by its reputation, endowed with authority so monumental that a reader is tempted to overlook the poem itself, to slight its grisly comedy or miss its mordant and ferocious wit, its dazzling series of surprises, its sheer wildness and irredeemable opacity. While Eliot's status as an international celebrity has plainly waned since his death in 1965—what other poet could give a lecture in a basketball arena holding fourteen thousand spectators, as Eliot did in 1956?—his most important poem still retains its lacerating power to startle and disturb.

ELIOT'S CAREER BEFORE *THE WASTE LAND*

Thomas Stearns Eliot was born in St. Louis, Missouri, on 26 September 1888, the last of six children. He had four sisters, the oldest of whom was nineteen years his senior, and one brother, Henry, who was nine years older. His mother and father were already in their forties by the time Eliot was born. His father, Henry Ware Eliot, was a successful businessman and president of the Hydraulic-Press Brick Company. But Eliot seems never to have been very close to him. Instead it was to his mother, Charlotte, that Eliot was drawn. Proud of her intelligence, she had not been able to attend university and instead had earned her living as a teacher until she met her husband. She had also written poetry. Her thwarted ambitions were transferred to her son, who was nurtured to become a scholar, perhaps even a poet. From what little can be discerned, Eliot was a shy and bookish boy, one who felt somewhat out of place wherever he was. His family maintained a strong sense of its origins in New England—his grandfather had moved from there to St. Louis in 1834—a sense which made him feel out of place in the South. But he was no less aware of his Missouri drawl when the family took its annual vacation in Gloucester, Massachusetts.[2] He was also isolated by a physical handicap, a congenital double hernia, which meant he had to wear a truss for most of his life and could not participate in sports. Eliot later recalled that his family had "lived on in a neighborhood which had become shabby to a degree approaching sluminess, after all our friends and acquaintances had moved further west."[3] The area was being taken over by poor African Americans, and Eliot's life-long appreciation of popular song and his responsiveness to the seedy side of urban life owed something to this background.[4]

When he was seven or eight, Eliot began to attend a local private school. In the autumn of 1898 he began to attend Smith Academy, a prepa-ratory school for Washington University, a prestigious university in St. Louis, which Eliot's grandfather had helped found. By January 1899, he already had brought out eight issues of his own magazine, the *Fireside,* a childish production that featured adventure stories, rhyming verses, and puns. Though he finished Smith Academy in 1905, his mother decided to wait a year before sending him to Harvard, a year he spent at Milton Academy, a private school outside Boston. There he met Scofield Thayer, a wealthy young man who later became co-owner and leading editor of the *Dial,* the journal in which *The Waste Land* was first published in the United States.

In the autumn of 1906 Eliot began his undergraduate studies at Har-vard. In his second year he decided to complete his course for a bachelor's degree in three years rather than the conventional four. His courses cov-ered a wide range of topics: German grammar, constitutional government, Greek literature, medieval history, English literature, French literature, ancient philosophy, modern philosophy, and comparative literature. But much that Eliot wanted to learn could not be discovered in the classroom. He was actively reading on his own. He later recalled the Scottish poet John Davidson (1857–1908), and especially his poem "Thirty Bob a Week," with its stark presentation of a city clerk. He had "found inspiration in the content of the poem," Eliot later recalled, "and in the complete fitness of content and idiom: for I also had a good many dingy urban images to reveal."[5] More important, however, was his discovery of Arthur Symons, whose study of *The Symbolist Movement in Literature* he purchased in December 1908. The book was "one of those which have affected the course of my life," he said many years later.[6] Above all it led Eliot to the discovery of the French poet Jules Laforgue (1860–1887), the author who was "the first to teach me how to speak, to teach me the poetic possibilities of my own idiom of speech."[7] Eliot promptly ordered the three volumes of Laforgue's *Oeuvres complètes*, which reached him in the spring of 1909. In Laforgue's poetry Eliot found much that he could adapt to his own use: the couplets turned by neat rhymes, the counterpoint achieved by interweaving stanzas with different imaginative weight and line length, and a tone that was questioning, quizzical, ironical, inconclusive. Within months the poems which Eliot was publishing in the *Harvard Advocate* were plainly showing the influence of Laforgue, even announcing it in their titles: "Nocturne" in November 1909, "Humouresque (after J. Laforgue)" and "Spleen" in January 1910. But influence should not be taken to imply passive imitation. "People are only influenced in the direction in which they want to go," Eliot wrote much later, "and influence consists largely in making them conscious of their wishes to proceed in that direction."[8] But what was the direction in which Eliot wanted to go? Conrad Aiken, whom Eliot met in the academic year 1909–1910, when he stayed on at Harvard for an extra year to study for an M.A., later recalled their conversations: "What did we talk about? or what didn't we? It was the first 'great' era of the comic strip, of Krazy Kat, and Mutt and Jeff, and Rube Goldberg's inspired lunacies: it was also perhaps the most creative period of American slang, and in both these departments of invention he took enormous pleasure."[9] Eliot's interest in "American slang" and "the comic strip," his openness to vernacular culture, may go a long way toward explaining why even the poems which most directly evince the influence of Laforgue possess a colloquial vigor that sets them apart.

Having finished his M.A., Eliot spent the summer of 1910 patiently transcribing all the poems he had been writing, assembling them into a volume which he titled *Inventions of the March Hare*, a collection which has recently been published in its entirety.[10] Then he set off for Paris, much to his mother's consternation.[11] In Paris he was fortunate to meet and exchange conversation lessons with Henri Alain-Fournier (1886–1914), the

young writer whose modern classic *Le grand Meaulnes* was to be published
in 1912. Alain-Fournier, who shared Eliot's interest in Jules Laforgue, was
the brother-in-law and close friend of Jacques Rivière (1886–1925), editor
of the *Nouvelle revue française*, a literary journal which, though founded
only in 1909, was already considered the most important review in Paris.
Eliot met Rivière on one occasion, but nothing further came of their encounter.[12] Eliot's other friendship in Paris was forged with Jean Verdenal
(1890–1915), a young medical student who lived in the same *pension* as
Eliot and shared his literary interests. It may have been Verdenal who introduced Eliot to the work of Charles Maurras (1868–1952), a conservative
ideologue who in 1899 had created an organization called L'Action française, a nationalist and royalist group that responded to the ongoing crisis
in French cultural life precipitated by the Dreyfus affair. How deeply
Maurras influenced Eliot has been a subject of much debate.[13]

In January and February 1911, while still living in Paris, Eliot went to
hear five lectures by the French philosopher Henri Bergson at the Collège
de France, and he later said that he had experienced a "temporary conversion to Bergsonism."[14] Meanwhile, he was writing more poems, including
"Entretiens dans un parc," "Interlude: In a Bar," "Bacchus and Ariadne,"
and "The Smoke That Gathers Blue and Sinks."[15] A few months later, in
April, he journeyed to London for the first time, taking in many traditional
sites: the National Gallery, the British Museum, Hampton Court, and, as
he noted in a letter to a friend, "the City—Thoroughly" (*LOTSE*, 19). Eliot,
of course, was referring to the financial district of London, known as the
City, the principal locale for *The Waste Land*. In July, before returning to
the United States, he took a trip to Munich, where he somehow met a former lady of the imperial court of Vienna: a memory of their conversation
would also enter into *The Waste Land* (see ll. 15–17 and notes; see Figs. 1,
2, 3). While in Munich, Eliot also completed the final version of "The Love
Song of J. Alfred Prufrock," and a few months later he completed "Portrait
of a Lady"—the two most important works of his early maturity. Already
by now, at the age of twenty-three, Eliot had found his voice—or rather,
voices. For Eliot possessed an uncanny gift for juxtaposing snippets of
wistful lyricism against moments of mordant self-reflection, and setting
off both these against dry, matter-of-fact records of urban decay.

"I had at that time," Eliot later recalled of his year in Paris, "the idea
of giving up English and trying to settle down and scrape along in Paris."[16]

But he had plainly changed his mind by the time he left. Eliot was never very confident of his own powers; his acute self-awareness entailed acute self-doubt. Who could assure him that his poems were anything more than highly intelligent jeux d'esprit? And there was pressure from his family to take up a safe and respectable profession. Eliot chose to become an academic, and enrolled as a graduate student in the philosophy department at Harvard. It was to be his home, or perhaps his prison, for the next three years. He took a variety of courses, some of which left an impress on *The Waste Land*. In his first year he studied Sanskrit in C. R. Lannon's course in Indic philology. In his second he studied Indian philosophy in classes taught by James Haughton Woods. He also took a course on Buddhism, given by Masaharu Anesaki. In "The Fire Sermon" and "What the Thunder Said," parts III and V of *The Waste Land*, Eliot was to draw on key texts which he had encountered in these classes, including the Upanishads and a sermon by the Buddha. In his third year Eliot took a course entitled "A Comparative Study of Various Types of Scientific Method," taught by Josiah Royce, as well as another on symbolic logic taught by the distinguished philosopher Bertrand Russell, whom he impressed.[17] Critics have long debated the significance of these courses for Eliot's poetic and intellectual development. Eliot's was a restless mind, simultaneously seeking out religious certainties from remote cultures and exploring the skepticism inherent in comparative approaches. One thing is certain: apart from some ribald ballads, Eliot wrote very little during his three years at Harvard. And as soon as he left, he began to write again.

In early 1914 Eliot was awarded a Sheldon Fellowship in Philosophy, which meant that he could travel to Merton College, Oxford, for a year. He planned to spend the summer in Marburg, Germany, honing his German-language skills, then go on to England. He arrived in Germany in July, but the outbreak of World War I meant that, as a foreign national, he had to leave the country. He went to London, planning then to go on to Oxford. By chance his old friend from Harvard, Conrad Aiken, was residing in London. Still interested in Eliot's early poems, Aiken had recently shown "Prufrock" and "La figlia che piange" to Harold Monro, proprietor of the Poetry Bookshop in London and editor of *Poetry and Drama*, then the principal journal for new poetry in England. Monro had dismissed them as "absolutely insane."[18] Undaunted, Aiken urged Eliot to visit someone else whom he had met over the summer, the American poet Ezra Pound. "You go to Pound. Show him your poems," Aiken reportedly said.[19] On 22 September, Eliot called on Pound and introduced himself. His life, though he did not know it, was about to be transformed.

At Pound's request, Eliot promptly sent him a selection of poems. By the end of the month Pound already had promised Eliot that he would get "Prufrock" published in *Poetry*, the Chicago magazine started in 1912 by Harriet Monroe, already the most prominent journal for new poetry in English. "He wants me to bring out a Vol. after the War," Eliot enthused to Aiken in late September 1914, adding ruefully: "The devil of it is that I have done nothing good since J. A[lfred] P[rufrock]. and writhe in impotence" (*LOTSE*, 58). Pound immediately grasped Eliot's importance, and he was soon laboring to get all his early poems into print. More important, his encouragement had rekindled Eliot's ambitions; once again he entertained the idea of becoming a poet, not a philosopher. "Then in 1914 . . . my meeting with Ezra Pound changed my life. He was enthusiastic about my poems, and gave me such praise and encouragement as I had long since ceased to hope for. Pound urged me to stay . . . and encouraged me to write verse again" (*LOTSE*, xvii).

Eliot moved to Merton College, Oxford, for the autumn term of 1914, but he was soon bored and returned to London in January 1915. He returned again to Oxford for the spring term, where he encountered his old friend Scofield Thayer. Sometime in the first week of March, Thayer introduced Eliot to Vivien Haigh-Wood, an intelligent, attractive young woman who dressed well and liked to dance. She was nervous and high-strung, and often suffered from headaches, cramps, and an irregular and overfrequent menstrual cycle. Eliot, who had confessed that he was still a virgin in December 1914, later recalled that he was simply "too shy and unpractised" to engage in a "flirtation or mild affair" (*LOTSE*, xvii). Instead, the two married. Their wedding, which transpired without their having informed their parents, took place on 26 June 1915. One contemporary observer, Aldous Huxley, thought their relationship was a matter of sexual attraction: "I met Mrs. E. for the first time and perceived that it is almost entirely a sexual nexus between Eliot and her: one sees it in the way he looks at her —she's an incarnate provocation."[20] Eliot, in old age, gave a rueful assessment. "I came to persuade myself that I was in love with her simply because I wanted to burn my boats and commit myself to staying in England. And she persuaded herself (also under the influence of Pound) that she would save the poet by keeping him in England." He concluded grimly: "To her the marriage brought no happiness . . . to me, it brought the state of mind out of which came *The Waste Land*" (*LOTSE*, xvii).

Meanwhile, Eliot was beginning to acquire a reputation, as Ezra Pound hectored and cajoled editors into publishing his poems. In June 1915 Harriet Monroe published "Prufrock" in *Poetry*. In July, Wyndham Lewis published four "Preludes" and "Rhapsody on a Windy Night" in the second issue of *Blast*. In September "Portrait of a Lady" was published by Alfred Kreymborg in the brief-lived New York review *Others*. Pound, meanwhile, had already sent Harriet Monroe another three poems which Eliot had composed earlier in the year while at Oxford, and in October "The Boston Evening Transcript," "Aunt Helen," and "Cousin Nancy" appeared in *Poetry*. In November, Pound brought out a collection of contemporary verse in which he reprinted four poems by Eliot ("Prufrock," "Portrait of a Lady," "Aunt Helen," and "The Boston Evening Transcript") and included one new work, "Hysteria." It was the first appearance of Eliot's poetry in book form.

Now married, Eliot set out to reorganize his life. In late July he returned to the United States, but he stayed for only three weeks. His parents wanted him to finish his graduate studies, and he evidently agreed to complete his thesis. When he returned to England in August, he found that Vivien was ill and, as he had already anticipated, that they were desperately short of money. Bertrand Russell stepped in to help, offering them the use of a bedroom in his flat till they could afford their own. Eliot began to teach at a grammar school in High Wycombe, a small town some forty miles outside London, which obliged him to rent a room there and return to London for long weekends. The pay was £140 a year and a daily meal. Russell had provided introductions to editors, and Eliot started to take up book reviewing in earnest, hoping to supplement his teaching salary; in the course of 1916 he published twenty-one reviews, chiefly on philosophical books. Russell proved still more generous, giving Eliot £3,000 in engineering debentures; the income from these averaged £150 per year. At last, by Christmas 1915 the Eliots moved out of Russell's flat. They spent three months at the home of Vivien's parents in Hampstead, and finally, in March 1916, got a flat of their own at 18, Crawford Mansions. It was small and cramped, and Eliot complained about it repeatedly in the years ahead. Beginning in January 1916, he took a teaching position at Highgate Junior School; it was much closer to central London and paid £20 a year more. Eliot kept the position for the rest of the year. But these temporary solutions to the problems of housing and domestic finances could not disguise the toll they were taking on his writing: in 1916 he published only four poems; two dating back to his time at Harvard ("Conversation Gallante" [1909] and "La figlia che piange" [1911]), and one to the brief interlude when he had been writing at Oxford in early 1915, just before he met Vivien ("Morning at the Window"). Only one, "Mr. Apollinax," was a contemporary composition.

At the end of 1916 Eliot resigned from his teaching position. For a few months he tried to survive as a freelance writer, but it proved impossible. In March 1917 he began to work for Lloyds Bank, where he would spend the next eight years of his life. Lloyds was already a huge corporation, the second largest of the "Big Six" British clearing banks which had emerged after decades of intensive merger and acquisition activity.[21] The acquisition process was just drawing to an end during Eliot's years at the bank, as Lloyds absorbed four banks during the period 1918–1923. The result was an immensely powerful concentration of capital, and the bank was now seeking to expand into the international arena. (In 1911 Lloyds had purchased Armstrong & Co., with branches in Paris and Le Havre, and in 1917 it joined forces with National Provincial Bank to create the Lloyds and National Provincial Foreign Bank, a new firm that by 1938 had twelve branches on the Continent, serving British nationals and companies in Europe.) Indirectly, it was this expansion which led to Eliot's employment. For it was a friend of Vivien's family, L. E. Thomas, then the chief general manager of National Provincial Bank, who gave Eliot a letter of introduction to Lloyds Bank, and accordingly Eliot was duly assigned to the Colonial and Foreign Department. Its offices were at 17 Cornhill Street (see Fig. 8), in the heart of the City, one of several abutting buildings owned by Lloyds which faced Cornhill and Lombard Streets. (In 1926, just after Eliot's departure, Lloyds tore down the older buildings and erected the head office it still occupies today.)

The British banks concentrated in the City were the heart of global capital, and Eliot's experience of their operations is perceptible throughout *The Waste Land,* which repeatedly conflates financial and sexual economies into an amorphous world of uncontrolled circulations. If *The Waste Land* is situated anywhere, it is in the City: King William Street (see Fig. 5), Moorgate, London Bridge (see Fig. 4), St. Mary Woolnoth (a church situated just opposite the Lombard Street facade of Lloyds Bank; see Figs. 6, 7), St. Magnus Martyr (another church, this one adjacent to London Bridge; see Figs. 12–14), Lower Thames Street (see Figs. 12–13), the Cannon Street Hotel (see Fig. 10), Queen Victoria Street—all are City locations evoked in the poem. Every day, from 9:30 to 5:30, working one Saturday in four, Eliot labored in his office, a tiny cog in the great machine of capital.

Eliot was one of 7,400 employees engaged by Lloyds Bank. During the First World War women clerks had first appeared at Lloyds. By late 1918 they totaled 3,300, nearly 45 percent of the bank's total labor force. With demobilization they were soon being dismissed, and after 1920 they were engaged only for typing or filing. By 1925 there were 1,500 left, all of them single (until 1949, women had to resign when they married). *The Waste Land* was unprecedented in placing an anonymous typist within the domain of serious poetry, as it does in part III; until then such subjects had been treated only in light or humorous verse.[22]

Eliot worked in the Colonial and Foreign Department for three years; in 1919 he was transferred to the Information Department, and in 1923 he returned to the Colonial and Foreign Department. There he tracked current movements in exchange rates against the background of economic and political developments. At the Information Department, as he told his mother, his work kept him busy:

> In the first place my work on German Debts has been very heavy. Next week I shall have an assistant and a typist to write my letters and do card indexing, but last week I have had to struggle through chaos myself, receiving hundreds of reports from Branches of the bank, classifying them, picking out the points that needed immediate attention, interviewing other banks and Government Departments, and trying to elucidate knotty points in that appalling document the Peace Treaty.
> (*LOTSE*, 369)

Eliot's salary nearly doubled from the moment he entered Lloyds. In 1917 he was earning £270 per year; by late 1918 his income had increased to £350 (*LOTSE*, 259), and by 1922 to £455. Part of this increase was merely a function of the postwar inflation, but part indicated real esteem for his services. Employees at the bank recalled him as a stylish dresser. One reminiscence, probably apocryphal, records that "he would often in the middle of dictating a letter, break off suddenly, grasp a sheet of paper, and start writing quickly when an idea came to him."[23]

The City in which Eliot worked differed sharply from the area as we know it today. Many of its thoroughfares had quite recently been remodeled to conform to the grand manner of Edwardian commercial developments. Jerry White has neatly described this style, "eclectic in its borrowings from classical architecture, and from Wren and the French Baroque, as grandiose as the London County Council's height restrictions would permit, with a buttoned-up pomposity of bearing which the odd flutter of decorative fancy did little to relieve, making offices look like rich men's mansions and calling them, with false modesty, 'Houses.'"[24] Between 1900 and 1914 many areas in the northern part of the City were largely rebuilt in this "Grand Manner," including Finsbury Square, Finsbury Pavement, Finsbury Circus, Moorgate (mentioned in *The Waste Land*), and London Wall. King William Street (also mentioned in *The Waste Land*) was remodeled around 1912 to accommodate new offices for insurance companies, while Gracechurch Street was remodeled to house banks. One effect of all this activity was to drive out residents; between 1901 and 1911 a quarter of the City's population was lost. "The City," one contemporary commented, "becomes more and more a collection of office buildings."[25] The sense of inhuman desolation which suffuses *The Waste Land*, its depiction of the City as haunted terrain in which "a spectre stops the passerby in full daylight" (note to line 60), owes much to this perceptible dwindling of living inhabitants, their homes consumed by a voraciously expanding commercial life. Although the City was an extreme case, it epitomized a process taking place throughout the whole of inner London. In the Edwardian period all but two of the twenty-eight metropolitan boroughs showed a net decline in population, as residents increasingly moved to new suburbs. The little warren of small shops and warehouses that clung to Lower Thames Street, at the foot of London Bridge (see Figs. 12, 13), was virtually a prehistoric relic by the time that Eliot wrote the plangent verses which commemorate them in *The Waste Land* (see lines 259–263).

Not that a loss of residents meant a decline in crowds in the City. Quite the contrary. Between 1891 and 1911 the number of employees in the City increased from 301,000 to 364,000, while "visitors" to the City meant that over a million people per day entered and left the square mile. What enabled the movement of such large numbers of people was a revolution

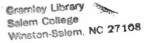

in urban transportation which took place between 1900 and 1914. Electrification of the railways, especially the Tube or underground system, was rapid. Inaugurated in June 1900, it was already complete by 1906. In 1903 the London County Council, which held a monopoly of tramways in inner London, began its electrification program for trams, and by 1914 electric trams were seen on most main roads throughout north, south, and east London. The era of the London motor bus got under way at about the same time, in 1907, when the London General Omnibus Company (LGOC) introduced its first electric trams. In 1911 the last horse-drawn service for the LGOC was closed. By that date, too, the motor taxi had also more or less completely displaced the horse-drawn hansom cab. Hansoms still existed, but increasingly they were rarities to be pointed out and gawked at. In *The Waste Land* "the sound of horns and motors" is omnipresent, while "the human engine waits / Like a taxi throbbing waiting," and "trams and dusty trees" cast inert gloom.

The year 1917 marked not only Eliot's entry into Lloyds, but also his first book publication. *Prufrock and Other Observations* was issued in June by the Egoist Press, the book publishing wing of the *Egoist,* a journal which combined feminist and individualist strains of thought. The press run was only five hundred copies, and reviews were not numerous. One reviewer dismissed Eliot as "one of those clever young men who find it amusing to pull the leg of a sober reviewer. . . . The subjects of the poems, the imagery, the rhythms have the wilful outlandishness of the young revolutionary idea."[26] But May Sinclair (1870–1946), an established English novelist, urged that "Prufrock" and "Portrait of a Lady" were "masterpieces." "Eliot's genius," she wrote, was "disturbing": "It is elusive; it is difficult; it demands a distinct effort of attention." Yet she concluded that "if there is anything more astounding and more assured than his performance it is his promise."[27] Edgar Jepson (1863–1938), an American novelist who resided in London, also praised the volume: "It is new in form, as all genuine poetry is new in form; it is musical with a new music, and that without any straining after newness. The form and music are a natural, integral part of the poet's amazingly fine presentation of his vision of the world."[28] Positive reviews did little for the book's sales: by 1919 it had sold enough copies to just cover expenses, and the publisher was able to pay back £1 and 15 s. of the £5 which Ezra Pound had lent the firm in support of publication costs. Pound asked that the outstanding amount be given to Eliot as royalties. By 1921 the book had sold 371 copies, with Eliot receiving £10.[29]

In June 1917 Eliot was appointed assistant editor of the *Egoist*, a position he held until the end of 1918. His salary was £36 per year, £12 of which was secretly provided by Ezra Pound from money furnished by John Quinn, an American lawyer and patron of letters. Eliot's life now assumed a steady routine of work. He rose two hours early in the morning to concentrate on his own writing; then worked an eight-hour day at the bank; then returned home to write reviews and fulfill his editorial duties for the *Egoist*. He also cultivated an increasingly wide circle of acquaintances. He met Richard Aldington, a young poet also associated with the *Egoist*. Through Bertrand Russell he was introduced to Lady Ottoline Morrell, a noted hostess. He was introduced to Virginia and Leonard Woolf and by late 1918 was being invited to their home in Richmond, Hogarth House. He got to know Sydney Schiff, a wealthy patron of the arts who was creating a new journal, *Arts and Letters*. Predictably, his activities were so many that he found it difficult to concentrate on writing poetry. To get over his writer's block he began to write in French, and in July 1917 he published three poems in French, and a fourth in English, in the *Little Review*. It was the first verse he had written in more than a year.

For Eliot 1918 was "a most exhausting year, alarms, illness, movings, and military difficulties" (*LOTSE*, 259–260). In the early part of the year, Vivien and he were both so tired that they decided to take a small cottage in Marlow, some forty miles outside of London, in June. They leased it for five years and sublet their flat in London, but now Eliot had to meet the added expenses of a long commute. Throughout the year he continued to ask for money from his mother, father, and brother Henry. In July he conceived the idea of enlisting in the U.S. military, and so began a protracted affair of bureaucratic delays and conflicting accounts of what he had to do to enlist. In October, Eliot moved back into the flat at 18 Crawford Mansions, while Vivien stayed on in Marlow for a few weeks more. Soon they were both ill with influenza, and Vivien's nerves were so bad that she could "hardly sleep at all" (*LOTSE*, 259). Though Eliot had managed in the spring to write four poems, which were published in the September issue of the *Little Review*, that was the extent of his output for the year. (The four were "Sweeney among the Nightingales," "Dans le restaurant,"

"Mr. Eliot's Sunday Morning Service," and "Whispers of Immortality.") To do better, he resolved to cut back on writing for the *Egoist*, allegedly on the advice of his doctor.

Despite having written only eight poems in two years, by late 1918 Eliot was involved in two book projects. One was for an edition of prose and verse which he had submitted in mid-October 1918 to Alfred Knopf, a young American publisher who had recently published a book by Pound. Eliot was unhappy with the projected volume but eager to have something published in the United States so that he could show his parents "that I have not made a mess of my life, as they are inclined to believe" (*LOTSE*, 266). But before Knopf could reach a decision, Eliot's father died on 7 January 1919. Eliot was stricken with grief, but still more determined to have a book published in the United States.

The other project was a small edition of his most recent poems, to be published by the Hogarth Press of Leonard and Virginia Woolf. The book contained only seven poems, and the edition, published in May 1919, comprised "fewer than 250" copies.[30] Still, it was a sign that Eliot was beginning to make a reputation for himself among a small, discerning public. And there were to be more such signs in the course of 1919. In March, Eliot was invited to become assistant editor of a literary journal that was being revived with new capital, the *Athenaeum*, edited by John Middleton Murry. Eliot turned down the position. He preferred the security offered by his position at Lloyds, and he wanted to remain independent of the infighting which comes with journalism: "I only write what I want to—*now*—and everyone knows that anything I do write is good. I can influence London opinion and English literature in a better way. I am known to be disinterested. . . . There is a small and select public which regards me as the best living critic, as well as the best living poet, in England" (*LOTSE*, 280). To another correspondent he explained:

> There are only two ways in which a writer can become important—to write a great deal, and have his writings appear everywhere, or to write very little. It is a question of temperament. I write very little, and I should not become more powerful by increasing my output. My reputation in London is built upon one small volume of verse, and is kept up by printing two or three more poems in a year. The only thing that matters is that

these should be perfect in their kind, so that each should be an event. (*LOTSE*, 285)

In April, Eliot published his first essay in the *Athenaeum*, a journal which enjoyed a much higher circulation than the *Egoist*. In September he was asked to contribute book reviews and an occasional leading article to the *Times Literary Supplement*, as he promptly informed his mother: "This is the highest honour possible in the critical world of literature, and we are pleased" (*LOTSE*, 337).

There were further developments. As soon as he had published the small collection of *Poems* with the Hogarth Press in May 1919, Eliot agreed to let John Rodker publish a deluxe and limited edition of all his poems under the title *Ara Vos Prec*. The volume was to reprint the twelve poems contained in *Prufrock and Other Observations* and the seven poems recently published in *Poems*, as well as three new poems to be published in periodicals in May and September 1919 ("A Cooking Egg," "Burbank with a Baedeker; Bleistein with a Cigar," and "Sweeney Erect"); it was also to include two previously unpublished poems, "Ode" and "Gerontion." Two of the new poems, "Burbank with a Baedeker" and "Gerontion," plainly invoked topoi of contemporary anti-Semitism. Unmentioned in contemporary reviews of Eliot's work, the subject has since become an object of considerable controversy.[31] Meanwhile, the protracted negotiations with the American publisher Knopf, originally for a book of poems and essays, had finally led to a result. Knopf would publish a book of poems only. *Poems*, the title given to the American edition of *Ara Vos Prec*, would appear at the same time as its English counterpart, in February 1920.

"Also," as Eliot explained to his mother in July 1919, "as a result of my Athenaeum articles, I have had proposals for books from two publishers . . . and hope to arrange something with one or the other" (*LOTSE*, 310). The proposal that came to fruition was for a collection of essays, an opportunity for Eliot to gather and revise the best of his growing number of reviews. The result was *The Sacred Wood*, published in England in November 1920, only nine months after *Ara Vos Prec*, and in the United States in February 1921, one year after Knopf's release of *Poems*. Inevitably *The Sacred Wood* was invoked to explain the poems, and by late 1920 Eliot was increasingly recognized as an up-and-coming poet and critic, a subject of growing controversy. In the span of a little more than eighteen months, from

March 1919 to November 1920, Eliot's status had undergone a remarkable change.

One other event that took place in 1919 was to prove significant. On 5 November, Eliot wrote a letter to the New York lawyer and cultural patron John Quinn, enumerating his current projects: "I am at work now on an article ordered by the *Times,* and when that is off I hope to get started on a poem that I have in mind" (*LOTSE,* 344). It was his earliest reference to *The Waste Land.* The date of this reference is crucial. For a great deal of critical debate about *The Waste Land* has turned on its relationship to Jessie Weston's contemporary study of the medieval Grail legends, a debate prompted partly by Eliot himself in the very first sentence of the notes which accompany the poem: "Not only the title, but the plan and a good deal of the incidental symbolism of the poem were suggested by Miss Jessie L. Weston's book . . ." But Weston's book was not published till late January 1920, more than two months after Eliot's letter to Quinn. Whatever role it played in the poem's conception and composition, it formed no part of the "poem I have in mind" in 1919.

Throughout 1920 Eliot was prevented from working on the long poem by a combination of events. Writing *The Sacred Wood* proved far more difficult than he had anticipated. He had originally hoped to complete it by the end of May, but the final manuscript was not posted to the publisher until 9 August, more than two months late. Then there was the flat at Crawford Mansions, which he and Vivien had "come to loathe on account of the noise and sordidness." In June he began searching for another and was horrified to learn that many were priced at "two to four times what we pay now" (*LOTSE,* 390). Housing exemplified in acute form the general surge in prices which followed in the immediate aftermath of the war. By the end of October, Eliot finally agreed on the rental terms for a new flat at 9, Clarence Gate Gardens, and by the end of November he moved in. But a third event further consumed his time, an enormous stomach abscess which nearly killed Vivien's father, requiring an emergency operation and weeks of painful recovery attended by Vivien. Finally, throughout 1920 Eliot complained of poor health, tiredness, and exhaustion— sometimes his own, sometimes Vivien's, often that of both. Eliot's regrets over not working on his projected poem recur throughout the year. To a novelist who was finding it difficult to concentrate he wrote in January 1920: "I have been trying to start work myself, and it is very difficult when *both* people in a household are run down" (*LOTSE*, 355). To his brother he wrote in September: "I have not done any writing for months, and now we are both sleeping very badly. . . . I feel maddened now because I want to get settled quietly and write some poetry" (*LOTSE*, 407). A week later he wrote to his mother: "I do not suppose that I shall be properly settled at work again till November; I have several things I want to do; and I want a period of tranquility to do a poem that I have in mind" (*LOTSE*, 408). "Am I writing much?" he asked himself, echoing a friend's question. "Only signing my name to leases and agreements" (*LOTSE*, 409). In October he advised his mother regretfully: "I have of course been unable to write, or even read and think, for some weeks" (*LOTSE*, 412). "You see," he explained to one correspondent, "we began looking for a flat in June, and since then I have simply not had the time to do a single piece of work . . . But I want to get to work on a poem I have in mind" (*LOTSE*, 419). By December even the success of *The Sacred Wood* was beginning to irritate him: "I am rather tired of the book now, as I am so anxious to get on to new work, and I should more enjoy being praised if I were engaged on something which I thought better or more important. I think I shall be able to do so soon" (*LOTSE*, 424). Eliot began writing *The Waste Land* two months later.

COMPOSITION OF THE POEM

To a reader encountering Eliot's masterpiece for the first time, it can be disconcerting to discover that the poem is known in two different forms. But so it has been since 1971, when Valerie Eliot (the poet's second wife) first published *The Waste Land: A Facsimile and Transcription of the Original Drafts* (hereafter *TWL:AF*, followed by page references), a volume which contained photographic reproductions and transcriptions of all the poem's extant prepublication materials.[32] For good or ill, these have become central to critical discussion of the poem. The problem with them, as almost every reviewer noted at the time, was that they are all undated, virtually inviting scholars to offer speculative chronologies that might reconstruct the sequence in which Eliot wrote the poem's various parts. For more than thirty years it was widely agreed that part III, or some portion of part III, was the first to be composed, and it was thought that this contained the poem's original nucleus or program, a plan which had then dissolved or fallen away in the course of writing the rest of the poem.[33] But this chronology was purely speculative and based solely on the published facsimiles, rather than study of the manuscripts themselves. More specifically, it was based on recognizable differences between the typewriter that had been used to type part III and the machine that had been used to type parts I and II. Unless one compared these typewriters with the machines used in other documents produced by Eliot, however, it was merely guesswork to assign priority to one over the other. It was not until 2004 that a scholar systematically compared the typewriters and the papers used in the prepublication manuscripts with those that had been used in Eliot's letters, student papers, essays, and poems during the period 1913–1922, a documentary base comprising over 1,200 leaves of paper. The result was unequivocal: the typewriter used for part III was a new one that first appeared in early September 1921, while the typewriter used for parts I and II was one that Eliot had been regularly using for the last seven years. Moreover, because the comparison also extended to the kinds of paper that Eliot used during this span of ten years, it was possible to achieve a much more finely calibrated understanding of which portions were written in which sequence, and so resolved a long-standing debate.[34] As a consequence, we now have a more finely calibrated understanding of how the poem came to be written.

Eliot began writing his long poem in late January or early February 1921, and over the next three months he completed parts I and II, more or less as we know them today. These he typed up in a fair copy sometime between 9 and 22 May (see *TWL:AF*, 6–21), part of an effort to put his affairs in order before his mother, his brother Henry, and his sister Marian were to arrive for an extended visit in early June. But in early May Eliot also received a typescript copy of the "Circe" episode of Joyce's *Ulysses*. It impressed him enormously, and in response he wrote a new beginning to part I (*TWL:AF*, 4–5), one which portrays several incidents in the course of a drinking binge that takes place one night in Boston. The protagonists go to a vaudeville show, stop in a brothel, and later are saved from being arrested by a policeman through the intervention of Mr. Donavan, a respectable citizen who has influence down at City Hall. The episode loosely recalls the closing portions of the "Circe" episode, with Mr. Donavan playing much the same role as Corny Kelleher. The entire passage, consisting of fifty-five lines, was probably added to the typescript of part I in late May, when Eliot also gave the entire poem a provisional title, "He Do the Police in Different Voices."

On 10 June, Eliot's family arrived in London, where they stayed for ten weeks before leaving on 20 August. Eliot's mother and his older sister Marian stayed in the Eliots' flat in Clarence Gate Gardens, while Eliot and Vivien moved into some portion of a flat at 12, Wigmore Street, then taken by Lucy Thayer, sister of Scofield Thayer (editor of the *Dial*) and a friend of Vivien's since 1915. Henry, meanwhile, was lodged in a separate room at 41, Gordon Square.[35] But with Vivien still feeling poorly, as she had been since February, it was decided in early July that she would go out "to a place in the country on Chichester harbour" (*LOTSE,* 459), while Henry left Gordon Square and joined Eliot in the flat at Wigmore Street.

It was at this moment that Lady Rothermere, the wife of a wealthy newspaper magnate, first broached a plan for launching a new literary and cultural journal to be edited by Eliot, an idea that eventually led to the creation of the *Criterion*. In the short term, it threatened much correspondence to work out the terms of her support and Eliot's participation, and by mid-July, Vivien was called back from the country to help. Now Vivien, Eliot, and his brother Henry were "encamped in an attic with a glass roof" (*LOTSE,* 461) at Wigmore Street, as Vivien put it; or as Eliot put it, in "very confined and uncomfortable quarters for three people" (*LOTSE,* 461). There they stayed for the next five weeks until the Eliot family departed. When they left, Henry took away Eliot's old typewriter, the one he had used since early 1914 at Harvard, and left in its place his own much newer machine as a present. It was during this ten-week period that Eliot composed lines 185–258, or most of the first half of part III, which at this point were introduced not by lines 173–184 as we know them today but by a very different passage of seventy-two lines which recount the doings of a wealthy socialite named Fresca in couplets that attempt to imitate Pope.

Eliot and Vivien spent yet another week at Wigmore Street after his family had departed, and moved back to Clarence Gate Gardens only on the weekend of 27–28 August. Both Eliot and Vivien were increasingly ill. To Mary Hutchinson he wrote on 1 September: "Also I am feeling completely exhausted—the departure of my family laid us both out—and have had some splitting headaches" (*LOTSE,* 467). And six days later he reported to Richard Aldington: "My wife has been very ill, we have had to have new consultations, and to make matters worse we have been moving from Wigmore Street back here" (*LOTSE,* 468). There were also pressing commitments for journalism. In early September he wrote his regular "London

Letter: September, 1921," for the *Dial*, his first essay typed on the new type-writer that Henry had left him. On 16 September he "finished an article, unsatisfactory to myself, on the metaphysical poets" (*LOTSE*, 469–470) —his review of Herbert J. C. Grierson's anthology, *Metaphysical Lyrics and Poems of the Seventeenth Century: Donne to Butler*—which appeared the next month in the *Times Literary Supplement* (see 192–201 this volume). By the end of September, Eliot's condition was so poor that Vivien arranged for him to see a "nerve specialist," who promptly advised Eliot to "go straight away for three months complete rest and change and . . . live according to a strict regimen which he has prescribed" (*LOTSE*, 471). Eliot requested a leave of absence from Lloyds Bank, which promptly granted it. But because plans for the *Criterion* had now advanced and called for Eliot to produce a first number in only three months' time, or in January 1922, he took a further ten days to postpone the journal's planned appearance and wrap up affairs in London. It was during this interval, on 10 October, that Ezra Pound came from Paris to London, where he stayed for eight days with his mother-in-law, Olivia Shakespeare, at 12, Brunswick Gardens in Kensington. Pound met Eliot on the evening of 12 October (Wednesday), and reported to his wife, Dorothy, on 14 October: "Eliot at last ordered away for 3 months—he seems rejuvinated [*sic*] at prospect."[36]

Finally, on 15 October, Eliot left for Margate, a seaside resort town located some seventy miles east of London. He was accompanied by Vivien, who stayed with him at the Albemarle Hotel in Cliftonville, an area just outside the main resort. Vivien remained for a little more than two weeks, until 31 October, then returned to London, leaving him alone. But already by 26 October she had reported that Eliot was "getting on *amazingly*," looking "younger, and fatter and nicer" (*LOTSE*, 479). Eliot stayed for another twelve days in the solitude of a seaside resort grown quiet after its high season. While there he composed three drafts for his long poem, "O City, City" (*TWL:AF*, 36–37), "The river sweats" (*TWL:AF*, 48–49), and "Highbury bore me" (*TWL:AF*, 50–51). These he conceived as forming a "part of Part III" when he described them to a friend and admirer in a letter which has been conjecturally dated to 11 November (*LOTSE*, 484–485).[37] Together the three drafts make up lines 259–311 of the published poem and form the conclusion to part III. In addition, Eliot composed a brief fragment of thirteen lines beginning "London, the swarming life" (*TWL:AF*, 36–37) and two independent poems, "Elegy" and "Dirge" (*TWL:AF*, 116–

119). The independent poems were the result of Eliot's growing concern that his long poem might not be long enough to make an independent book, and from October 1921 to January 1922 he repeatedly considered the idea of having a small group of poems which would fill out the space. With these manuscripts in hand, Eliot returned to London late on 12 November.

He stayed less than a week, until 18 November. Knowing that he would soon be leaving for Lausanne, where he was to stay for six weeks and receive treatment from the Swiss psychiatrist Roger Vittoz, Eliot attempted to assemble a working draft of part III of the poem as so far composed. He began to prepare a typescript (*TWL:AF*, 22–35, carbon 38–47), the first part of the poem typed with the newer typewriter which his brother Henry had left him in August. The typescript incorporated the passage beginning "London, the swarming life," which he had just composed while in Margate, now inserted before what is line 215 of the published poem. But his plan went awry: evidently he simply didn't have time to finish typing all of part III and got only about halfway through, as far as what is now line 258. In addition, he typed up a third independent poem titled "Exequy" (*TWL:AF*, 100–103). It would go nicely with "Elegy" and "Dirge," the two independent poems he had composed while in Margate. Meanwhile, for the moment the introduction to part III remained the passage already mentioned, the seventy-two lines of Popean couplets depicting the wealthy socialite Fresca (*TWL:AF*, 23–27, carbon 38–41).

On 19 November, Eliot left for Paris, again accompanied by Vivien. In Paris they stayed at the Hotel Pas du Calais, 59, rue des Saints Pères, in the Sixth Arrondissement. Eliot may not have stayed more than a day, and some evidence suggests that he had left the city already by 21 November. Ezra and Dorothy Pound were in town, but having just moved into a new studio at 70 bis, rue Notre Dames des Champs, were busy painting the walls and constructing furniture. Pound and Eliot certainly met during the brief period when Eliot was in the city, but it is unlikely that Pound would have had enough time to go through *The Waste Land*.[38] "Eliot seemed fairly well when I saw him on his way through Paris last week," he wrote to one correspondent on 5 December.[39] Vivien, meanwhile, was left behind in Paris on her own, and in the weeks that followed received little companionship from the Pounds, who were preoccupied with other matters. On 13 December, Dorothy Pound was hospitalized for an abscess on her left forefinger, which required surgery to cut off the tip bone, and she remained in the hospital until 27 December.[40]

In Lausanne, Eliot stayed at the Hotel St. Luce, a tranquil pension, from 22 November until 2 January. Lausanne, he wrote, was a "very quiet town, except when children come downhill on scooters over the cobbles. Mostly banks and chocolate shops" (*LOTSE*, 490). It was amid these that Eliot finished his draft of *The Waste Land*. He wrote a draft of part IV which ran to ninety-two lines (compared with ten in the published version of the poem), and also a draft of part V, which was virtually identical with the final, published version (*TWL:AF*, 54–61, 70–81). In addition, he became concerned by the lack of a vivid connection between the ending of part III, dominated by the taut series of three lyrics sung by the Thames-daughters (echos of the Rhine maidens in Wagner's Ring cycle), which he had drafted when alone in Margate in early November, and the beginning of part III (*TWL:AF*, 22–23 and 26–27), with its caustic account of the doings of Fresca, a passage he had drafted earlier in the summer while his family was visiting. They seemed too disjunct, and Eliot responded by drafting an additional passage of seventeen lines designed to link them more firmly (*TWL:AF*, 28–29). Since the evocation of the Thames-daughters entailed obvious reference to water, Eliot decided to expand another, quite minor reference to water in part III's beginning (*TWL:AF*, 26–27, ll. 56–57). On the partial typescript for part III which he had prepared in London in mid-November, he now placed a large asterisk and the command "insert" directly opposite a passage which recounted Fresca's reading habits (*TWL:AF*, 26–27), her daily immersion "in a soapy sea / of Symonds–Walter Pater–Vernon Lee." Then he began a new draft which transformed Fresca into a version of Venus rising from the sea:

> From which, a Venus Anadyomene
> She stept ashore to a more varied scene,
> Propelled by Lady Katzegg's guiding hand,
> She knew the wealth and fashion of the land.
> (*TWL:AF*, 28–29)

And so it went for another thirteen lines, all in what Pound would later call the "too loose" manner of Eliot's pastiche of Pope (*TWL:AF*, 38–39). Our concern, however, is not with the passage's success or failure but with the kind of order that was dictating the poem's composition: for that order was fundamentally contingent and retrospective. It was not, in other words, an order being achieved as the realization of a plan or program, dictated by some predetermined notion of mythic structure or ritual pattern. What *The Waste Land* achieved were relative and incremental orders of coherence, orders fundamentally local and retrospective in nature. And because the orders of coherence which dictated the poem's composition were so local, it meant that substantial parts of the poem could be eliminated without doing damage to the whole. Which is precisely what happened next.

Eliot arrived in Paris on 2 January 1922, bringing with him the sheaf of typescripts, drafts, and autograph fair copies which he had assembled over the previous eleven months. Deeply uncertain about the worth of his entire project, he submitted these to Ezra Pound for advice and suggestions for improvement. What transpired is widely recognized as one of the greatest acts of editorial intervention on record. With uncanny insight, Pound urged Eliot to remove the large tracts of narrative which furnished the beginning to parts I, III, and IV of the poem. From part I he deleted the fifty-four-line sequence which depicted a rowdy night on the town in Boston; from part III he expunged the lengthy beginning which described the activities of Fresca, at that point a passage which ran to eighty-nine lines; and from part IV he slashed away the detailed exposition of the final voyage of Phlebas, another eighty-three lines. In addition, he pruned twenty-seven lines from the central scene in part III, the tryst of the unnamed typist and "the young man carbuncular." To top it off, he made another two hundred minor editorial changes, typically deleting or questioning isolated words and phrases.

The process was only slightly more complicated than the above summary suggests. At one point, on the autograph fair copy of what was then the beginning to part IV, Pound wrote in black ink, "Bad—cant attack until I get typescript" (*TWL:AF*, 54–55). During his first reading of the poem, in other words, Pound had gone through parts I, II, and III, then had asked Eliot to furnish him with a typescript version of parts IV and V. Eliot promptly obliged while still in Paris (*TWL:AF*, 62–69, 82–89), using Pound's own typewriter to do so, which now became the third of the three typewriters which were used for the prepublication manuscripts. Pound then went on to finish his second editorial intervention with the poem, which chiefly consisted of removing the first eighty-four lines of part IV. What emerged was very close to the poem as we know it today, with one significant exception. Pound's deletion of the original beginning to part III, which he had made during his first editorial intervention, meant that it effectively lacked an introduction, seeming to start much too abruptly. While still in Paris, therefore, Eliot drafted a ten-line passage which would serve as part III's opening, a slightly abbreviated version of lines 173–184 in the published poem, a plangent and deeply personal farewell to the nymphs, young men, and even the urban detritus which have populated the poem (*TWL:AF*, 24–25).

Writing and editing Eliot's long poem was one thing; publishing it would be another. Eliot's stay in Paris, by sheer chance, overlapped with that of Horace Liveright, a young American publisher who was director of the firm Boni and Liveright. Liveright was making an acquisition tour in Europe, trying to secure publishing contracts with younger writers of promise, and only months earlier he had published one of Pound's best collections of recent verse, *Poems, 1918–1921*. During his five days in Paris, Liveright visited Pound daily, and on the evening of 3 January he had an extraordinary dinner with Eliot, Pound, and James Joyce to discuss a milestone publishing program. To Joyce, still seeking an American publisher for *Ulysses*, he offered $1,000 against royalties, provided only that legal opinion deemed the work publishable. To Pound he offered a contract guaranteeing $500 annually for two years in addition to translator's fees for any work from French agreed upon by both parties. To Eliot he offered $150 advance against 15 percent royalties for *The Waste Land* and promised publication in the autumn list. As yet he had not read the poem, and his view of it was wholly mediated by Pound.[41]

Eliot evidently made a fair copy of the poem for Liveright over the next few days and sent it to him at his hotel in London, the next stop on Liveright's tour. On 11 January, in a brief note addressed to Pound, Liveright expressed some worry: "I'm disappointed that Eliot's material is as short. Can't he add anything?" he asked Pound. Eliot's worst fear, that his long poem would be too short to stand as an independent volume, was now being realized. Ultimately, it was this fear which led him to create the notes for the poem. Anxious, yet also pleased with the results of Pound's editing, Eliot proceeded to return to London on Sunday, 16 January, together with Vivien. The next day he resumed his work at Lloyds Bank.

PUBLICATION OF THE POEM, COMPOSITION OF THE NOTES

Back in London, Eliot now made a complete but still provisional typescript of the poem, nineteen pages in length, which he sent to Pound in Paris. "MUCH improved," commented Pound. He had only two reservations. He disliked the epigraph which Eliot had added to the poem (*TWL:AF*, 2–3), a passage taken from Joseph Conrad's novel *The Heart of Darkness*, and he opposed Eliot's plan to include three additional poems at the end, the independent works which Eliot had hoped would assuage Liveright's concerns about length. "The thing runs from April . . . to shantih without [a] break. That is 19 pages, and let us say the longest poem in the English landwidge. Don't try to bust all records by prolonging it three pages further," he wrote on 24 January (*LOTSE*, 497).[42]

Eliot, meanwhile, continued to have doubts about the shape of the poem and to fret over its publication. On 20 January he wrote to Scofield Thayer, an old friend who was now co-owner and the guiding editor of the American magazine the *Dial*, to offer him first publication of the poem in periodical form. The poem, at this moment, was undergoing Pound's third editorial intervention, as Eliot carefully noted. ("It will have been three times through the sieve by Pound as well as myself so should be in a final form" [*LOTSE*, 502].) Describing the work, Eliot briefly characterized it as "a poem of about four hundred and fifty lines, *in four parts*" (*LOTSE*, 502; italics mine). Remarkable though it seems to us, Eliot was planning to issue the poem without part IV. Six days later, however, when writing again to Pound on 26 January, Eliot had second thoughts, asking: "Perhaps better omit Phlebas also???" (*LOTSE*, 504). Pound replied with characteristic vigor: "I DO advise keeping Phlebas. In fact I more'n advise. Phlebas is an integral part of the poem; the card pack introduces him, the drowned phoen. sailor, and he is needed ABsoloootly where he is. Must stay in" (*LOTSE*, 505).

Even after he had acceded to Pound's demand that the ten lines of "Phlebas" or part IV be restored, Eliot faced the question that had intermittently troubled him: the poem was too short to make up an independent book. Adding notes, it now occurred to him, might resolve the problem, and even if they didn't suffice to make it a book suitable for Liveright, they might be enough to justify a small volume which could be published as a deluxe or limited edition. On 16 February, having learned from his friend Conrad Aiken about Maurice Firuski, a publisher of deluxe editions who was situated in Cambridge, Massachusetts, Eliot wrote to pursue this prospect:

> Your name has been given me by Conrad Aiken. . . . I understand that you issue these books in limited editions, and that for the volumes you take in this series you give a sum down in advance royalty.
>
> My poem is of 435 lines; with certain spacings essential to the sense, 475 book lines; furthermore, it consists of five parts, which would increase the space necessary; and with title pages, some notes that I intend to add, etc., I guess that it would run to from 28 to 32 pages.

But Firuski was slow to reply, and by 12 March Liveright had confirmed his interest in publishing the poem as a book. For the moment, at least, an American book publication seemed secure. More troubling was the poem's appearance in a periodical.

The source of the trouble, from Eliot's viewpoint, was Scofield Thayer. Thayer was enormously wealthy, the heir to a fortune in the woolen industry. His co-owner in the *Dial,* James Sibley Watson, Jr., was also wealthy, the heir of a fortune built up through early investments in Western Union, the American telegraph company. Together the two men were subsidizing the *Dial* at the rate of $73,300 per year, a remarkable figure when one recalls that a teacher in this period typically earned $1,100 per year. Thayer had followed Eliot's literary career with interest, and his sister was a friend of Eliot's wife, Vivien. Beginning in 1921 Thayer had contracted Eliot to write an occasional feature on cultural news from London, a "London Letter" that would inform American readers about topics of current discussion. He had also asked Eliot to give him a first option of publication for any new poetry he might produce.

Eliot, we have seen, had written Thayer about *The Waste Land* already on 20 January 1922, only four days after he had returned from Paris. Thayer promptly replied and offered Eliot $150, or £30, for the poem. But Eliot did not answer him until 8 March, when he telegraphed Thayer that he could not accept less than £50 ($250). Four days later, on 12 March, Thayer responded by renewing his offer of $150, advanced without his having yet seen the manuscript. On 16 March, Eliot, in turn, withdrew his offer of the poem entirely. He had heard "on good authority that you paid £100 to George Moore for a short story, and I must confess that this influenced me in declining $150 for a poem which has taken me a year to write and which is my biggest work . . . and certainly if I am to be offered only 30 to 35 pounds for such a publication it is out of the question" (*LOTSE*, 515). Ezra Pound, he went to say, supported his decision.

Thayer was furious. And since Pound was also being paid by the *Dial* to write a "Paris Letter," and was more vulnerable because he had no income outside his literary earnings, Thayer demanded that he explain himself on 10 April. Pound offered a muddled account, but one that sufficed to assuage Thayer for the moment. The critical question of where *The Waste Land* would be published, however, was left unresolved. On 6 May, Pound himself intervened: he wrote to a friend and urged her to take up the question with John Peale Bishop, then the managing editor of *Vanity Fair* and an aspiring poet, one familiar with Eliot's work and aware of the potential importance of a long poem by him. As it so happened, Bishop was sailing to Paris within a matter of weeks and would have the opportunity to meet with Pound himself.

Pound and Eliot, meanwhile, arranged to meet in Verona, a town in northern Italy that was on Pound's itinerary in a tour that he was making and conveniently close to Lugano, Switzerland, where Eliot himself was taking a brief holiday. They met on 2 June and had further discussions about the poem's potential publishers. By now Eliot was planning to publish the poem in the first issue of his own journal, the *Criterion*, in October, thus securing serial publication in Britain. But who would publish a periodical version of the poem in the United States? Three candidates were still in play: the *Dial*, provided that Thayer could be persuaded to pay more; *Vanity Fair*, which possessed a much larger circulation than the *Dial*; and the *Little Review*, an avant-garde magazine associated with Pound—a journal that could pay little and had very small circulation but would at least issue the poem without question.

Back in New York, however, Thayer's co-owner had decided to intervene on his own, hopeful that he could forestall *Vanity Fair* from triumphing over the *Dial*. James Sibley Watson, Jr., sailed for Europe, determined to meet Pound and, through him, gain access to Eliot. On 19 July, a Wednesday, he met with Pound over lunch in Paris. He "wants T's poem for Dial," Pound explained to his wife, who was then away in London. The trajectory of their conversation over lunch can be readily imagined. As Pound had already written to Thayer back in March, his view of Eliot's poem was un-compromising: "His poem is as good in its way as Ulysses in its way, and there is so DAMN little genius, so DAMN little work that one can take hold of and say, 'This at any rate stands, makes a definite part of literature.'" Pound's comparison of *The Waste Land* to *Ulysses* must have been especially telling to one such as Watson, a man keenly interested in new books who had just traveled from New York to Paris. For *Ulysses,* at this time, was not just a set of words, a text that could be easily purchased at any local book-shop. It existed in only one form, in the deluxe and limited edition of one thousand copies that Sylvia Beach had published in Paris some five months earlier, and that edition had already become a precious commodity whose value was soaring in the market for rare books and fine editions.[43] When Watson arrived in Paris, copies that had originally been priced at 150 francs (£3 and 3s, or about $15) were fetching 500 francs (£10, or nearly $50) in the Paris market. Watson was quite conversant with these figures; after all, he himself had already gone to Sylvia Beach's shop in Paris to pick up his own copy of *Ulysses* (no. 33, signed by Joyce; originally priced at 350 francs, now worth 1,165 francs), one he had been prudent enough to order in advance. Moreover, the price of the book was still rising, and by early August, when Watson left Paris it was to double yet again both in Paris and in London. In this atmosphere of feverish speculation, to compare *The Waste Land* to *Ulysses* was to say a great deal indeed.

Pound probably proposed his own very practical solution to the impasse between Eliot and Thayer. Back in March he had suggested to Thayer that Eliot be given what he called "the December award," his term for the an-nual Dial Award which the magazine had first instituted a year earlier: a prize of $2,000 (£400) for distinguished services in the cause of modern letters. The prize would be the unofficial price for the poem, while the offi-cial one would remain the $150 which Thayer had first offered. Watson was taken with this idea. He promptly flew to Berlin, where Thayer was staying, and secured his agreement, though as yet neither man had read a word of the poem. Then he returned to Paris, once again to seek out Pound.

The two men met for a second time on Thursday, 27 July, and Pound now agreed to write to Eliot and broach the new proposal. It was a propo-sition that Eliot could not easily resist. After all, the Dial Award nearly equaled his annual salary at Lloyds Bank, and it would be a curious man who would not like to see his annual income suddenly doubled. "I will let you have a copy of the Waste Land for confidential use as soon as I can make one," he replied to Pound the next day. "I gather from your remarks that Watson is at present in Paris. I have no objection to either his or Thayer's seeing the manuscript" (*LOTSE,* 552). But in fact it took Eliot more than two weeks to make a copy of the poem and send it to Watson in Paris. When Watson finally received it, on 16 August, he informed his colleague Thayer in Berlin:

> In response to Pound's letter Eliot has assumed a more con-
> ciliatory attitude and has sent on a copy of Wasteland for our
> perusal. I am forwarding it to you. . . . Anyway I wrote him
> more plainly about the prize and await his answer. I found
> the poem disappointing on first reading but after a third shot
> I think it up to his usual—all the styles are there, somewhat
> toned down in language [autograph addition:] *adjectives!* and
> theatricalized in sentiment—at least I thought.

The protracted negotiations with the *Dial* were intersecting with three other developments. One was the proposal first launched by Pound back in May, that the poem be published in *Vanity Fair.* On 1 August, Edmund Wilson, who had succeeded John Peale Bishop as the journal's managing editor, had written a letter to Eliot, offering to publish anything new he might have in hand. Meanwhile, on 3 August, Bishop himself had met with Pound in Paris, an encounter which he promptly described to Wilson in New York:

> Pound I met the other afternoon. I found him extended on
> a bright green couch, swathed in a hieratic bathrobe made of
> a maiden aunt's shit-brown blanket. . . . However, he was quite
> gracious, and the twinkle of his eyes whenever he makes a
> point is worth something. . . . Here's the thing however—
> Eliot is starting a quarterly review: he is to run "Waste Land,"
> the new series of lyrics in his first number: he and Thayer have
> split and the *Dial* will not publish it. Perhaps you might want
> to arrange for the American publication. Pound says they are
> as fine as anything written in English since 1900.

Wilson's letter probably reached Eliot in London by 10 August, but it was not till 14 August that he replied:

Thank you for your letter of the 1st. inst., I should be very glad
to do for you such an article as you suggest. For the next two
months I shall be far too busy to attempt such a thing, but
I think that I should be able to provide one during October
or November if that is satisfactory to you. As for a poem, I am
afraid that is quite impossible at present as I have only one
for which I have already contracted.

Eliot, plainly, was not being straightforward. As yet he had made no
contractual arrangement for publishing *The Waste Land* in a periodical.
(Indeed, it was not till the next day, 15 August, that Eliot wrote to Watson
in Paris, accepting Watson's plan to give him the Dial Award and making
some additional suggestions.) Eliot, in fact, rejected the offer from *Vanity
Fair* for two reasons. First, its rate of payment could never equal the sum
that came with the Dial Award. *Vanity Fair* was a commercial enterprise
that paid current market rates, not a publication subsidized by lavish patronage. Second, though *Vanity Fair* had ten times the circulation (96,500)
of the *Dial* (9,500), it represented a level of commercial success and popular acceptance that threatened to undermine the status that Eliot was trying to establish for his work. He wanted his poem to be successful, but
not too successful.

The second development was the poem's publication in book form,
which was slowly gathering momentum. Eliot had been pleased when
Liveright in mid-March had first confirmed his interest in publishing the
poem, but had grown alarmed when Liveright finally sent him a contract
in mid-June, worried by the vagueness of its terms. In response he had
turned to John Quinn, the New York lawyer and cultural patron who had
generously handled Eliot's contract with his previous American publisher,
Knopf, without charging a fee. To Quinn he wrote on 25 June, describing
his new work: "I have written . . . a long poem of about 450 words [lines],
which, with notes that I am adding, will make a book of 30 to 40 pages"
(*LOTSE*, 530). Even now, more than five months after the poem had been
finished, Eliot had still not completed the notes. Indeed, his syntax leaves
it unclear whether he had even begun: at best he was in the middle of the
process, with still some distance to go. Moreover, if the book was to be included in the autumn list, the deadline for submission of a final manuscript
was fast approaching: "Liveright said he would print it for the autumn if

he had the poem by the end of July" (*LOTSE*, 531). When Liveright, around 9 July, sent Eliot a letter indicating that he had agreed to the revised contract proposed by Quinn, Eliot hurriedly addressed the problem of a typescript in another letter to John Quinn, dated 19 July: "As it is now so late I am enclosing the typescript to hand to him when the contract is complete, or to hold if he does not complete. I had wished to type it out fair, but I did not wish to delay it any longer. This will do for him to get on with, and I shall rush forward the notes to go at the end" (*LOTSE*, 547). Eliot's comments make it clear that even as late as 19 July, six months after the poem had been finished, he had not completed the notes. Plainly it was a task which he approached with diffidence, not to say indifference. Exactly when Eliot completed them is unclear. "I suppose that the poem is now going to press," he told one correspondent on 15 August (*LOTSE*, 560), a statement which seems to imply that the notes had been completed by then. Only now, some eighteen months after Eliot had first begun the poem in February 1921, did it assume the shape that we know today.

Still waiting back in Paris, Watson finally received Eliot's reply to his proposal outlining receipt of the Dial Award as an unofficial payment for the poem: "Subject to Mr. Liveright's consent, I would let the *Dial* publish the poem for $150, not before November 1st. In this event I would forego the $150 advance from Mr. Liveright, and he would delay publication as a book until the new year. Possibly he would be glad to do this, on the possibility of the book's getting the prize, which might increase the sales" (*LOTSE*, 560). Armed with this letter, Watson set sail for New York on 18 August. "So the matter is still in the air," he wrote a day later to his colleague in Berlin, Scofield Thayer. But the final pieces in the jigsaw puzzle soon fell into place.

On 21 August, Eliot wrote to John Quinn, outlining the *Dial*'s proposal and leaving open the door for Quinn to alter the contract. "A few days ago I had an attractive proposal from Mr. Watson of the *Dial* who are very anxious to publish the poem. . . . They suggested getting Liveright to postpone the date of publication as a book" (*LOTSE*, 564). Meanwhile, the indefatigable Watson landed in New York on 29 August and promptly set out to reach terms with Liveright. "Watson has just come back," wrote his assistant two days later to Scofield Thayer in Berlin, "and the Eliot affair is taking up much of our time." Watson soon convinced Liveright that the publicity generated by the Dial Award would enhance rather than detract from sales of the book. But Liveright demanded that the *Dial* purchase 350 copies of the book at the same price charged to booksellers, and Watson promptly agreed, effectively guaranteeing that Liveright would at least break even. A few days later, on 7 September, Watson's assistant Gilbert Seldes met with Liveright in the office of John Quinn to sign letters of agreement.

By that date, Liveright's proofs of the poem were already en route to Eliot in London. On 15 September, Eliot could tell Pound, in a brief postscript to a letter about other matters: "Liveright's proof is excellent" (*LOTSE*, 570). Eliot was much less happy with the printer who produced the *Criterion* version of the poem in London. To Richard Cobden-Sanderson, the *Criterion*'s publisher, he wrote on 27 September, "I am also sending you the manuscript and the proof of the first part of my poem, so that you may have a record of the undesired alterations made by the printers" (*LOTSE*, 574). On 3 October, Eliot wrote him again: "You will see that I am enclosing the corrected proof of the rest of *The Waste Land*. I shall ring you up tomorrow morning at about eleven and will explain why I have done so" (*LOTSE*, 576). But at last the long travails of the poem were drawing to a close. Two weeks later the first number of the *Criterion* appeared, on 16 October, containing the first publication of *The Waste Land*, without notes. Publication of the poem in the November number of the *Dial*, again without notes, took place a few days later. When the December number of the *Dial* came out four weeks later, around 20 November, it announced Eliot's receipt of the Dial Award, an event that received a substantial amount of media coverage. A short time later, about 1 December, the poem appeared for the first time as a book, complete with notes, issued by the American firm of Boni and Liveright.

One small matter remained. On 23 October, Eliot sent all the extant manuscripts of *The Waste Land* to John Quinn as a present, a token of his gratitude to Quinn for having arranged his contracts with Knopf, Liveright, and the *Dial*. Eliot thought the manuscript important for what it said not about himself but about Pound: "In the manuscript of *The Waste Land* which I am sending you, you will see the evidences of his work, and I think that his manuscript is worth preserving in its present form solely for the reason that it is the only evidence of the difference which his criticism has made to this poem" (*LOTSE*, 572). Quinn received the manuscript in January 1923. When he died the next year, it was inherited by his sister,

Julia Anderson, who in turn bequeathed it to her daughter, Mary. For many years it was simply left in storage among the many cases of Quinn's papers. The manuscript was rediscovered only in the early 1950s, and in 1958 was sold to the Berg Collection of the New York Public Library, though the acquisition was not publicly announced until 1968. Three years later, in 1971, Valerie Eliot published photographic reproductions and transcriptions of the manuscript.

READING *THE WASTE LAND*

John Peale Bishop, a young and aspiring American poet who had recently resigned as managing editor of *Vanity Fair,* was living in Paris in November 1922. In August, we have seen, he had briefly met Ezra Pound to discuss the possibility of *Vanity Fair'*s publishing Eliot's new poem; now he was settling in to do some writing of his own. On 3 November, just over two weeks after *The Waste Land* had been published, he wrote to his friend Edmund Wilson and described his projected work:

> I am trying to work out an elaborate form which will be partly lyrical, partly descriptive, partly dramatic. . . . I need not say the chief difficulty is to eradicate T. S. Eliot from all future work.
> . . . I have read *The Waste Land* about five times a day since the copy of the *Criterion* came into my hands. It is IMMENSE. MAGNIFICENT. TERRIBLE. I have not yet been able to figure it all out; especially the fortune telling episode, the king my brother and the king my father, and the strange words that look like Hindu puzzle to me. I have not of course had the advantage of the notes which you say the book version will contain. Perhaps you can enlighten me on the following points: Mr. Eugenides (his significance), Magnus Martyr, Phlebas the Phoenician. The red rock is I take it the modern world both intellectual and mechanical. But the cock crowing, presaging the dawn and rain? And what is the experience referred to in the last section with all the DAs in it? Do you recognize *Le Prince d'Aquitaine de la tour abolie* or *shantih?*
>   I don't think he has ever used his stolen lines to such terrible effect as in this poem. And the HURRY UP PLEASE IT'S TIME makes my flesh creep.[44]

Bishop's letter is important because, apart from Watson's letter to Thayer in mid-August 1921, it is the only evidence that we have of a contemporary reader's first experience of the poem. Bewilderment and admiration vie with a keen sense of the poem's terrifying power.

But Bishop was not alone in sensing the poem's power. An anonymous reviewer in the *Times Literary Supplement* urged:

> Mr. Eliot's poem is also a collection of flashes, but there is no effect of heterogeneity, since all these flashes are relevant to the same thing and together give what seems to be a complete expression of this poet's vision of modern life. We have here range, depth, and wonderful expression. What more is necessary to a great poem? This vision is singularly complex and in all its labyrinths utterly sincere. It is the mystery of life that it shows two faces, and we know of no other poet who can more adequately and movingly reveal to us the inextricable tangle of the sordid and the beautiful that makes up life.[45]

On the other side of the Atlantic, Burton Rascoe promptly hailed it as "perhaps the finest poem of this generation," and went on:

> At all events it is the most significant in that it gives voice to the universal despair or resignation arising from the spiritual and economic consequences of the war, the cross purposes of modern civilization, the cul-de-sac into which both science and philosophy seem to have got themselves and the breakdown of all great directive purposes which give joy and zest to the business of living. It is an erudite despair. . . . His method is highly elliptical, based on the curious formula of Tristan Corbière, wherein reverential and blasphemous ideas are juxtaposed in amazing antitheses, and there are mingled all the shining verbal toys, impressions and catch lines of a poet who has read voraciously and who possesses an insatiable curiosity about life. . . . The final intellectual impression I have of the poem is that it is extremely clever (by which I do not mean to disparage it; on the contrary): it is a rictus which masks a hurt romantic with sentiments plagued by crass reality; and it is faulty structurally for the reason that, even with the copious

(mock and serious) notes he supplies in elucidation, it is so
idiosyncratic a statement of ideas that I, for one, cannot follow
the narrative with complete comprehension. The poem however, contains enough sheer verbal loveliness, enough ecstasy,
enough psychological verisimilitude, and enough even of
a readily understandable etching of modern life, to justify
Mr. Eliot in his idiosyncracies.[46]

Rascoe's reference to "the copious . . . notes" shows that he had been reading Liveright's edition, not the November 1922 issue of the *Dial* that he
was ostensibly reviewing. But more important was the way he juxtaposed
"the copious . . . notes" with his charge that the poem was "faulty struc-
turally" and his confession that he could not "follow the narrative with
complete comprehension"—a juxtaposition that sketched the fault lines
of much subsequent debate about the poem, continuing to the present.
For to Rascoe, as to many later readers and critics, the notes hinted at lev-
els of narrative and structural coherence which jarred with his experience
of the poem. To read the poem was to plummet through a series of sketches,
scenes, glimpses, and gleams of lyrical intensity bereft of the spatiotemporal
and logical-causal connections typical of narrative—a dreamworld experience that startled and disturbed; to read the notes was to find reference
to "the plan," an arcane but ultimately identifiable logic which was dictating
the poem's entangled movements, perhaps even a narrative structure discernible behind its unruly opacity. The tension between these poles of interpretation was replayed over and over in early reviews and critical discussions of the poem. Conrad Aiken, for example, reached "the conclusion
that the poem succeeds—as it brilliantly does—by virtue of its incoherence,
not of its plan; by virtue of its ambiguities, not of its explanations." With
great prescience, Aiken foresaw the trajectory of critical discussion of the
poem: "It is perhaps important to note that Mr. Eliot, with his comment
on the 'plan,' and several critics, with their admiration of the poem's woven
complexity, minister to the idea that *The Waste Land* is, precisely, a kind
of epic in a walnut shell: elaborate, ordered, unfolded with a logic at every
joint discernible; but it is also important to note that this idea is false."[47]

Aiken and Rascoe, in taking up such questions with an air of serious
interest, were typical of American reviewers. In the period that immediately followed the poem's publication in 1922 and 1923, there were at least

forty-six reviews of *The Waste Land* in the United States, more or less equally divided between positive and negative ones. In Britain, by contrast, there were only twelve, and ten of them were hostile.[48] A similar disparity appears in the poem's sales figures. Horace Liveright, writing in February 1923, noted that "The Waste Land has sold 1000 copies to date and who knows, it may go up to 2000 or 3000." In fact, it went up to 5,000.[49] The Hogarth Press edition in Britain fared much less well. Its 443 copies, published on 12 September 1923, did not sell out until 11 February 1925, seventeen months later.[50] The Dial Award had turned the poem into a subject of debate in contemporary media coverage in the United States, lending it an urgency that it did not possess in Britain. But the problem that had preoccupied the American reviewers, a perceived tension between the experience of the text and the experience suggested by the notes, only became more acute in the years ahead because of Eliot's subsequent allegiances.

In 1928, only six years after he had published *The Waste Land,* Eliot issued *For Lancelot Andrewes,* a collection of eight recent essays preceded by a preface in which Eliot announced that he was now a "classicist in literature, a royalist in politics, and anglo-catholic in religion."[51] It was a deliberately provocative statement, and since then it has often been quoted as if it sufficed to characterize the whole of Eliot's work and life. It was an impression that Eliot himself did much to foster in subsequent years. In 1932 he published his *Selected Essays, 1917–1932,* a selective compilation of book reviews and essays which he had been writing since 1919. The first essay in the book was "Tradition and the Individual Talent," a work from 1919 in which Eliot had urged that the personality of the individual artist be submerged in his work, or even expunged, in response to the claims of a vague tradition. Perhaps innocently, Eliot even misdated the essay, assigning it to 1917 and so making it stand as the gateway to all of his subsequent work, including *The Waste Land.*[52] Of the ten essays that Eliot wrote while composing *The Waste Land,* only three were included in the *Selected Essays,* those which most reinforced the impression that Eliot had always been a "classicist in literature." Suppressed were the other seven essays from the same period (all reprinted for the first time in this volume), which had reveled in the vernacular pleasures of British music hall and caricature, and had sketched an aesthetics that could be called "classicist" only by a remarkable extension of the term. Similarly, the *Selected Essays* gave special prominence to a piece which Eliot had recently written in 1930 on Baudelaire, one in which he damned the French poet for "having an imperfect, vague romantic conception of Good."[53] Silently erased was the contrast between this theological estimate of the French poet and the unstinting admiration for him shown in the suppressed essays of 1921. Eliot's conversion to Christianity and his growing allegiance to conservative political and social views constituted a profound change in his thought, but the extent of that change was concealed under the slowly mounting edifice of neoclassicism.

In the new climate of taste, one that Eliot himself did much to usher in, there was no longer a tension between the text of *The Waste Land* and the claims to coherence implied by the notes' reference to "the plan." The problem that had preoccupied the poem's early reviewers vanished from sight. The most influential critic to erase that tension was Cleanth Brooks, an American critic from the conservative South, who in 1939 published an essay that profoundly shaped the course of criticism on the poem for the next forty years. Brooks set out to show that the poem was "a unified whole," that every detail in it contributed to a work of extraordinary structural, thematic, and poetic integrity. Characteristically, Brooks's starting point was the first of the poem's notes, the one which urged: "Not only the title, but the plan and a good deal of the incidental symbolism of the poem were suggested by Miss Jessie L. Weston's book . . . " No less characteristically, Brooks urged that the theme of the poem could best be reconstructed from Eliot's 1930 essay on Baudelaire, the one in which he had repudiated the French poet's "imperfect, vague romantic conception of Good." That a term such as "Good" nowhere appears in Eliot's writings from the period when he was composing *The Waste Land* deterred Brooks not a moment. As for critics who had earlier described a poem far more wild and unruly than the one delineated by Brooks, they were merely victims of "the myth" that had quickly grown up around the poem.[54]

Eliot himself, in his very late years, was relaxed enough that he could be more candid about the notes and their status. Though his late memory garbled a few points of chronology and omitted some details, its general tenor was accurate, and it is worth citing in full. In 1956, when discussing ways in which critics might be misled, Eliot said:

Here I must admit that I am, on one conspicuous occasion,
not guiltless of having led critics into temptation. The notes to

The Waste Land I had at first intended to put down all the references for my quotations, with a view to spiking the guns of critics of my earlier poems who had accused me of plagiarism. Then, when it came to print *The Waste Land* as a little book— for the poem on its first appearance in the *Dial* and the *Criterion* had no notes whatever—it was discovered that the poem was inconveniently short, so I set to work to expand the notes, in order to provide a few more pages of printed matter, with the result that they became the remarkable exposition of bogus scholarship that is still on view to-day. I have sometimes thought of getting rid of these notes; but now they can never be unstuck. They have had almost greater popularity than the poem itself—anyone who bought my book of poems, and found that the notes to *The Waste Land* were not in it, would demand his money back. . . . No, it is not because of my bad example to other poets that I am penitent; it is because my notes stimulated the wrong kind of interest among the seekers of sources. It was just, no doubt, that I should pay my tribute to the work of Miss Jessie Weston; but I regret having sent so many enquirers off on a wild goose chase after Tarot cards and the Holy Grail.[55]

When one interviewer, three years later, asked Eliot whether Pound's excisions had changed "the intellectual structure of the poem," Eliot answered: "No. I think it was just as structureless, only in a more futile way, in the longer version." The implicit acknowledgment that the "shorter version," or the published text of *The Waste Land*, was "structureless," was a long way from the claim that it was governed by a "plan." "In *The Waste Land*," Eliot went on in the same interview, "I wasn't even bothering whether I understood what I was saying." But that hardly mattered, he now thought. "These things, however, become easier to people with time. You get used to having *The Waste Land*, or *Ulysses*, about."[56]

By the early 1970s the dominance of the New Criticism, which had been epitomized by Cleanth Brooks, was drawing to a close, and already one could detect beginnings of the turn to structuralism that was to be signaled by the publication of Jonathan Culler's book *Structuralist Poetics* (1975).[57] In the late 1970s and the 1980s structuralism was rapidly displaced by poststructuralism and deconstruction, then by various kinds of feminism and the rise of New Historicism, critical paradigms that stressed not the wholeness and unity of the text but its dividedness, the contradictory impulses at work beneath the surface of all language. By 1989 one critic could characterize *The Waste Land* as a poem "riddled with absences" and everywhere marked by "ruptures" and "discontinuities."[58] Nothing could have been farther from the "unified whole" which Cleanth Brooks had postulated. At the same time, however, the New Critical reading of the poem has never entirely vanished and continues to hold sway over the imagination of many critics. One sees its tenacious hold at work in the writing of one recent scholar who repeatedly notes "the poem's marmoreal reserve" and "monumental impregnability."[59] The notion of the neoclassical monument, so alien to the experience of the poem which its earliest readers described, still exerts its power over such accounts.

The reader who is about to encounter the poem for the first time, then, faces a range of critical questions awaiting him or her. Does a single or unified consciousness preside over the poem, an identifiable speaker or protagonist, or is the attempt to discern one a means of skirting the poem's fabulous, even fantastic dimensions? Is the poem prodded forward by a narrative which is fitfully glimpsed but nevertheless readily discerned, or are the many shards of narrative that plainly appear and reappear only a way of insinuating that the poem is guided by some other, more arcane logic? And is that logic the outcome of a plan or program that governed the poem's construction, or is it only that of a wild, irredeemable pathos? And why is the poem so insistent about its topicality, its embeddedness in the streets, the buildings, even the bodies that occupy London's financial district? Do the economies of finance and sexuality meet and blur, as if linked by some nameless yet powerful currency? And what authority should a reader ascribe to the notes? The demise of critical consensus about the poem means that today, more than ever before, those questions are open to fresh interrogation.

Of course those are only a few of the countless questions that arise from reading the poem, and it would be presumptuous to sketch the answers to them here. To a reader approaching the poem for the first time, one can only suggest what lies ahead by invoking the terms that John Peale Bishop used when he first read the poem so long ago in 1922: "IMMENSE. MAGNIFICENT. TERRIBLE." Perhaps the ultimate testimony to the poem's wild power is the fact that it has, for so long, survived the attention of its warmest admirers.

Notes

1. Donald Hall, *Remembering Poets: Reminiscences and Opinions* (New York: Harper and Row, 1978), 78, 91–92.
2. Peter Ackroyd, *T. S. Eliot: A Life* (New York: Simon and Schuster, 1984), 24. I have relied on Ackroyd's life of Eliot throughout this account of Eliot's early years, and on Lyndal Gordon's *T. S. Eliot: An Imperfect Life* (New York: Vintage, 1998).
3. T. S. Eliot, "The Influence of Landscape upon the Poet," *Daedalus: Journal of the American Academy of Arts and Sciences* 89, no. 2 (Spring 1960): 420–422.
4. For an account of Eliot's lifelong engagement with vernacular and popular culture, see David Chinitz, *T. S. Eliot and the Cultural Divide* (Chicago: University of Chicago Press, 2003).
5. T. S. Eliot, Preface to *John Davidson: A Selection of His Poems*, ed. Maurice Lindsay (London: Hutchinson, 1961), xi–xii.
6. T. S. Eliot, Review, "*Baudelaire and the Symbolists: Five Essays*, by Peter Quennell," *Criterion* 9, no. 2 (January 1930): 357.
7. T. S. Eliot, "What Dante Means to Me" (1950), in *To Criticize the Critic* (New York: Farrar, Straus, 1965), 125.
8. T. S. Eliot, "A Commentary," *Criterion* 26, no. 65 (July 1937): 667.
9. Conrad Aiken, "King Bolo and Others," in Tambimuttu and David March, eds., *T. S. Eliot: A Symposium* (London: Frank and Cass, 1965; orig. pub. 1948), 20–23, quotation p. 21.
10. See T. S. Eliot, *Inventions of the March Hare*, ed. Christopher Ricks (New York: Harcourt, Brace, 1996).
11. Charlotte Eliot to T. S. Eliot, 3 April 1910: "I cannot bear to think of your being alone in Paris, the very words give me a chill," in Valerie Eliot, ed., *The Letters of T. S. Eliot*, vol. 1, *1898–1922*, 10. Hereafter references to this edition are given with the abbreviation *LOTSE* and placed in parentheses within the text.
12. T. S. Eliot, "Rencontre," *Nouvelle Revue Française* 12, no. 139 (1 April 1925): 657–658.
13. Alfred Dreyfus (1853–1914), a Jew who was a captain in the French army, was falsely accused and convicted of treason in 1894. After various intellectuals called for a new trial, Dreyfus was again found guilty and sentenced in 1899, but then pardoned by the president of the French Republic. In 1904 he applied for a revision of the 1899 verdict, and in July 1906, it was definitively quashed. The twelve-year affair revealed a virulent strain of anti-Semitism in French society, and Maurras was often charged with pandering to it. During World War II he collaborated with the Vichy government and afterward he was condemned to prison for life. Eliot gave a lecture on Maur-

ras in late 1916, in which he gave an overview of Maurras's "protest against all the conditions in art and society which seemed to be due to the [French] Revolution." Maurras's reaction was "fundamentally sound, but marked by extreme violence and intolerance." In February 1934, Maurras's followers were involved in violent street protests, and Eliot deprecated the violence but also seemed to excuse it. (See T. S. Eliot, "A Commentary," *Criterion* 13, no. 52 [April 1934]: 451–454.) Scholars disagree about the extent of Eliot's interest in Maurras. For the argument that already by 1916 Eliot had developed a "classical, royalist, and religious point of view" derived from Maurras, see Ronald Schuchard, *Eliot's Dark Angel* (Oxford: Oxford University Press, 1999), 25–69, which reprints the synopsis of Eliot's 1916 lecture on Maurras (from which I have quoted in the text [quotation p. 29]), and uses the phrase I have quoted within this note (52). I disagree with this view. On Eliot and anti-Semitism, see below, n. 31.

14. T. S. Eliot, *A Sermon, Preached in Magdalene College Chapel, 7 March 1948* (Cambridge: Cambridge University Press, 1948), 5.

15. See Eliot, *Inventions of the March Hare*, 48–51, 68–70.

16. T. S. Eliot, "The Art of Poetry, I: T. S. Eliot," *Paris Review* 21 (Spring–Summer, 1959), rpt. in George Plimpton, ed., *Writers at Work: The Paris Review Interviews, Second Series* (Harmondsworth: Penguin, 1977), 99.

17. See Grover Smith, ed., *Josiah Royce's Seminar, 1913–1914: As Recorded in the Notebooks of Harry Todd Costello* (New Brunswick, N.J.: Rutgers University Press, 1963).

18. Conrad Aiken to Joy Grant, 31 August 1962, quoted in Joy Grant, *Harold Monro and the Poetry Bookshop* (London: Routledge Kegan Paul, 1967), 101.

19. Eliot, "Art of Poetry, I," 95.

20. Aldous Huxley, letter to Ottoline Morrell, 21 June 1917, quoted in Robert Gathorne-Hardy, ed., *Ottoline at Garsington: Memoirs of Lady Ottoline Morrell, 1915–1918* (New York: Knopf, 1975), 207.

21. In the following account of Lloyds, and Eliot at Lloyds, I am indebted to J. R. Winton, *Lloyds Bank, 1918–1969* (Oxford, New York: Oxford University Press, 1982), 1–43.

22. Examples include T. W. H. (Thomas William Hodgson) Crosland (1865–1924), "To the American Invader," in his *Outlook Odes* (London: At the Unicorn, 1902), 30–32; Enoch Miner [pseud.: Topsy Typist], *Our Phonographic Poets. Written by Stenographers and Typists upon Subjects Pertaining to Their Arts. Compiled by "Topsy Typist"* (New York: Popular Publishing, 1904); Samuel Ellsworth Kiser, *Love Sonnets of an Office Boy* (Chicago: Forbes, 1907), twenty-eight sonnets addressed to the office typewriter girl; Andrew Lang, "Matrimony," in *The Poetical Works of Andrew Lang*, ed. Leonora Blanche Lang (London: Longmans, 1923), 3: 179–180.

23. Quoted in Winton, *Lloyds Bank*, 40.

24. Jerry White, *London in the Twentieth Century* (London: Penguin Viking, 2002), 9.

25. Quoted ibid., 12; my remarks throughout this paragraph and the next derive from White.

26. Unsigned Review, *Literary World* 83, no. 107 (5 July 1917), rpt. in Michael Grant, ed., *T. S. Eliot: The Critical Heritage* (London: Routledge, 1982), 1: 74.

27. May Sinclair, "*Prufrock and Other Observations:* A Criticism," *Little Review* 4 (December 1917), rpt. ibid., 1: 83–88.

28. Edgar Jepson, "Recent United States Poetry," *English Review* 27 (May 1918), rpt. ibid., 1: 91–92.

29. Jane Lidderdale and Mary Nicholson, *Dear Miss Weaver: Harriet Shaw Weaver, 1876–1961* (New York: Viking, 1970), 256.

30. Donald Gallup, *T. S. Eliot: A Bibliography*, rev. ed. (New York: Harcourt, Brace, 1969), 25 (A3).

31. The most recent installment of the debate concerning Eliot and anti-Semitism is found in *Modernism/Modernity* 10, no. 1 (January 2003): 1–70. This includes an important essay by Ronald Schuchard, "Burbank with a Baedeker, Eliot with a Cigar: American Intellectuals, Anti-Semitism, and the Idea of Culture" (1–26), six responses to it by other scholars (27–56), and a reply by Schuchard (57–70). See also Anthony Julius, *T. S. Eliot, Anti-Semitism, and Literary Form* (Cambridge: Cambridge University Press, 1995), and Christopher Ricks, *T. S. Eliot and Prejudice* (Berkeley: University of California Press, 1988), chapter 2, "Anti-Semitism," 25–76.

32. Valerie Eliot, ed., *The Waste Land: A Facsimile and Transcript of the Original Drafts* (New York: Harcourt, Brace, 1971).

33. See Hugh Kenner, "The Urban Apocalypse," in A. Walton Litz, ed., *Eliot in His Time: Essays on the Occasion of the Fiftieth Anniversary of* The Waste Land (Princeton: Princeton University Press, 1973), 23–49, and Grover Smith, "The Making of *The Waste Land,*" *Mosaic* 6, no. 1 (1972): 127–141.

34. See Lawrence Rainey, *Revisiting "The Waste Land"* (New Haven: Yale University Press, 2005), chapter 1, "With Automatic Hand: Writing *The Waste Land,*" 1–70, 153–201.

35. Unpublished letter from T. S. Eliot to Mary Hutchinson, [15 June 1921; postmark 16 June 1921], University of Texas, Harry Ransom Humanities Research Center.

36. Unpublished letter from Ezra Pound to Dorothy Pound, 14 [October 1921], Indiana University, Lilly Library, Pound Mss. III.

37. Valerie Eliot assigns the letter to [4? November 1921]; for arguments urging that it be assigned to [11 November 1921], see Rainey, *Revisiting "The Waste Land,*" 26.

38. Valerie Eliot assigns Eliot's departure from Paris to "22? November" (*LOTSE*, xxxvi). But a difficulty for this date is posed by Eliot's letter to the editor of the *Times Literary Supplement*, which was datelined Lausanne and published on 24 November. Surely it had to have been set in type by 23 November at the latest, and it must have been posted at least one day earlier, on 22 November. It is too much to suppose that Eliot could have taken the train from

Paris to Lausanne, arrived, and then written and posted a letter the same
afternoon. More likely he left Paris on 21 November, perhaps even 20 November. Pound's letter to Scofield Thayer (quoted later in the text) indicates
that Eliot was simply "on his way through Paris," not staying for an extended
period.

39. Unpublished letter from Ezra Pound to Scofield Thayer, 5 December 1921,
Beinecke Library, *Dial* Papers.

40. Unpublished letters from Ezra Pound to his father, Homer Pound, 3 December [1921] and 25[–26] December 1921; Beinecke Library, YCAL Mss. 43.

41. For details of the poem's publication I draw on my account in *Revisiting
"The Waste Land,"* chapter 2, "The Price of Modernism: Publishing *The
Waste Land,"* 71–101, where all quotations and claims are annotated. To
repeat them here would be superfluous.

42. The letter is dated "24 Saturnus" by Pound, who follows an arcane calendar
("The Little Review Calendar") that he published in the *Little Review* 7, no. 2
(Spring 1922): 2. The month Saturnus was meant to correspond with was
January. Mrs. Eliot, in her edition of *LOTSE,* mistakenly assigns the letter
to December 1921, following D. D. Paige, the editor of Ezra Pound, *Selected
Letters, 1907–1941* (New York: New Directions, 1971), 169. Though Paige's
error was first noticed back in 1972 by Hugh Kenner in "The Urban Apocalypse," 44, n. 7, it evidently had not come to Mrs. Eliot's attention before
she published her edition of the letters in 1988.

43. For details regarding the publication of *Ulysses,* here and below, I draw on
my earlier account, "Consuming Investments: Joyce's *Ulysses,"* in *Institutions
of Modernism: Literary Elites and Public Culture* (New Haven: Yale University
Press, 1998), 42–76 and 186–194, where all these claims are footnoted.

44. Unpublished letter from John Peale Bishop to Edmund Wilson, 3 November
1922, Beinecke Rare Book and Manuscript Library, Edmund Wilson Papers.

45. Unsigned review of the first issue of the *Criterion* and review of *The Waste
Land, Times Literary Supplement,* no. 1084 (26 October 1922), 690; rpt. in
Grant, *T. S. Eliot,* 1: 134–135.

46. Burton Rascoe, "A Bookman's Day Book," *New York Tribune,* 5 November
1922, section V, p. 8.

47. Conrad Aiken, "An Anatomy of Melancholy," *New Republic* 33 (7 February
1923): 294–295, rpt. in Grant, *T. S. Eliot,* 1: 156–161, quotation p. 161.

48. The twelve English reviews are listed in the Bibliography of this volume,
pages 256–257; forty-eight American reviews are listed on pages 257–259,
and these reviews mention four others which have not been identified.

49. Letter from Horace Liveright to Ezra Pound, 5 February 1923, Bloomington,
Indiana University, Pound Manuscripts. The figure of five thousand copies
is given by Tom Dardis, *Firebrand: The Life of Horace Liveright* (New York:
Random House, 1995), 97.

50. The Hogarth Press figures were given by Leonard Woolf to I. M. Parsons,
who reports them in "T. S. Eliot's Reputation," *Critical Quarterly* 8 (1966): 180.

51. T. S. Eliot, *For Lancelot Andrewes* (London: Faber and Gwyer, 1928), ix.
52. On the misdating of "Tradition and the Individual Talent" in the first edition of Eliot's *Selected Essays*, see Donald Gallup, *T. S. Eliot: A Bibliography*, rev. ed. (New York: Harcourt, 1969), 47, A21.a.
53. The Baudelaire essay stands conspicuously as the first in a section treating modern authors, a position it still occupies today. The sentence by Eliot quoted here is found in his *Selected Essays* (New York: Harcourt, 1950), 380.
54. Cleanth Brooks, "*The Waste Land:* Critique of the Myth," in *Modern Poetry and the Great Tradition* (Chapel Hill: University of North Carolina Press, 1939), 136–172; "unified whole" appears on 136, the references to Weston and the Baudelaire essay on 137.
55. T. S. Eliot, "The Frontiers of Criticism," in *On Poetry and Poets* (London: Faber, 1957), 109–110, ellipsis mine. Ezra Pound, writing in 1939, remembered the genesis of the notes in similar terms, and he highlighted their effect on the poem's reception: "The bearing of this poem was not overestimated, nevertheless the immediate reception of it even by second rate reviewers was due to the purely fortuitous publication of the notes, and not to the text itself. Liveright wanted a longer volume and the notes were the only available unpublished matter." Ezra Pound, "T. S. Eliot," in Frances Steloff and Kay Steele, eds., *We Moderns* (New York: Gotham Book Mart, 1939), 24.
56. T. S. Eliot, "The Art of Poetry, I: T. S. Eliot" (see n. 15), 96, 105.
57. Jonathan Culler, *Structuralist Poetics* (Ithaca, N.Y.: Cornell University Press, 1975).
58. Wayne Koestenbaum, "*The Waste Land:* T. S. Eliot's and Ezra Pound's Collaboration on Hysteria," in *Double Talk: The Erotics of Male Literary Collaboration* (London: Routledge, 1989), 112, 113.
59. Christine Froula, "Corpse, Monument, *Hypocrite Lecteur:* Text and Transference in the Reception of *The Waste Land*," *Text: An Interdisciplinary Annual of Textual Studies* 9 (1996): 304–314.

A Note on the Text

SINCE THE STORY OF *The Waste Land's* publication has already been recounted in the Introduction, we can turn directly to the implications of that publication history in assessing the poem's text. *The Waste Land* appeared in three more or less contemporaneous versions: first, on 16 October, without notes, in the October issue of the *Criterion* (the English journal edited by Eliot himself); then around 20 October, again without notes, in the November issue of the *Dial* (an American journal co-owned by Scofield Thayer and James Sibley Watson, Jr.); and finally around 1 December, now with notes, in a small book issued by the American publisher Boni and Liveright.

Recounting the publication in this way seemingly assigns priority to the *Criterion's* version of the poem—the first to be published and the one that Eliot could most directly supervise. But in fact the situation was more complicated. The first manuscript which Eliot sent to press was the one which, on 19 July, he posted to John Quinn to consign to Liveright when he signed the revised contract that Quinn was then drawing up. ("I only hope the printers are not allowed to bitch the punctuation and the spacing, as that is very important for the sense," Eliot had added [*LOTSE*, 547].) True, the manuscript sent to Quinn still lacked the notes. Those Eliot finally completed and forwarded to Liveright sometime before 15 August, the day he told James Sibley Watson: "I suppose that the poem is now going to press" (*LOTSE*, 560). The combined manuscript, text and notes, underwent a brisk production process, for only one month later, on 15 September, Eliot could tell Ezra Pound his assessment of Liveright's work: "Liveright's proof is excellent" (*LOTSE*, 570). Thus, though Liveright's version of *The Waste Land* was the last to be published, it was the first to be produced. Its production process was so swift because, throughout August and into the first week of September, Liveright assumed he would be the poem's only publisher in the United States, and by contract he was obliged to issue it in his autumn list, or in October or November at the latest. It was only in the very last days of August that Liveright received Watson's proposal that the poem first be published (without notes) in the *Dial*, then be issued as a book (with notes) by Liveright. Moreover, the letter of agreement that sanctioned this arrangement was not signed till 7 September.

The date is important. Normally during this period, transatlantic mail between New York and London required nine days. In effect, the contract between the *Dial* and Liveright was signed so late (7 September) that the *Dial* did not have time to request a setting copy from Eliot. To request a setting copy (nine days), await its arrival (nine days), produce and send off a proof of it (at least nine days), and then receive and execute corrections (another nine days) would have required a minimum of thirty-six days.[1] In fact, the *Dial*'s publication of the poem, about 20 October 1922, took place only forty-three days after the journal finalized its letter of agreement with Liveright on 7 September. The *Dial*, in other words, lacked the time to request, or produce a proof based on, an authoritative setting text of the poem. It had no choice except to use a version of the text furnished by Liveright. True, Eliot had sent a manuscript of the text to James Sibley Watson when he was still in Paris, back in mid-August; but that was a reading copy, not one meant to serve as setting copy.[2] Moreover, in the copious records of the *Dial*, no document mentions a setting copy furnished by Eliot or proofs overseen by him. Instead, the poem's hurried production at the *Dial* and the lack of any documents that register Eliot's involvement combine to confirm evidence gleaned by collating the two texts: the *Dial* text is derived from that of Liveright and has no independent authority. Its variants are of interest to the extent that they represent a well-intentioned typesetter's efforts to make sense of the Liveright text, but they have no independent authority. Eliot never saw them until publication and was never consulted about them.

On the other side of the Atlantic, Eliot's involvement was more active in the production of the *Criterion*'s version of the text. But it was also decidedly negative. To Richard Cobden-Sanderson, the publisher of the *Criterion*, Eliot wrote on 27 September (twelve days after he had told Pound that Liveright's proof was "excellent"), "I am also sending you the manuscript and the proof of the first part of my poem, so that you may have a record of the undesired alterations made by the printers" (*LOTSE*, 574).[3] And on 3 October, Eliot wrote Cobden-Sanderson again: "You will see that I am enclosing the corrected proof of the rest of *The Waste Land*. I shall ring you up tomorrow morning at about eleven and will explain why I have done so" (*LOTSE*, 576). Eliot's consternation is palpable in these comments, and readily understandable if we collate the *Criterion* text with that of Boni and Liveright. Consider a sample passage, the first two verse-paragraphs which form the opening to part III and contain thirty lines (ll. 173–202). The *Criterion* version introduces nine variants in spelling, spacing, punctuation, and font: in four places it adds commas (ll. 187, 188, 200, 201), in another it changes the font and in yet another it adds a blank line (202, 198–199), in still two more it alters punctuation (180, 192), and in one last it emends a spelling ("gashouse" to "gas-house" at 190). All minor changes, it is true, but eight of the nine are changes of precisely the sort that Eliot had hoped to avoid ("the punctuation and the spacing . . . very important for the sense" [*LOTSE*, 547]). The result is an overall change in the flow and pace of the text. The printer who set the *Criterion* text was officious, trying to make an unruly *Waste Land* conform much more closely to conventional usage. In comparison, the *Dial* printing of the same passage introduces only two changes, minor alterations in punctuation which are merely matters of house style (the period, or full stop, is eliminated after "Mrs." in lines 198 and 199, consistent with similar changes in lines 57 and 209).[4]

Nor was it just in 1922 that Eliot considered the Liveright printing "excellent" and dismissed the *Criterion* one as filled with "undesired alterations." In 1923, when the poem was issued in book form for the first time in England by the Hogarth Press, Eliot chose the Liveright text as setting copy. Still more tellingly, two years later, when the poem was collected for the first time in Eliot's *Poems, 1909–1925* (London: Faber and Gwyer, 1925), he again chose the Liveright as setting copy. That he preferred it over the *Dial*, *Criterion*, and Hogarth printings is beyond doubt, and the present edition follows him in adopting the Liveright as its base text. (It was also in this 1925 edition, it should be noted, that Eliot added the dedication to Ezra Pound which has appeared with the poem ever since, a dedication he had first written in the inscribed copy of the Boni and Liveright edition of the poem which he gave to Pound in 1923.)

Adopting the Boni and Liveright text *(B)* as setting copy for both the 1923 Hogarth *(H)* and the 1925 Faber edition of *Poems, 1909–1925 (F),* as Eliot did, entailed an obvious though not insurmountable problem. It meant that any corrections which he made in the 1923 Hogarth would automatically disappear unless he actively intervened to make them a second time in 1925. Or to put it differently, any real or manifest error which *B* contained would automatically recur not just once in *H* but again in *F,* unless Eliot actively noted and corrected it. How extensive was the problem? Not very. The Boni and Liveright text contained eight errors and one potential variant, affecting a total of seventeen lines. (The reason for the discrepancy between these figures [nine and seventeen] is that two of the errors in *B* recurred five times each; if we subtract the four "repeats" of the two errors [eight "repeats"] from the seventeen lines, then our two figures coincide.)

If we set aside questions of font changes for the moment, the eight errors were:

1. l. 42 "Od'" instead of the correct "Öd'" or "Oed'"
2. l. 111 "tonight" instead of what was then current English usage, "to-night"
3. l. 112 "Why do you never speak." instead of the obviously correct "Why do you never speak?"
4. l. 131 "'What shall I do now? What shall I do?'" instead of the correct reading, "'What shall I do now? What shall I do?" (no closing quotation mark)
5. ll. 141, 152, 165, 168, 169 missing apostrophes in the words "it's"
6. ll. 149, 153, 154, 163, 164 missing apostrophes in the words "won't" or "don't"
7. l. 161 "alright" instead of "all right"
8. l. 259 "O City city" instead of "O City City"

Of these eight errors, Eliot noted and corrected five in *H* (2, 3, 5, 6, and 8 above). But of course his corrections were automatically undone in *F* because it reverted to *B* as setting text. This time, in *F*, he remembered to execute only two of the five corrections he had earlier made (2 and 6 above), and he added one more (7 above), in effect adding a sixth correction to *B*. Further, in *F* he also altered the spelling of "aetherial" to the more common "aethereal" in line 415, even though "aetherial" had been his own usage in the autograph and typescript fair copies which he had shown to Ezra Pound (*TWL:AF*, 78–79, 88–89). This edition, then, follows Eliot in adopting *B* as setting text, admitting the six corrections which he made in 1923 *(H)* and 1925 *(F)*, admitting also the one alteration ("aethereal") he made in 1925, and of course admitting the other, far more significant alteration which he made in 1925, the addition of the dedication to Ezra Pound.

An attentive reader will have noticed that two of *B*'s obvious errors (1, 4 above) still await attention. In the second of these, *B* reads, " 'What shall I do now? What shall I do?' " The officious printers of the *Dial* and the *Criterion* both noticed the unnecessary closing quotation marks (or inverted commas) in this passage and deleted them; but the marks returned in *H* and *F*, and Eliot failed to catch the mistake. Worse still, the error persisted in all subsequent printings. The closing quotation marks are not found in the typescript which Eliot showed Pound in Paris (*TWL:AF*, 12 and 18), however, and its authority and common sense dictate their removal.

The same is true for the last of *B*'s obvious mistakes (1 above), the ridiculous "Od'" instead of "Öd'" or "Oed'." Although the mistake was corrected in the *Dial*, that text has no authority. The mistake was not corrected in the *Criterion*, nor in *H* or *F*. Yet Eliot was certainly an adept reader and writer of German, one who knew where German words required an umlaut. Indeed, in 1922 (when *The Waste Land* was going to press) he wrote three letters in German to Hermann Hesse and Ernst Curtius which are uniformly correct in their use of umlauts.[5] Moreover, when he first wrote this passage in his own hand, an autograph addition made to the typescript of part I which he showed to Ezra Pound, he wrote "Öd'" (see *TWL:AF*, 6). The authority for this emendation, then, derives from Eliot's own usage in the *Waste Land* manuscripts.

It should be noted that the variant reading "Oed'" appears for the first time in Eliot's *Collected Poems, 1909–1935* (1936). It has long been known that Eliot made a number of corrections in a proof copy of *Collected Poems, 1909–1935* which is held in the library of King's College, Cambridge—

corrections which, for reasons that are not known, were not entered into the text.[6] The authority of that edition, therefore, is troubled and cannot be admitted as an authority for this edition. The spelling "Oed'" is not the one that Eliot himself used when he wrote the poem, and it may be no more than the expedient of a typesetter who had no umlauts at hand. (It has stood in all editions ever since.) But the question of the authority which lies behind *Collected Poems, 1909–1935* raises one other, more important question.

Line 428 of the Boni and Liveright edition reads, *"Quando fiam ceu chelidon*—O swallow swallow." The text reads the same in every early printing: in the *Dial*, in the *Criterion*, in the 1923 Hogarth, and in the 1925 Faber edition of *Poems, 1909–1925*. It also reads that way in the 1932 American edition of *Poems, 1909–1925*. Only in 1936, in *Collected Poems, 1909–1935*, does the text suddenly undergo a change, with the first words now reading: *"Quando fiam uti chelidon."* But the authority of that edition is deeply suspect, as we have already seen. Moreover, there can be no doubt whatever about which version of this passage Eliot had in mind when he wrote the poem: in both his autograph fair copy of part V and the typescript fair copy of it which he prepared for Ezra Pound while he was in Paris in early 1922, Eliot unequivocally wrote and typed *"ceu chelidon,"* not *"uti chelidon"* (see *TWL:AF*, 80–81, 88–89).

Further, there is something fussy, even a bit pedantic, about this alteration. While the change from *ceu* to *uti* makes no difference in the passage's meaning, the latter is the more widely accepted scholarly reading of the Latin text.[7] A similar change takes place many years later in the 1962 Mardersteig edition of *The Waste Land*. Whereas line 202 in all the early editions reads, *"Et O ces voix d'enfants, chantant dans la coupole!"* the Mardersteig edition, which Eliot himself supervised, emends the punctuation to read: "Et, o ces voix d'enfants chantant dans la coupole." This reading brings the quotation into accord with the published readings of Verlaine's text but out of accord with the poet's ear.[8] Much the same takes place with the alteration of *ceu* to *uti*, an alteration which has behind it only the dubious authority of *Collected Poems, 1909–1935*, even though it has been followed by all later editions. If it was Eliot's change, then it was Eliot acting as the officious custodian of his monument, and acting against the poet's ear.

Two more, quite minor changes must be noted, both in the poem's notes. The introductory headnote in both the Boni and Liveright and the

Hogarth editions mistakenly reports that Jessie Weston's book was published by Macmillan. In a presentation copy of the Hogarth which Eliot gave "to Mother from Tom. 14.ix.23," he corrected "Macmillan" to "Cambridge Univ. Press."[9] A briefer version of this change, simply to "Cambridge," was made in the Faber *Poems, 1909–1925*, remained in all subsequent editions, and is followed here. Also, in both the Boni and Liveright and Hogarth editions, the notes to lines 196 and 197 were reversed. They are silently corrected here.

Apart from these two obvious corrections to Eliot's notes, there are numerous matters of consistency in citing titles and punctuation which were left uncorrected not only in B and H but also in F and many subsequent editions. Eliot was plainly diffident about the notes and never devoted his attention to proofreading them. To cite one example, although the titles of books and other major works are routinely rendered in italics throughout the notes, the titles of Wagner's *Tristan und Isolde* and Dante's *Inferno* (notes to lines 31, 63, and 64) were left in roman in B, H, F, and many later editions, including *The Complete Poems and Plays*. But to leave the notes in this state merely creates or perpetuates pointless distractions. Moreover, it can be argued, whereas the text of the poem proper shows signs of Eliot's active editorial intervention in B, H, and F, the text of the notes does not, and is therefore devoid of his or any other authority. Errors of this kind, therefore, have been corrected, and the corrections have been duly noted in the Historical Collation that follows.

This edition, then, follows Eliot in adopting B as setting text; it admits the six corrections which he made to the text proper in 1923 *(H)* and 1925 *(F)* and the one alteration ("aethereal") he made in 1925 *(F)*; it admits the other alteration that he also made in 1925, the addition of the dedication to Ezra Pound; it also admits the alteration to the first note which he made in 1925 *(F)*; and it admits two further emendations (lines 14, 131) on the authority of the *Waste Land* manuscripts which Eliot wrote or typed and showed to Ezra Pound in early 1922. It rejects the (generally dubious) authority of all editions from 1936 on, including that of the autograph manuscript which Eliot prepared in 1960, which, after line 137, contained a line ("The ivory men make company between us") that had been in early typescripts of the poem but which never appeared in any printing prepared during Eliot's lifetime, including the 1962 Mardersteig, which Eliot himself on one occasion referred to as "the standard text."[10] In short, it presents the text that most closely conforms to Eliot's intentions during the period when he was actively concerned with and intervening in the text's shape and evolution.

A final point must be added concerning the poem's lineation. In the Boni and Liveright edition, what are lines 346 and 347 in *Collected Poems, 1909–1962* and many other editions were counted as a single line. Though the Hogarth edition did not include line numbers, it evidently presupposed the same lineation as Boni and Liveright, since the notes to all lines after these two used the same numerical references as did Boni and Liveright. The lineation also remained the same in *Poems, 1909–1925,* and it is therefore this earlier lineation which is followed here. To enhance ease of reference, however, the line number is given at every fifth line, rather than every tenth line as was done in all numbered editions during Eliot's lifetime.

Notes

1. True, the *Dial* could have saved eight days in requesting a setting copy from Eliot by telegraphing him, cutting down the minimum time to produce the poem from thirty-six to twenty-eight days. But since James Sibley Watson was presiding over the poem's publication in the *Dial,* having so actively intervened to secure it for the journal, he may also have recalled his experience with Eliot earlier in the summer. Though Eliot had promised Ezra Pound on 28 July that he would make a new copy of *The Waste Land* for Watson to read while still in Paris (*LOTSE,* 552), it was not till 16 August that the copy had finally arrived. If a similar delay of nineteen days were to occur now, Watson may have calculated, even a production process reduced to twenty-eight days would not have sufficed for the *Dial* to meet its schedule.
2. Four prepublication typescripts of the poem are known to exist. One is found among the *Dial* papers at the Beinecke Rare Book and Manuscript Library of Yale University. Another is housed in the James Sibley Watson, Jr., papers at the Berg Collection of the New York Public Library. A third is found among the papers of Jeanne Robert Foster at the Houghton Library of Harvard University. A fourth is housed in the John Hayward Collection at the library of King's College, Cambridge University. None of these served as setting copies, and all of them have a great many nonauthorial variants that are devoid of any authority.
3. The printers of the *Criterion* were Hazel, Watson & Viney, Ltd., located in Aylesbury, Buckinghamshire. See unpublished letter from T. S. Eliot to F. S. Flint, 22 September 1922, University of Texas, Harry Ransom Center for the Humanities.
4. Consider one other portion of the text, the poem's first part, in which Eliot had detected an alarming number of "undesired alterations made by the

printers" of the *Criterion*. Despite his efforts to remove these, the *Criterion* still has eleven variants when collated against the Boni and Liveright text. Two of these are substantives (*B*'s "And went on in sunlight" at line 10 becomes *C*'s "And went on in the sunlight," while *B*'s "One must be so careful these days" at line 58 becomes *C*'s "One must be so careful in these days"). Five are the result of quotation marks or inverted commas having been added to speeches (ll. 15, 16, 46, 47, 59), and two more are minor alterations of punctuation (the em dash is removed from line 37, the first exclamation point in line 76 is changed to a comma). One is a change of font (lines 31–34 are changed from italics to roman), and one is the addition of a blank line of space between lines 41 and 42. The *Dial,* instead, makes nine changes to the Boni and Liveright text. Three result from attempting to rationalize the treatment of quotations in a foreign language. Whereas the Boni and Liveright text had given lines 31–34 in italics but also used roman for lines 11, 42, and 76, the *Dial* text aimed for consistency and placed them all in italics (the *Criterion* text had tried to achieve consistency by the reverse procedure, putting lines 31–34 in roman). Another variant results from a similar attempt to rationalize capitalization. Since "hyacinth" was lowercase in lines 35 and 36, the *Dial* made "hyacinth" in lines 37 lowercase as well. Two more were spelling changes, altering the British usage "cruellest" to the American "cruelest" and correcting Liveright's erroneous German "Od'" to "Öd'." Yet another two were alterations of punctuation, eliminating the apparently superfluous comma at the end of line 26 and (in conformity with house style) dropping the period after "Mrs." One was a more serious error, the dropping of the blank line between lines 42 and 43. Minute variants in the spelling of three other words in the notes are recorded in the historical collation.

5. Unpublished letters from T. S. Eliot to Hermann Hesse, 24 and 31 May 1922, Schweizerisches Literaturarchiv; unpublished letter from T. S. Eliot to Ernst Curtius, 9 July 1922, Universitätsbibliothek, Bonn.

6. See A. D. Moody, *Thomas Stearns Eliot: Poet* (Cambridge: Cambridge University Press, 1979), 303.

7. "More widely accepted scholarly reading" understates the case. I know of no edition of the poem which reads "ceu." But the problem is more complicated than a simple opposition between "ceu" and "uti." Briefly, there are three manuscripts which contain the *Pervigilium Veneris*. One is the Codex Pithoeanus, named after Pierre Pithou (1539–1595), a French humanist who published the first edition of the poem in 1577. Another is the Codex Salmasianus, so called from the Latin form (*Salmasius*) of the name of Claude de Saumaise (1588–1653), a French scholar who owned it. In 1871 a third manuscript was discovered, now in Vienna and hence known as the Codex Vindobonensis, which is a copy of a lost manuscript, one made by the humanist Jacopo Sannazaro (1457–1530) sometime between 1503 and 1505. The three have different readings of the opening words to this line:

Pithoeanus: quando faciam ut celidon
Salmasianus: quando fiam ut caelidon
Vindobonensis: quando faciam ut chelidon

Since the Codex Salmasianus is older than Pithoeanus by two centuries, scholars have generally preferred its reading of *fiam* over *faciam*. Since *chelidon* (or "swallow") is the more correct and attested way of rendering this Greek word in ancient or late antique Latin, they have overwhelmingly chosen it over *celidon* and *caelidon,* a decision supported after 1871 by the testimony of Vindobonensis. The critical problem is the line's third word, *ut,* which makes no sense metrically. Another syllable is needed. In 1644 Andreas Rivinus (or Andreas Bachmann, 1601–1656) suggested *uti* as a speculative emendation. A slender majority of scholars have since adopted this reading, which makes good sense; yet *ceu* would also be a plausible emendation, though it would depart more sharply from the testimony of the manuscripts. I have examined some thirty editions of the poem and not found one which reads *ceu*. But *ceu* is clearly the reading, or even misreading, that Eliot had stored in his memory when he wrote *The Waste Land,* and throughout the period 1922–1925, when he was still actively involved with the text's evolution.

8. Moody, *Eliot,* 307.
9. Daniel Woodward, "Notes on the Publishing History and Text of *The Waste Land,*" *Papers of the Bibliographical Society of America* 58 (1964): 262.
10. Letter from T. S. Eliot to Daniel Woodward, 26 June 1963, cited in Woodward, "Notes," 264.

THE WASTE LAND

The Waste Land

"Nam Sibyllam quidem Cumis ego ipse oculis meis vidi in ampulla
pendere, et cum illi pueri dicerent: Σίβυλλα τί θέλεις; respondebat
illa: ἀποθανεῖν θέλω."

For Ezra Pound
il miglior fabbro

I. THE BURIAL OF THE DEAD

April is the cruellest month, breeding
Lilacs out of the dead land, mixing
Memory and desire, stirring
Dull roots with spring rain.
Winter kept us warm, covering   5
Earth in forgetful snow, feeding
A little life with dried tubers.
Summer surprised us, coming over the Starnbergersee
With a shower of rain; we stopped in the colonnade,
And went on in sunlight, into the Hofgarten,   10
And drank coffee, and talked for an hour.
Bin gar keine Russin, stamm' aus Litauen, echt deutsch.
And when we were children, staying at the archduke's,
My cousin's, he took me out on a sled,
And I was frightened. He said, Marie,   15
Marie, hold on tight. And down we went.

In the mountains, there you feel free.
I read, much of the night, and go south in the winter.

What are the roots that clutch, what branches grow
Out of this stony rubbish? Son of man,   20
You cannot say, or guess, for you know only
A heap of broken images, where the sun beats,
And the dead tree gives no shelter, the cricket no relief,
And the dry stone no sound of water. Only
There is shadow under this red rock,   25
(Come in under the shadow of this red rock),
And I will show you something different from either
Your shadow at morning striding behind you
Or your shadow at evening rising to meet you;
I will show you fear in a handful of dust.   30

    Frisch weht der Wind
    Der Heimat zu,
    Mein Irisch Kind,
    Wo weilest du?

"You gave me hyacinths first a year ago;   35
"They called me the hyacinth girl."
—Yet when we came back, late, from the Hyacinth Garden,
Your arms full, and your hair wet, I could not
Speak, and my eyes failed, I was neither
Living nor dead, and I knew nothing,   40
Looking into the heart of light, the silence.
Öd' und leer das Meer.

Madame Sosostris, famous clairvoyante,
Had a bad cold, nevertheless
Is known to be the wisest woman in Europe,   45
With a wicked pack of cards. Here, said she,
Is your card, the drowned Phoenician Sailor,
(Those are pearls that were his eyes. Look!)
Here is Belladonna, the Lady of the Rocks,
The lady of situations.   50

Here is the man with three staves, and here the Wheel,
And here is the one-eyed merchant, and this card,
Which is blank, is something he carries on his back,
Which I am forbidden to see. I do not find
The Hanged Man. Fear death by water.   55
I see crowds of people, walking round in a ring.
Thank you. If you see dear Mrs. Equitone,
Tell her I bring the horoscope myself.
One must be so careful these days.

Unreal City,   60
Under the brown fog of a winter dawn,
A crowd flowed over London Bridge, so many,
I had not thought death had undone so many.
Sighs, short and infrequent, were exhaled,
And each man fixed his eyes before his feet.   65
Flowed up the hill and down King William Street,
To where Saint Mary Woolnoth kept the hours
With a dead sound on the final stroke of nine.
There I saw one I knew, and stopped him, crying: "Stetson!
"You who were with me in the ships at Mylae!   70
"That corpse you planted last year in your garden,
"Has it begun to sprout? Will it bloom this year?
"Or has the sudden frost disturbed its bed?
"Oh keep the Dog far hence, that's friend to men,
"Or with his nails he'll dig it up again!   75
"You! hypocrite lecteur! —mon semblable, —mon frère!"

II. A GAME OF CHESS
The Chair she sat in, like a burnished throne,
Glowed on the marble, where the glass
Held up by standards wrought with fruited vines
From which a golden Cupidon peeped out   80
(Another hid his eyes behind his wing)
Doubled the flames of sevenbranched candelabra
Reflecting light upon the table as
The glitter of her jewels rose to meet it,

From satin cases poured in rich profusion;   85
In vials of ivory and coloured glass
Unstoppered, lurked her strange synthetic perfumes,
Unguent, powdered, or liquid—troubled, confused
And drowned the sense in odours; stirred by the air
That freshened from the window, these ascended   90
In fattening the prolonged candle-flames,
Flung their smoke into the laquearia,
Stirring the pattern on the coffered ceiling.
Huge sea-wood fed with copper
Burned green and orange, framed by the coloured stone,   95
In which sad light a carvèd dolphin swam.
Above the antique mantel was displayed
As though a window gave upon the sylvan scene
The change of Philomel, by the barbarous king
So rudely forced; yet there the nightingale   100
Filled all the desert with inviolable voice
And still she cried, and still the world pursues,
"Jug Jug" to dirty ears.
And other withered stumps of time
Were told upon the walls; staring forms   105
Leaned out, leaning, hushing the room enclosed.
Footsteps shuffled on the stair.
Under the firelight, under the brush, her hair
Spread out in fiery points
Glowed into words, then would be savagely still.   110

"My nerves are bad to-night. Yes, bad. Stay with me.
"Speak to me. Why do you never speak? Speak.
"What are you thinking of? What thinking? What?
"I never know what you are thinking. Think."

I think we are in rats' alley   115
Where the dead men lost their bones.

"What is that noise?"
                        The wind under the door.

"What is that noise now? What is the wind doing?"
Nothing again nothing.   120
"Do
"You know nothing? Do you see nothing? Do you remember
"Nothing?"
I remember
Those are pearls that were his eyes.   125
"Are you alive, or not? Is there nothing in your head?"
But
O O O O that Shakespeherian Rag—
It's so elegant
So intelligent   130

"What shall I do now? What shall I do?
"I shall rush out as I am, and walk the street
"With my hair down, so. What shall we do tomorrow?
"What shall we ever do?"
The hot water at ten.   135
And if it rains, a closed car at four.
And we shall play a game of chess,
Pressing lidless eyes and waiting for a knock upon the door.

When Lil's husband got demobbed, I said—
I didn't mince my words, I said to her myself,   140
HURRY UP PLEASE IT'S TIME
Now Albert's coming back, make yourself a bit smart.
He'll want to know what you done with that money he gave you
To get yourself some teeth. He did, I was there.
You have them all out, Lil, and get a nice set,   145
He said, I swear, I can't bear to look at you.
And no more can't I, I said, and think of poor Albert,
He's been in the army four years, he wants a good time,
And if you don't give it him, there's others will, I said.
Oh is there, she said. Something o' that, I said.   150
Then I'll know who to thank, she said, and give me a straight look.
HURRY UP PLEASE IT'S TIME
If you don't like it you can get on with it, I said,

Others can pick and choose, if you can't.
But if Albert makes off, it won't be for lack of telling.   155
You ought to be ashamed, I said, to look so antique.
(And her only thirty-one.)
I can't help it, she said, pulling a long face,
It's them pills I took, to bring it off, she said.
(She's had five already, and nearly died of young George.)   160
The chemist said it would be all right, but I've never been the same.
You *are* a proper fool, I said.
Well, if Albert won't leave you alone, there it is, I said,
What you get married for if you don't want children?
HURRY UP PLEASE IT'S TIME   165
Well, that Sunday Albert was home, they had a hot gammon,
And they asked me in to dinner, to get the beauty of it hot—
HURRY UP PLEASE IT'S TIME
HURRY UP PLEASE IT'S TIME
Goonight Bill. Goonight Lou. Goonight May. Goonight.   170
Ta ta. Goonight. Goonight.
Good night, ladies, good night, sweet ladies, good night, good night.

III. THE FIRE SERMON

The river's tent is broken: the last fingers of leaf
Clutch and sink into the wet bank. The wind
Crosses the brown land, unheard. The nymphs are departed.   175
Sweet Thames, run softly, till I end my song.
The river bears no empty bottles, sandwich papers,
Silk handkerchiefs, cardboard boxes, cigarette ends
Or other testimony of summer nights. The nymphs are departed.
And their friends, the loitering heirs of city directors;   180
Departed, have left no addresses.
By the waters of Leman I sat down and wept . . .
Sweet Thames, run softly till I end my song,
Sweet Thames, run softly, for I speak not loud or long.

But at my back in a cold blast I hear   185
The rattle of the bones, and chuckle spread from ear to ear.

A rat crept softly through the vegetation
Dragging its slimy belly on the bank
While I was fishing in the dull canal
On a winter evening round behind the gashouse   190
Musing upon the king my brother's wreck
And on the king my father's death before him.
White bodies naked on the low damp ground
And bones cast in a little low dry garret,
Rattled by the rat's foot only, year to year.   195
But at my back from time to time I hear
The sound of horns and motors, which shall bring
Sweeney to Mrs. Porter in the spring.
O the moon shone bright on Mrs. Porter
And on her daughter   200
They wash their feet in soda water
Et O ces voix d'enfants, chantant dans la coupole!

Twit twit twit
Jug jug jug jug jug jug
So rudely forc'd.   205
Tereu

Unreal City
Under the brown fog of a winter noon
Mr. Eugenides, the Smyrna merchant
Unshaven, with a pocket full of currants   210
C.i.f. London: documents at sight,
Asked me in demotic French
To luncheon at the Cannon Street Hotel
Followed by a weekend at the Metropole.

At the violet hour, when the eyes and back   215
Turn upward from the desk, when the human engine waits

Like a taxi throbbing waiting,
I Tiresias, though blind, throbbing between two lives,
Old man with wrinkled female breasts, can see
At the violet hour, the evening hour that strives   220
Homeward, and brings the sailor home from sea,
The typist home at teatime, clears her breakfast, lights
Her stove, and lays out food in tins.
Out of the window perilously spread
Her drying combinations touched by the sun's last rays,   225
On the divan are piled (at night her bed)
Stockings, slippers, camisoles, and stays.
I Tiresias, old man with wrinkled dugs
Perceived the scene, and foretold the rest—
I too awaited the expected guest.   230
He, the young man carbuncular, arrives,
A small house agent's clerk, with one bold stare,
One of the low on whom assurance sits
As a silk hat on a Bradford millionaire.
The time is now propitious, as he guesses,   235
The meal is ended, she is bored and tired,
Endeavours to engage her in caresses
Which still are unreproved, if undesired.
Flushed and decided, he assaults at once;
Exploring hands encounter no defence;   240
His vanity requires no response,
And makes a welcome of indifference.
(And I Tiresias have foresuffered all
Enacted on this same divan or bed;
I who have sat by Thebes below the wall   245
And walked among the lowest of the dead.)
Bestows one final patronising kiss,
And gropes his way, finding the stairs unlit . . .

She turns and looks a moment in the glass,
Hardly aware of her departed lover;   250
Her brain allows one half-formed thought to pass:

"Well now that's done: and I'm glad it's over."
When lovely woman stoops to folly and
Paces about her room again, alone,
She smoothes her hair with automatic hand,   255
And puts a record on the gramophone.

"This music crept by me upon the waters"
And along the Strand, up Queen Victoria Street.
O City City, I can sometimes hear
Beside a public bar in Lower Thames Street,   260
The pleasant whining of a mandoline
And a clatter and a chatter from within
Where fishmen lounge at noon: where the walls
Of Magnus Martyr hold
Inexplicable splendour of Ionian white and gold.   265

The river sweats
Oil and tar
The barges drift
With the turning tide
Red sails   270
Wide
To leeward, swing on the heavy spar.
The barges wash
Drifting logs
Down Greenwich reach   275
Past the Isle of Dogs.
              Weialala leia
              Wallala leialala
Elizabeth and Leicester
Beating oars   280
The stern was formed
A gilded shell
Red and gold
The brisk swell
Rippled both shores   285

Southwest wind
Carried down stream
The peal of bells
White towers
　　　　Weialala leia　　　　　　　　　　　　　　290
　　　　Wallala leialala

"Trams and dusty trees.
Highbury bore me. Richmond and Kew
Undid me. By Richmond I raised my knees
Supine on the floor of a narrow canoe."　　　　　295

"My feet are at Moorgate, and my heart
Under my feet. After the event
He wept. He promised 'a new start.'
I made no comment. What should I resent?"

"On Margate Sands.　　　　　　　　　　　　　　300
I can connect
Nothing with nothing.
The broken fingernails of dirty hands.
My people humble people who expect
Nothing."　　　　　　　　　　　　　　　　　　305
　　　　la la

To Carthage then I came

Burning　burning　burning　burning
O Lord Thou pluckest me out
O Lord Thou pluckest　　　　　　　　　　　　　310

burning

IV. DEATH BY WATER
Phlebas the Phoenician, a fortnight dead,
Forgot the cry of gulls, and the deep sea swell
And the profit and loss.

A current under sea   315
Picked his bones in whispers. As he rose and fell
He passed the stages of his age and youth
Entering the whirlpool.
                    Gentile or Jew
O you who turn the wheel and look to windward,   320
Consider Phlebas, who was once handsome and tall as you.

V. WHAT THE THUNDER SAID
After the torchlight red on sweaty faces
After the frosty silence in the gardens
After the agony in stony places
The shouting and the crying   325
Prison and palace and reverberation
Of thunder of spring over distant mountains
He who was living is now dead
We who were living are now dying
With a little patience   330

Here is no water but only rock
Rock and no water and the sandy road
The road winding above among the mountains
Which are mountains of rock without water
If there were water we should stop and drink   335
Amongst the rock we cannot stop or think
Sweat is dry and feet are in the sand
If there were only water amongst the rock
Dead mountain mouth of carious teeth that cannot spit
Here one can neither stand nor lie nor sit   340
There is not even silence in the mountains
But dry sterile thunder without rain
There is not even solitude in the mountains
But red sullen faces sneer and snarl
From doors of mudcracked houses   345
                         If there were water
And no rock
If there were rock

And also water
And water
A spring   350
A pool among the rock
If there were the sound of water only
Not the cicada
And dry grass singing
But sound of water over a rock   355
Where the hermit-thrush sings in the pine trees
Drop drop drip drop drop drop drop
But there is no water

Who is the third who walks always beside you?
When I count, there are only you and I together   360
But when I look ahead up the white road
There is always another one walking beside you
Gliding wrapt in a brown mantle, hooded
I do not know whether a man or a woman
—But who is that on the other side of you?   365
What is that sound high in the air
Murmur of maternal lamentation
Who are those hooded hordes swarming
Over endless plains, stumbling in cracked earth
Ringed by the horizon only   370
What is the city over the mountains
Cracks and reforms and bursts in the violet air
Falling towers
Jerusalem Athens Alexandria
Vienna London   375
Unreal

A woman drew her long black hair out tight
And fiddled whisper music on those strings
And bats with baby faces in the violet light
Whistled, and beat their wings   380
And crawled head downward down a blackened wall
And upside down in air were towers

Tolling reminiscent bells, that kept the hours
And voices singing out of empty cisterns and exhausted wells.

In this decayed hole among the mountains 385
In the faint moonlight, the grass is singing
Over the tumbled graves, about the chapel
There is the empty chapel, only the wind's home,
It has no windows, and the door swings,
Dry bones can harm no one. 390
Only a cock stood on the rooftree
Co co rico   co co rico
In a flash of lightning. Then a damp gust
Bringing rain

Ganga was sunken, and the limp leaves 395
Waited for rain, while the black clouds
Gathered far distant, over Himavant.
The jungle crouched, humped in silence.
Then spoke the thunder
DA 400
Datta: what have we given?
My friend, blood shaking my heart
The awful daring of a moment's surrender
Which an age of prudence can never retract
By this, and this only, we have existed 405
Which is not to be found in our obituaries
Or in memories draped by the beneficent spider
Or under seals broken by the lean solicitor
In our empty rooms
DA 410
Dayadhvam: I have heard the key
Turn in the door once and turn once only
We think of the key, each in his prison
Thinking of the key, each confirms a prison

Only at nightfall, aethereal rumours   415
Revive for a moment a broken Coriolanus
DA
Damyata: The boat responded
Gaily, to the hand expert with sail and oar
The sea was calm, your heart would have responded   420
Gaily, when invited, beating obedient
To controlling hands

I sat upon the shore
Fishing, with the arid plain behind me
Shall I at least set my lands in order?   425

London Bridge is falling down falling down falling down
Poi s'ascose nel foco che gli affina
Quando fiam ceu chelidon — O swallow swallow
Le Prince d'Aquitaine à la tour abolie
These fragments I have shored against my ruins   430
Why then Ile fit you. Hieronymo's mad againe.
Datta. Dayadhvam. Damyata.

    Shantih   shantih   shantih

Notes

Not only the title, but the plan and a good deal of the incidental symbolism
of the poem were suggested by Miss Jessie L. Weston's book on the Grail legend:
From Ritual to Romance (Cambridge). Indeed, so deeply am I indebted, Miss
Weston's book will elucidate the difficulties of the poem much better than my
notes can do; and I recommend it (apart from the great interest of the book itself)
to any who think such elucidation of the poem worth the trouble. To another
work of anthropology I am indebted in general, one which has influenced our
generation profoundly; I mean *The Golden Bough;* I have used especially the two
volumes *Adonis, Attis, Osiris.* Anyone who is acquainted with these works will
immediately recognise in the poem certain references to vegetation ceremonies.

I. THE BURIAL OF THE DEAD

Line 20. Cf. Ezekiel II, i.

23. Cf. Ecclesiastes XII, v.

31. V. *Tristan und Isolde,* I, verses 5–8.

42. Id. III, verse 24.

46. I am not familiar with the exact constitution of the Tarot pack of cards, from
which I have obviously departed to suit my own convenience. The Hanged
Man, a member of the traditional pack, fits my purpose in two ways: because
he is associated in my mind with the Hanged God of Frazer, and because
I associate him with the hooded figure in the passage of the disciples
in Part V. The Phoenician Sailor and the Merchant appear later; also the
"crowds of people," and Death by Water is executed in Part IV. The Man
with Three Staves (an authentic member of the Tarot pack) I associate,
quite arbitrarily, with the Fisher King himself.

60. Cf. Baudelaire:

> "Fourmillante cité, cité pleine de rêves,
> "Où le spectre en plein jour raccroche le passant."

63. Cf. *Inferno* III, 55–57:

> "Si lunga tratta
> "di gente, ch'io non avrei mai creduto
> "che morte tanta n'avesse disfatta."

64. Cf. *Inferno* IV, 25–27:

> "Quivi, secondo che per ascoltare,
> "non avea pianto, ma' che di sospiri,
> "che l'aura eterna facevan tremare."

68. A phenomenon which I have often noticed.

74. Cf. The Dirge in Webster's *White Devil.*

76. V. Baudelaire, Preface to *Fleurs du Mal.*

II. A GAME OF CHESS

77. Cf. *Antony and Cleopatra,* II, ii, l. 190.

92. Laquearia. V. *Aeneid,* I, 726:

> "dependent lychni laquearibus aureis
> incensi, et noctem flammis funalia vincunt."

98. Sylvan scene. V. Milton, *Paradise Lost*, IV, 140.
99. V. Ovid, *Metamorphoses*, VI, Philomela.
100. Cf. Part III, l. 204.
115. Cf. Part III, l. 195.
118. Cf. Webster: "Is the wind in that door still?"
126. Cf. Part I, ll. 37, 48.
138. Cf. the game of chess in Middleton's *Women Beware Women*.

III. THE FIRE SERMON
176. Spenser, *Prothalamion*.
192. Cf. *The Tempest*, I, ii.
196. Cf. Marvell, "To His Coy Mistress."
197. Cf. Day, *Parliament of Bees*:

> "When of the sudden, listening, you shall hear,
> "A noise of horns and hunting, which shall bring
> "Actaeon to Diana in the spring,
> "Where all shall see her naked skin . . ."

199. I do not know the origin of the ballad from which these lines are taken;
it was reported to me from Sydney, Australia.
202. V. Verlaine, "Parsifal."
210. The currants were quoted at a price "carriage and insurance free to
London"; and the Bill of Lading etc. were to be handed to the buyer
upon payment of the sight draft.
218. Tiresias, although a mere spectator and not indeed a "character," is yet the
most important personage in the poem, uniting all the rest. Just as the one-
eyed merchant, seller of currants, melts into the Phoenician Sailor, and
the latter is not wholly distinct from Ferdinand Prince of Naples, so all the
women are one woman, and the two sexes meet in Tiresias. What Tiresias
sees, in fact, is the substance of the poem. The whole passage from Ovid
is of great anthropological interest:

> ". . . Cum Iunone iocos et maior vestra profecto est
> Quam, quae contingit maribus," dixisse, "voluptas."
> Illa negat; placuit quae sit sententia docti
> Quaerere Tiresiae: venus huic erat utraque nota.
> Nam duo magnorum viridi coeuntia silva
> Corpora serpentum baculi violaverat ictu
> Deque viro factus, mirabile, femina septem
> Egerat autumnos; octavo rursus eosdem
> Vidit et "est vestrae si tanta potentia plagae,"
> Dixit, "ut auctoris sortem in contraria mutet,
> Nunc quoque vos feriam!" percussis anguibus isdem
> Forma prior rediit genetivaque venit imago.

Arbiter hic igitur sumptus de lite iocosa
Dicta Iovis firmat; gravius Saturnia iusto
Nec pro materia fertur doluisse suique
Iudicis aeterna damnavit lumina nocte,
At pater onmipotens (neque enim licet inrita cuiquam
Facta dei fecisse deo) pro lumine adempto
Scire futura dedit poenamque levavit honore.

221. This may not appear as exact as Sappho's lines, but I had in mind the "longshore" or "dory" fisherman, who returns at nightfall.

253. V. Goldsmith, the song in *The Vicar of Wakefield*.

257. V. *The Tempest*, as above.

264. The interior of St. Magnus Martyr is to my mind one of the finest among Wren's interiors. See *The Proposed Demolition of Nineteen City Churches* (P. S. King & Son Ltd.).

266. The song of the (three) Thames-daughters begins here. From line 292 to 306 inclusive they speak in turn. V. *Götterdämmerung*, III, i: the Rhine-daughters.

276. V. Froude, *Elizabeth*, Vol. I, ch. iv, letter of De Quadra to Philip of Spain: "In the afternoon we were in a barge, watching the games on the river. (The queen) was alone with Lord Robert and myself on the poop, when they began to talk nonsense, and went so far that Lord Robert at last said, as I was on the spot there was no reason why they should not be married if the queen pleased."

293. Cf. *Purgatorio*, V. 133:

"Ricorditi di me, che son la Pia;
"Siena mi fe', disfecemi Maremma."

307. V. St. Augustine's *Confessions*: "to Carthage then I came, where a cauldron of unholy loves sang all about mine ears."

308. The complete text of the Buddha's Fire Sermon (which corresponds in importance to the Sermon the Mount) from which these words are taken, will be found translated in the late Henry Clarke Warren's *Buddhism in Translation* (Harvard Oriental Series). Mr. Warren was one of the great pioneers of Buddhist studies in the occident.

312. From St. Augustine's *Confessions* again. The collocation of these two representatives of eastern and western asceticism, as the culmination of this part of the poem, is not an accident.

V. WHAT THE THUNDER SAID
In the first part of Part V three themes are employed: the journey to Emmaus, the approach to the Chapel Perilous (see Miss Weston's book) and the present decay of eastern Europe.

357. This is *Turdus aonalaschkae pallasii*, the hermit-thrush which I have heard in Quebec County. Chapman says (*Handbook of Birds of Eastern North America*) "it is most at home in secluded woodland and thickety retreats. . . . Its notes are not remarkable for variety or volume, but in purity and sweetness of

tone and exquisite modulation they are unequaled." Its "water-dripping song" is justly celebrated.

360. The following lines were stimulated by the account of one of the Antarctic expeditions (I forget which, but I think one of Shackleton's): it was related that the party of explorers, at the extremity of their strength, had the constant delusion that there was *one more member* than could actually be counted.

366–76. Cf. Hermann Hesse, *Blick ins Chaos:* "Schon ist halb Europa, schon ist zumindest der halbe Osten Europas auf dem Wege zum Chaos, fährt betrunken im heiligen Wahn am Abgrund entlang und singt dazu, singt betrunken und hymnisch wie Dmitri Karamasoff sang. Ueber diese Lieder lacht der Bürger beleidigt, der Heilige and Seher hört sie mit Tränen."

401. "Datta, dayadhvam, damyata" (Give, sympathise, control). The fable of the Thunder is found in the *Brihadaranyaka-Upanishad,* 5, I. A translation is found in Deussen's *Sechzig Unpanishads des Veda,* p. 489.

407. Cf. Webster, *The White Devil,* V. vi:

> ". . . they'll remarry
> "Ere the worm pierce your winding-sheet, ere the spider
> "Make a thin curtain for your epitaphs."

411. Cf. *Inferno,* XXXIII, 46:

> "ed io sentii chiavar l'uscio di sotto
> "all'orribile torre."

Also F. H. Bradley, *Appearance and Reality,* p. 346.

> "My external sensations are no less private to myself than are my thoughts or my feelings. In either case my experience falls within my own circle, a circle closed on the outside; and, with all its elements alike, every sphere is opaque to the others which surround it. . . . In brief, regarded as an existence which appears in a soul, the whole world for each is peculiar and private to that soul."

424. V. Weston: *From Ritual to Romance;* chapter on the Fisher King.

427. V. *Purgatorio,* XXVI, 148.

> "'Ara vos prec, per aquella valor
> 'Que vos guida al som de l'escalina,
> 'Sovegna vos a temps de ma dolor.'
> Poi s'ascose nel foco che gli affina."

428. V. *Pervigilium Veneris.* Cf. Philomela in Parts II and III.

429. V. Gerard de Nerval, Sonnet "El Desdichado."

431. V. Kyd's *Spanish Tragedy.*

433. Shantih. Repeated as here, a formal ending to an Upanishad. "The Peace which passeth understanding" is a feeble translation of the content of this word.

1 The Arcade of the Hofgarten, Munich, c. 1910 (Courtesy Stadtarchiv München)

2 The Arcade Café in the Hofgarten, Munich, c. 1910 (Courtesy Stadtarchiv München)

3 Aerial view of the Hofgarten, Munich, c. 1910 (Courtesy Stadtarchiv München)

4 London Bridge, 1914 (© Museum of London)

5 King William Street, intersection with Eastcheap, London, c. 1920. The statue of King William IV was removed in 1935. (Courtesy Brian Girling Collection)

6 St. Mary Woolnoth, London, as it appeared in Eliot's time (From London County Council, *Proposed Demolition of Nineteen City Churches* [London: London County Council, 1920])

7 St. Mary Woolnoth, London, a more recent view (© Bob Mankeshaw LRPS, www.imagesofengland.org.uk)

8 Lloyds Bank, Cornhill Street facade, London, c. 1920 (Courtesy Guildhall Library, Corporation of London)

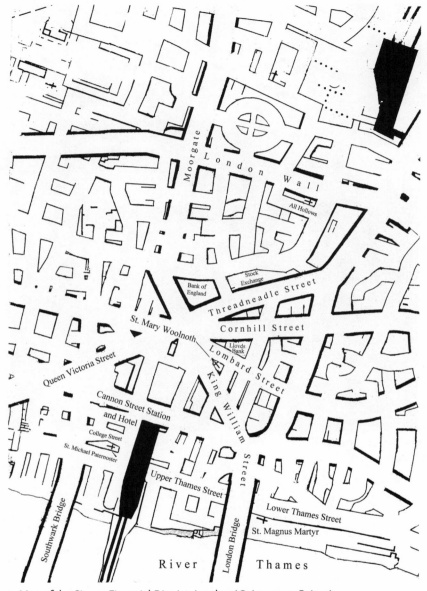

9 Map of the City, or Financial District, London (© Lawrence Rainey)

10 Cannon Street Station and Hotel, London, c. 1910 (Courtesy National Railway Museum, York)

11 Hotel Metropole, Brighton, c. 1910 (© The Royal Pavilion Libraries and Museums [Brighton and Hove])

12 Lower Thames Street, exterior of St. Magnus Martyr, London, c. 1920 (From London
County Council, *Proposed Demolition of Nineteen City Churches* [London: London County
Council, 1920])

13 Lower Thames Street, exterior of St. Magnus Martyr, London, c. 1910 (Courtesy Brian Girling Collection)

14 Interior of St. Magnus Martyr, London (Courtesy Kerry Downes)

15 Margate Sands, Margate (Courtesy Margate Local History Museum)

16 St. Michael Paternoster, London, 1920 (From London County Council, *Proposed Demolition of Nineteen City Churches* [London: London County Council, 1920])

Editor's Annotations to *The Waste Land*

Epigraph: "For on one occasion I myself saw, with my own eyes, the Cumaean
   Sibyl hanging in a cage, and when some boys said to her, 'Sibyl, what do you
   want?' she replied, 'I want to die.'" This account is given by Trimalchio, a
   character in the *Satyricon,* the satirical novel written by the Roman writer
   Petronius in the first century A.D. Trimalchio is a wealthy vulgarian who is
   hosting a dinner which occupies the novel's middle section; he is vying with
   his guests, trying to surpass their tales of wonder, but merely muddles up
   commonplace stories of Hercules and Ulysses before turning to his account
   of the Cumaean sibyl. His anecdote, in other words, is partly a species of
   braggadocio and may even be a lie, and it is partly an excuse for him to prove
   that he can speak, as well as read, Greek.

   There were as many as ten sibyls in the ancient world, prophetesses
whom the ancient Greeks and Romans consulted about the future, but the
most famous was the Cumaean Sibyl, whose oracular cavern was rediscovered by archaeologists at the site of ancient Cumae near Naples in 1934.
Her prophecies were delivered in Greek hexameter verses inscribed on palm
leaves and placed at the mouth of her cave. If no one came to collect them,
they were scattered by the winds and never read. One collection of such
verses was put in the charge of a special priestly college in Rome, guarded in
subterranean chambers beneath the temple of Jove on the Capitoline Hill.
After they were destroyed in 83 B.C. when the temple burned, a new collection was made to replace them.

   The Cumaean Sibyl figures prominently in Virgil's *Fourth Eclogue,*
where she delivers a prophecy which Christians later interpreted as foreshad-
owing the birth of Christ. She is also described at length in Virgil's *Aeneid*

VI, 1–155, where she tells Aeneas that he must find a golden bough in order
to enter the underworld. She also figures in Ovid's *Metamorphoses* XIV, 101–
153, the account to which Trimalchio alludes. Promised by Apollo that she
could have one wish fulfilled, whatever it might be, she chose to live as many
years as the grains of sand she could hold in her hand; but she forgot to
choose eternal youth, and was condemned to grow ever older and more
shriveled.

   In the prepublication version of *The Waste Land* the poem's epigraph
was taken from Joseph Conrad's *Heart of Darkness* (1900), as the narrator recounts the death of Kurtz: "Did he live his life again in every detail of desire,
temptation, and surrender during that supreme moment of complete knowledge? He cried in a whisper at some image, at some vision—he cried out
twice, a cry that was no more than breath—'The horror! the horror!'"

   Ezra Pound, writing to Eliot on 24 January 1922 (incorrectly assigned
to 24 December 1921 by Valerie Eliot in *LOTSE*, 497), wrote: "I doubt if Conrad is weighty enough to stand the citation." Eliot replied, probably on 26
January (incorrectly assigned by Valerie Eliot to [24? January]), "Do you mean
not use Conrad quot. or simply not put Conrad's name to it? It is much the
most appropriate I can find, and somewhat elucidative." Pound, responding
on 28 January, told Eliot to "Do as you like . . . re the Conrad; who am I to
grudge him his laurel crown." See *LOTSE*, 504–505.

Dedication: "the better craftsman" in Italian. Eliot dedicates the poem to Ezra
   Pound with the phrase that registers Dante's tribute to the Provençal poet
   Arnaut Daniel, who flourished between 1180 and 1200; see *Purgatorio* XXVI,
   117. The dedication first appeared in a presentation copy which Eliot gave
   Pound in January 1923; it was published for the first time in 1925 when *The
   Waste Land* was included in *Poems, 1909–1925*. For Pound's role in shaping
   the poem, see the Introduction, 23–25.

The Burial of the Dead: "The Order for the Burial of the Dead" prescribes the
   words and actions of a burial service within the Church of England; the text
   appears in the *Book of Common Prayer*.

1–2: Critics often compare this account of April with the opening to the General
   Prologue to *The Canterbury Tales* by Geoffrey Chaucer (1343?–1400), which
   adopts a more conventional and cheerful treatment of spring.

7 [a little life]: Perhaps an echo from "To Our Ladies of Death," a poem by James
   Thomson (1834–1882): "Our Mother feedeth thus our little life, / That we in
   turn may feed her with our death." Compare also Thomson's, "The City of
   Dreadful Night,"

   This little life is all we must endure,
   The grave's most holy peace is ever sure,
   We fall asleep and never wake again;
   Nothing is of us but the mouldering flesh,
   Whose elements dissolve and merge afresh
   In earth, air, water, plants, and other men.

Yet the phrase "a little life" is hardly unique to Thomson. It occurs repeatedly in Christian writing which compares the "little life" of man to the vast designs of God.

8 [Starnbergersee]: The German name for Lake Starnberger, which is located fifteen kilometers (roughly nine miles) from Munich. Eliot visited the city in 1911.

10 [Hofgarten]: "Court Garden" in German. The Hofgarten, which is located in the heart of Munich, dates to the seventeenth century and stands opposite the Residenz, a sprawling building that until 1918 was the home of the Wittelsbach family, the ruling house of Bavaria. One side of the Hofgarten abuts a tall arcade, the "colonnade" referred to in line 9 (see Fig. 1), while just beyond the arcade is the Arcade Café (see Fig. 2), situated within the Hofgarten (see Fig. 3).

12 [Bin gar keine Russin . . . echt deutsch]: "I am not a Russian, I come from Lithuania, a real German" (German).

15 [Marie]: In her notes to *The Waste Land: A Facsimile and Transcription of the Original Drafts* (hereafter *TWL:AF*), Valerie Eliot states that Eliot "met" the Countess Marie Larisch, though "when and where is not known," and that "his description of the sledding . . . was taken verbatim from a conversation he had with" her (p. 126). Marie Larisch (1858–1940) was the illegitimate daughter of Ludwig Wilhelm, heir to the throne of Bavaria, and Henriette Mendel, a commoner. In 1859 Marie's father renounced his claim to the throne and married her mother. Around 1874 Marie went to live with Ludwig's sister, her aunt, who was Empress Elizabeth of Austria, and she became a companion to the empress's son and the heir to the throne, Archduke Rudolf. In 1877 Marie married Georg, Count Larisch von Moennich. In 1889 the archduke was found dead, together with his mistress, and it became known that Marie had served as a go-between for them, leaving her in disgrace. To justify her conduct she later wrote *My Past: Reminiscences of the Courts of Austria and Bavaria, together with the True Story of Events Leading up to the Tragic Death of Rudolph, Crown Prince of Austria* (London: Bell and Sons; New York: Putnam, 1913). In 1950 the book was rediscovered by a scholar of Eliot's work, and for some twenty years, until Valerie Eliot published her account in 1971, it was thought to have served as a source for *The Waste Land*.

19–20 [What the roots . . . stony rubbish]: Perhaps an echo of Job 8:16–17. "He is green before the sun, and his branch shooteth forth in his garden. His roots are wrapped about the heap, and seeth the place of stones."

20 [Son of man]: Eliot's note cites Ezekiel 2:1. "And he said unto me, Son of man, stand upon they feet, and I will speak unto thee." Thereafter "son of man" becomes the form in which God addresses the prophet Ezekiel.

22 [broken images]: Perhaps an echo of Ezekiel 6:4, in which God judges the people of Israel for worshiping idols: "And your altars shall be desolate, and your images shall be broken: and I will cast down your slain men before your idols."

23 [And the dead tree . . . no relief]: Eliot's note cites Ecclesiastes 12:5, which describes the "evil days" that come when men are old and declining into darkness: "Also when they shall be afraid of that which is high, and fears shall
   be in the way, and the almond tree shall flourish, and the grasshopper shall
   be a burden, and desire shall fail: because man goeth to his long home, and
   the mourners go about in the streets." Compare Eliot's comments on Ecclesiastes in "Prose and Verse," 162–163.

26 [Come in . . . this red rock]: Perhaps an echo of Isaiah 2:10: "Enter into the
   rock and hide thee in the dust, for fear of the Lord." Or perhaps an echo of
   a more consoling prophecy in Isaiah 32:2: "And a man shall be as a hiding
   place from the wind, and a covert from the tempest; as rivers of water in a
   dry place, as the shadow of a great rock in a weary land."

28–29 [Your shadow . . . rising to meet you]: Perhaps an echo from a speech
   by the title character in the play *Philaster* by Francis Beaumont and John
   Fletcher (written around 1608–1610). Philaster is a young prince who, like
   Hamlet, has been unfairly dispossessed of his kingdom; he is in love with
   Arethusa, daughter of the king, the man who has dispossessed him. Megra,
   a lady of the court, has falsely accused Arethusa of having a love affair with
   someone else, and her charge has been reinforced by Dion, a trusted cour-
   tier who, wanting to force Philaster into open rebellion against the king,
   has sworn that he knows it to be true. Philaster believes the accusation, and
   longs to travel to "some far place / Where never womankind durst set her
   foot," a place where he will "preach to birds and beasts / What woman is
   and help to save them from you"—that is, from women in general. There
   he will deliver a homily to the animals which will show

> How that foolish man
> That reads the story of a woman's face
> And dies believing it is lost forever.
> How all the good you have is but a shadow
> I'th' morning with you and at night behind you,
> Past and forgotten. (III.ii.132–137)

As used by Eliot, the relevant phrases have been stripped of their amorous
and gender-bound context and applied to humans in general.

31–34 [*Frisch weht . . . weilest du*]: As Eliot notes, his quotation is from the opera
   Tristan und Isolde (1865) by Richard Wagner (1813–1883), I.i.5–8. "Fresh
   blows the wind / To the homeland / My Irish child, / Where are you tarry-
   ing?" (German). The scene opens on a ship that is transporting Isolde
   from Cornwall to Ireland, where she is to marry King Mark. She is accompanied by Tristan, the king's nephew. From the ship's rigging, a sailor's
   voice resounds with a melancholy song about an Irish woman left behind,
   which includes the lines transcribed by Eliot. Later in the opera, Isolde
   decides to kill both Tristan and herself with poison; but her companion,

Brangäne, substitutes a love potion for the poison, and the two fall hope-
lessly in love.

35 [hyacinths]: In Greek myth Hyacinth was a beloved companion of Apollo.
When the two engaged in a discus-throwing contest, Apollo's discus inadver-
tently killed his friend. Where drops of Hyacinth's blood touched the ground,
a purple flower miraculously arose, resembling a lily. Apollo inscribed his
grief upon the flower, which was said to have marks which looked like the
letters AI, ancient Greek for a cry of woe. The story is told in Ovid, *Metamorphoses* X, 162–219. Several different flowers seem to have been included
under this name in the ancient world, none of them the modern flower
which we call a hyacinth.

39–40 [I was neither / Living nor dead]: Perhaps an allusion to Dante, *Inferno*
XXXIV, 25. Dante recalls his state of mind when he first saw Satan at the
very bottom of the Inferno:

Com' io divenni allor gelato e fioco
nol dimandar, lettor, ch' i' non lo scrivo,
però ch' ogni parlar sarebbe poco.
Io non morì, e non rimasi vivo.

This can be translated:

How chilled and faint I turned then,
Do not ask, reader, for I cannot describe it,
For all speech would fail it.
I did not die, and did not remain alive.

41 [and I knew nothing]: Compare Job 8:9: "For we are but of yesterday, and know
nothing, because our days upon earth are a shadow."

42 [Öd' und leer das Meer]: "Desolate and empty the sea" (German). From Wagner's *Tristan und Isolde*, III.i.24. Tristan is lying grievously wounded outside
Kareol, his castle in Brittany, tended by his companion Kurwenal. He will
die unless Isolde can come and cure him with her magic arts. Tristan wakes
from his delirium; he is clinging to life only so that he can find Isolde and
take her with him into the realm of night. For a moment he thinks that he
sees Isolde's ship approaching; but a shepherd who is watching with him
pipes a sad tune: "Desolate and empty the sea."

43 [Madame Sosostris]: The name is obviously appropriate for someone who
equivocates, or whose answer to every question is a variant of "so so." Not
surprisingly, her friend is named Mrs. Equitone, a variant on the notion of
equivocation. To learned readers the name Sosostris may also recall the
Greek work for "savior," *soteros*, which survives in the English word soterio-
logical, of or having to do with the doctrine of salvation in Christian theol-
ogy. For many years scholars also thought that her name was suggested to
Eliot by a character in Aldous Huxley's novel *Chrome Yellow* (1921), in which

Mr. Scogan disguises himself as a gipsy fortune-teller named Sesostris and, at the village fête, reads the fortune of a simple young girl whom he means to seduce. This scholarly myth was first promulgated by Grover Smith, "The Fortuneteller in Eliot's *Waste Land*," *American Literature* 25 (1954): 490–492. To support his claim Smith cited a letter he had received from Eliot, dated 10 March 1952, in which Eliot had said it was "almost certain" that he had borrowed the name from *Chrome Yellow* ("almost certain" are the only words of the letter which are directly quoted). Smith then paraphrased the rest of the letter: "He has also said that, *being unconscious of the borrowing*, he was unaware of any connection between the name of the clairvoyant and that assumed by Mr. Scogan" (italics mine). Eliot had better reason than he knew for being "unaware of any connection" between the two characters, for he had probably drafted the scene with Madame Sosos4tris by early February 1921 and had certainly completed the typescript of parts I and II sometime in mid-May, while Huxley, who was living in Italy, did not even begin to write his novel until the beginning of June (see Sybille Bedford, *Aldous Huxley: A Biography*, vol. I, *1894–1939* [London: Chatto and Windus, 1973], 117, 119). Eliot and Huxley did not correspond during this period, as the two men were not close; and Eliot, writing in January 1921, had damned Huxley's recent long poem "Leda" as "a concession to the creamy top of the General Reading Public" (see London Letter, March 1921, 139).

Smith's mistaken claim was diffused in his subsequent monographs on Eliot: *T. S. Eliot's Poetry and Plays: A Study in Sources and Influence* (Chicago: University of Chicago Press, 1956), 76, a work that went through numerous impressions and a second edition in 1974, and *The Waste Land* (London: George Allen and Unwin, 1983), 47, 67–68. From these it became a standard note in all commentaries on the poem.

46 [pack of cards]: The tarot deck consists of twenty-two cards, one unnumbered and the rest numbered through twenty-one, which are added to a pack (British usage) or deck of fifty-six cards arranged in four suits (cups, wands, swords, and pentacles or pentangles). Jessie Weston suggested that these suits were repositories of primeval symbols of fertility corresponding to the four Grail talismans, grail-cup, lance, sword, and dish (*From Ritual to Romance*, 77–79). Scholars have expended vast amounts of ink on establishing precise connections between the tarot cards and Eliot's use of them, even though Eliot, in his notes to the poem, admitted that he had little familiarity with the tarot and had "departed" from it "to suit [his] own convenience."

47 [the drowned Phoenician Sailor]: There is no such card in the tarot deck, but this passage is thought to anticipate part IV of *The Waste Land*.

48 [Those are pearls . . . Look!]: From Shakespeare, *The Tempest* I.ii.399. The play begins with a storm scene and a shipwreck: young Prince Ferdinand and others from the court of Naples come to shore on an unnamed island inhabited by Prospero, the former ruler of Naples whose throne has been usurped by his brother Antonio, acting in concert with Ferdinand's father, Alonso. At

Prospero's behest the storm has been created by Ariel, a magical spirit of the island who serves him. When Ferdinand laments his father's supposed death —he is mistaken, for his father is still alive—Ariel tries to comfort him with a song (396–405):

Full fathom five thy father lies;
Of his bones are coral made;
Those are pearls that were his eyes;
Nothing of him that doth fade
But doth suffer a sea change
Into something rich and strange.
Sea nymphs hourly ring his knell:
      Burden. Ding-dong.
Hark! Now I hear them—ding-dong bell.

49 [Here is Belladonna . . . Rocks]: Belladonna is Italian for "beautiful woman." There is no such card in the tarot pack. Commentators have often urged that the phrase, "the Lady of the Rocks," has overtones of a passage in the essay by Walter Pater (1839–1894) on "Leonardo da Vinci" in *The Renaissance* (1873). Pater discusses da Vinci's painting *La Gioconda,* popularly known as the Mona Lisa: "She is older than the rocks among which she sits; like the vampire, she has been dead many times, and learned the secret of the grave; and had been a diver in deep seas, and keeps their fallen day about her; and trafficked for strange webs with Eastern merchants." But Eliot disliked Pater's prose style; see his comments on it in "Prose and Verse," 162.

51–52 [Here is the man . . . the one-eyed merchant]: The first two cards, the man with three staves and the wheel, are genuine tarot cards, but the one-eyed merchant is Eliot's invention.

60 [Unreal City]: The City is the name for the financial district (see Fig. 9) in London, located just beyond the north end of London Bridge. The area is home to the Royal Exchange, the Bank of England, and the head offices or headquarters of Britain's major commercial banks, including Lloyds Bank in Lombard Street, where Eliot worked from 1917 to 1925. The London Bridge that Eliot knew (see Fig. 4) was built between 1825 and 1831 to a design by John Rennie (1761–1821); it was dismantled in 1967 and replaced with the current structure.

      Eliot's note at this point invokes a poem by Charles Baudelaire (1821–1867), "Les sept viellards" (1859), which recounts a ghostly encounter in the street that sets the pattern for the incident which follows in this portion of *The Waste Land.*

Fourmillante cité, cité pleine de rêves,
Où le spectre en plein jour raccroche le passant!
Les mystères partout coulent comme des sèves
Dans les canaux étroits du colosse puissant.

Un matin, cependant que dans la triste rue
Les maisons, dont la brume allongeait la hauteur,
Simulaient les deux quais d'un rivière accrue,
Et que, décor semblable à l'âme de l'acteur,

Un brouillard sale et jaune inondait tout l'espace,
Je suivais, roidissant mes nerfs comme un héros
Et discutant avec mon âme déjà lasse,
Le faubourg secoué par les lourds tombereaux.

Tout à coup, un vieillard dont les guenilles jaunes
Imitaient la couleur de ce ciel pluvieux,
Et dont l'aspect aurait fait pleuvoir les aumônes,
Sans la méchanceté qui luisait dans ses yeux,

M'apparut. On eût dit sa prunelle trempée
Dans le fiel; son regard aiguisait les frimas,
Et sa barbe à long poils, roide comme une épée,
Se projetait, pareille à celle de Judas.

Il n'était pas voûté, mais cassé, son échine
Faisant avec sa jambe un parfait angle droit,
Si bien que son bâton, parachevant sa mine,
Lui donnait la tournure et le pas maladroit

D'un quadrupède infirme ou d'un juif à trois pattes.
Dans la neige et la boue il allait s'empêtrant,
Comme s'il écrasait des morts sous ses savates,
Hostile à l'univers plutôt qu'indifférent.

Son pareil le suivait: barbe, oeil, dos, bâton, loques,
Nul trait ne distinguait, du même enfer venu,
Ce jumeau centenaire, et ces spectres baroques
Marchaient du même pas vers un but inconnu.

À quel complot infâme étais-je donc en butte,
Ou quel méchant hasard ainsi m'humiliait?
Car je comptai sept fois, de minute en minute,
Ce sinistre vieillard qui se multipliait!

Que celui-là qui rit de mon inquiétude,
Et qui n'est pas saisi d'un frisson fraternel,
Songe bien que malgré tant de décrépitude
Ces sept monstres hideux avaient l'aire éternel!

Aurais-je, sans mourir, contemplé le huitième,
Sosie inexorable, ironique et fatal,
Dégoûtant Phénix, fils et père de lui-même?
—Mais je tournai le dos au cortège infernal.

Exaspéré comme un ivrogne qui voit double,
Je rentrai, je fermai ma porte, épouvanté,
Malade et morfondu, l'esprit fiévreux et trouble,
Blessé par le mystère et par l'absurdité!

Vainement ma raison voulait prendre la barre;
La tempête en jouant déroutait ses efforts,
Et mon âme dansait, dansait, vieille gabarre
Sans mâts, sur une mer monstrueuse et sans bords!

John Goudge (1921–) offered this translation of "The Seven Old Men" in his
Selected Poems of Charles Baudelaire (Walton-on-Thames: Outposts, 1979):

City swarming with people! City crowded with dreams!
Through the narrow back streets of this mighty colossus,
Like the sap in a tree, a dark mystery streams,
And ghosts clutch a man's sleeve, in broad day, as he passes.

One morning when the houses that lined the sad street
Hovered larger than life, so it seemed, in the mist,
And resembled the banks of a river in spate,
A stage set for the shade of a pantomimist,

In the foul, yellow fog that pervaded the whole
Atmosphere, I strode on, like a hero in battle,
Each nerve taut, and communed with my world-weary soul,
While the carts made the neighbourhood shake with their rattle.

All at once in the gloom, an old man came in sight,
Wearing tatters as yellow as thundery skies,
And a torrent of alms had showered down at his plight,
Were it not for the malice that gleamed in his eyes,

You'd have said that his beard was as long as a lance,
Jutting out, and the equal of Judas' quite,
That his eyeballs were bloating in bile, that his glance
Was so cold as to sharpen the sting of frostbite.

He was not so much crooked as broken, his spine
With his legs represented a perfect right-angle,
And his stick put the finishing touch to his mien,
For it gave him the gait of and made him resemble

A lame four-booted beast or a jew with three legs.
'Twas as though in the mud and the snow as he went,
He was trampling the dead underground with his clogs—
Rather hateful and spiteful than indifferent.

His twin followed him close, beard, back, stick, rages and eye,
By no mark could you tell one foul fiend from his brother.
These grotesque apparitions, pace for pace, went their way,
Each was bound for the same unknown end as the other.

Was it wicked mischance that had made me a fool?
By some infamous plot was I being seduced?
I know not, but I counted this sinister ghoul
Some seven times in seven minutes, by himself reproduced.

And the man who makes fun of my disquietude
And who feels not the chill of a brotherly shiver
Should mark well that despite such decrepitude
These grim brutes had the look of surviving for ever.

Had an eighth then appeared, I believe I'd have died—
One more pitiless twin sent to menace and mock
An incestuous phoenix, by himself multiplied—
But I took to my heels and presented my back

To this ghastly parade. As if drunk, vision doubled,
Panic-struck, I ran home, shut the door, turned the key;
I was ill, overcome, hot and cold, deeply troubled,
At once baffled and hurt by the absurdity.

And in vain did my reason attempt to take charge,
For its efforts were foiled by the tempest in me,
And my soul began dancing a jig, like a barge
Without masts on a monstrous and infinite sea.

62–63 [so many . . . so many]: Eliot's note cites Dante, *Inferno* III, 55–57: "such
a long stream / of people, that I would not have thought / that death had
undone so many." As soon as Dante passes through the gates of Hell, he
hears first "sighs, lamentations, and loud wailings" (III, 22), then "strange
tongues, horrible languages, words of pain, tones of anger, voices loud and
hoarse" (III, 25–27). In the gloom he discerns "a long stream of people."
He asks Virgil, his guide in the underworld, why these people are here, and
Virgil explains that in life these did neither good nor evil, thinking only of
themselves; like the Sibyl in the epigraph to *The Waste Land*, they "have no
hope of death, and so abject is their blind life that they are envious of every
other lot" (III, 46–48).

64 [Sighs . . .]: Eliot's note cites Dante, *Inferno* IV, 25–27: "Here, as far I could
tell by listening, / Was no lamentation more than sighs, / Which kept the air
forever trembling." Dante has entered the first circle of Hell, or Limbo, and
describes the sound that emanates from those who died without being bap-
tized, and who therefore must live forever with the torment of desiring to
see God, yet knowing that they never will.

66 [King William Street]: The thoroughfare (see Fig. 5) which runs from the
   north end of London Bridge directly into the City, or financial district, of
   London (see Fig. 9).

67 [St. Mary Woolnoth]: The church, a neoclassical work designed by Nicholas
   Hawksmoor (1661–1736), who was a prominent architect in the early eighteenth century, was erected from 1716 to 1724 (see Figs. 6, 7). It is located at
   the intersection of King William Street and Lombard Street; Eliot worked in
   the Lombard Street head office of Lloyds Bank (see Fig. 9), and to reach work
   had to pass St. Mary Woolnoth every morning. By his time the church had
   already become a relic, isolated and dwarfed by the larger office blocks of the
   City's banks, since people no longer resided within the City and the church
   had lost its parishioners.

70 [Mylae]: A city on the northern coast of Sicily, now called Milazzo, off the coast
   of which there occurred a naval battle between the Romans and the Cartha-
   ginians in 260 B.C., the first engagement in the first of the Punic Wars. The
   Romans won, destroying some fifty ships, an early step in their battle for
   commercial domination of the Mediterranean.

74–75 [Oh keep the Dog . . . again!]: Eliot's note directs the reader to *The White
   Devil* (1612), a play by John Webster (c. 1580–c. 1635). It dramatizes numerous acts of political and sexual betrayal, among which Flamineo murders his
   own brother Marcello. Their mother, in act V, scene iv, sings a demented
   dirge over Marcello's body (her song is given in italics, her spoken words in
   roman):

   Call for the Robin-Red-rest and the wren,
   Since o'er shady groves they hover,
   And with leaves and flowers do cover
   The friendless bodies of unburied men.
   Call unto his funeral Dole
   The ant, the field-mouse, and the mole
   To rear him hillocks, that shall keep him warm,
   And (when gay tombs are robbed) sustain no harm,
   But keep the wolf far thence, that's foe to men,
   For with his nails he'll dig them up again.
   They would not bury him 'cause he died in a quarrel
   But I have an answer for them.
   Let holy church receive him duly
   Since hee paid the church tithes truly.
   His wealth is summed, and this is all his store:
   This poor men get; and great men get no more.
   Now the wares are gone, we may shut shop.
   Bless you all, good people.

76 [hypocrite lecteur! . . . mon frère]: Eliot's note cites "Au Lecteur" ("To the

Reader") (1855), the first poem in *Les Fleurs du Mal* (Flowers of evil, 1857), by Charles Baudelaire.

La sottise, l'erreur, le péché, la lésine,
Occupent nos esprits et travaillent nos corps,
Et nous alimentons nos aimable remords,
Comme les mendiants nourrissent leur vermine.

Nos péchés sont têtus, nos repentirs sont lâches;
Nous nous faisons payer grassement nos aveux,
Et nous rentrons gaiement dans le chemin bourbeux,
Croyant par de vils pleurs laver toutes nos taches.

Sur l'oreiller du mal c'est Satan Trismégiste
Qui berce longuement notre esprit enchanté
Et le riche métal de notre volonté
Est tout vaporisé par ce savant chimiste.

C'est le Diable qui tient les fils qui nos remuent!
Aux objets répugnants nous trouvons des appas;
Chaque jour vers l'Enfers nous descendons d'un pas,
Sans horreur, à travers des ténèbres qui puent.

Ainsi qu'un débauché pauvre qui baise et mange
Le sein martyrisé d'une antique catin,
Nous volons au passage un plaisir clandestin
Que nous pressons bien forte comme une vieille orange.

Serré, fourmillant, comme un million d'helminthes,
Dans nos cerveaux ribote un peuple de Démons,
Et, quand nous respirons, la Mort dans nos poumons
Descend, fleuve invisible, avec de sourdes plaintes.

Se le viol, le poison, le poignard, l'incendie,
N'ont pas encore brodé de leur plaisants dessins
Le canevas banal de nos piteux destins,
C'est que notre âme, hélas! n'est pas assez hardie.

Mais parmi les chacals, les panthères, les lices,
Les singes, les scorpions, les vautours, les serpents,
Les monstres glapissants, hurlants, grognants, rampants,
Dans la ménagerie infâme de nos vices

Il en est un plus laid, plus méchant, plus immonde!
Quoiqu'il ne pousse ni grands gestes ni grands cris,
Il ferait volontiers de la terre un débris
Et dans un bâillement avalerait le monde;

C'est l'Ennui!—l'oeil chargé d'un pleur involontaire
Il rêve d'échafauds en fumant son houka.
Tu le connais, lecteur, ce monstre délicat,
—Hypocrite lecteur,—mon semblable,—mon frère!

The South African poet Roy Campbell (1901–1957) offered this translation of
"To the Reader" in his *Poems of Baudelaire: A Translation of Les Fleurs du mal*
(New York: Pantheon, 1952):

Folly and error, avarice and vice,
Employ our souls and waste our bodies' force.
As mangey beggars incubate their lice,
We nourish our innocuous remorse.

Our sins are stubborn, craven our repentance.
For our weak vows we ask excessive prices.
Trusting our tears will wash away the sentence,
We sneak off where the muddy road entices.

Cradles in evil, that Thrice-Great Magician,
The Devil, rocks our souls, that can't resist;
And the rich metal of our own volition
Is vaporised by that sage alchemist.

The Devil pulls the strings by which we're worked:
By all revolting objects lured, we slink
Hellwards; each day down one more step we're jerked
Feeling no horror, through the shades that stink.

Just as a lustful pauper bites and kisses
The scarred and shrivelled breast of an old whore,
We steal, along the roadside, furtive blisses,
Squeezing them, like stale oranges, for more.

Packed tight, like hives of maggots, thickly seething,
Within our brains a host of demons surges.
Deep down into our lungs at every breathing
Death flows, an unseen river, moaning dirges.

If rape or arson, poison or the knife
Has wove no pleasing patterns in the stuff
Of this drab canvas we accept as life—
It is because we are not bold enough!

Among the jackals, leopards, mongrels, apes,
Snakes, scorpions, vultures, that wish hellish din,
Squeal, roar, writhe, gambol, crawl, with monstrous shapes,
In each man's foul menagerie of sin—

> There's one more damned than all. He never gambols,
> Nor crawls, nor roars, but, from the rest withdrawn,
> Gladly of this whole earth would make a shambles
> And swallow up existence with a yawn . . .
>
> Boredom! He smokes his hookah, while he dreams
> Of gibbets, weeping tears he cannot smother.
> You know this dainty monster, too, it seems
> Hypocrite reader!—You!—My twin!—My brother!

A Game of Chess: The title is indebted to the play by Thomas Middleton (1580–
   1627), *A Game at Chess* (1624), in which chess becomes an allegory of the
   diplomatic games between England and Spain. Middleton also wrote *Women
   Beware Women* (date disputed, 1613–1614 or 1622–1624; first published
   1653), a play which Eliot cites in his note to line 137. In act II, scene ii, a
   game of chess is played between Livia, who is acting on behalf of the Duke of
   Florence, and the mother of Leantio, who is ostensibly watching over Leantio's young and beautiful wife. The game is a ruse to distract the mother,
   whose daughter-in-law is meanwhile being seduced by the duke on the balcony above. The dialogue about the chess game ironically comments on the
   different mating moves being performed overhead by the duke and the
   young wife.

77 [The chair she sat in . . . throne]: Eliot cites Shakespeare's *Antony and Cleopatra*
   II.ii.190. Enobarbus, a friend and follower of Marc Antony, describes Cleo-
   patra as she was when floating on her ship down the Cydnus River to
   Antony (ll. 192–206):

> The barge she sat in, like a burnished throne,
> Burned on the water: the poop was beaten gold;
> Purple the sails, and so perfumèd that
> The winds were lovesick with them; the oars were silver,
> Which to the tune of flutes kept stroke, and made
> The Water which they beat to follow faster,
> As amorous of their strokes. For her own person,
> It beggared all description: she did lie
> In her pavilion, cloth-of-gold of tissue,
> O'erpicturing that Venus where we see
> The fancy outwork nature. On each side her
> Stood pretty dimpled boys, like smiling Cupids,
> With divers-colored fans, whose wind did seem
> To glow the delicate cheeks which they did cool,
> And what they undid did.

92 [laquearia]: A Latin term, in the plural, for a paneled or fretted ceiling. Eliot's
   note refers to Virgil, the *Aeneid* I, 726–727. Aeneas and his crew have just
   arrived in Carthage after fleeing the ruins of Troy, destroyed by the Greeks

at the end of the Trojan War; Dido, the queen of Carthage, has given them a royal welcome and serves them dinner in a banquet hall of great luxury. The gods have fated her to fall in love with Aeneas during this meal, which will ensure that she provides him with aid and thus that he will go on to fulfill his destiny, the foundation of Rome; but to do this he will have to desert her, prompting her suicide. The story acquires irony from the reader's knowledge that Rome will eventually destroy Carthage. "Blazing torches hang down from the gilded ceiling, / And vanquish the night with their flames."

93 [coffered]: Decorated with sunken panels, though an undertone of "coffin" is audible.

98 [sylvan scene]: Eliot's note refers us to Milton's *Paradise Lost* IV, 140, a line that is found within a passage that describes Satan as he approaches paradise, where he will tempt Eve (131–141):

> So on he fares, and to the border comes
> Of *Eden*, where delicious Paradise,
> Now nearer, Crowns with her enclosure green,
> As with a rural mound the champaign head
> Of a steep wilderness, whose hairy sides
> With thicket overgrown, grotesque and wild,
> Access deni'd; and over head up grew
> Insuperable highth of loftiest shade,
> Cedar, and Pine, and Fir, and branching Palm,
> A Silvan Scene, a woody Theatre
> Of stateliest view.

100: Eliot's note cites Ovid's *Metamorphoses*, VI, 424–674, given here in the prose translation by Frank Justin (Cambridge: Harvard University Press, 1916):

> Now Tereus of Thrace had put these [warriors from Argos, Sparta, Mycenae, and other cities warring against Athens] to flight with his re-lieving troops, and by the victory had a great name. And since he was strong in wealth and in men, and traced his descent, as it happened, from Gradivus, Pandion, king of Athens, allied him to himself by wed-ding him to [his daughter] Procne. But neither Juno, bridal goddess, nor Hymen, nor the Graces were present at that wedding. The Furies lighted them with torches stolen from a funeral; the Furies spread the couch, and the uncanny screech-owl brooded and sat on the roof of their chamber. Under this omen were Procne and Tereus wedded; under this omen was their child conceived. Thrace, indeed, rejoiced with them, and they themselves gave thanks to the gods; both the day on which Pandion's daughter was married to their illustrious king, and that day on which Itys was born, they made a festival: even so is our true advantage hidden.
>
> Now Titan through five autumnal seasons had brought round the

revolving years, when Procne coaxingly to her husband said: "If I have
found any favour in your sight, either send me to visit my sister or let
my sister come to me. You will promise my father that after a brief stay
she shall return. If you give me a chance to see my sister you will confer
on me a precious boon." Tereus accordingly bade them launch his ship,
and plying oar and sail, he entered the Cecropian harbour and came to
land on the shore of Piraeus [the port of Athens]. As soon as he came
into the presence of his father-in-law they joined right hands, and the
talk began with good wishes for their health. He had begun to tell of his
wife's request, which was the cause of his coming, and to promise a
speedy return should the sister be sent home with him, when lo! Philomela entered, attired in rich apparel, but richer still in beauty; such as
we are wont to hear the naiads described, and dryads when they move
about in the deep woods, if only one should give to them refinement
and apparel like hers. The moment he saw the maiden Tereus was
inflamed with love, quick as if one should set fire to ripe grain, or dry
leaves, or hay stored away in the mow. Her beauty, indeed, was worth it;
but in his case his own passionate nature pricked him on, and, besides,
the men of his clime are quick to love: his own fire and his nation's
burnt in him. His impulse was to corrupt her attendants' care and her
nurse's faithfulness, and even by rich gifts to tempt the girl herself, even
at the cost of all his kingdom; or else to ravish her and to defend his
act by bloody war. There was nothing which he would not do or dare,
smitten by this mad passion. His heart could scarce contain the fires
that burnt in it. Now, impatient of delay, he eagerly repeated Procne's
request, pleading his own cause under her name. Love made him eloquent, and as often as he asked more urgently than he should, he would
say that Procne wished it so. He even added tears to his entreaties, as
though she had bidden him to do this too. Ye gods, what blind night
rules in the hearts of men! In the very act of pushing on his shameful
plan Tereus gets credit for a kind heart and wins praise from wickedness. Ay, more—Philomela herself has the same wish; winding her
arms about her father's neck, she coaxes him to let her visit her sister;
by her own welfare (yes, and against it, too), she urges her prayer.
Tereus gazes at her, and as he looks feels her already in his arms; as he
sees her kisses and her arms about her father's neck, all this goads him
on, food and fuel for his passion; and whenever she embraces her father
he wishes that he were in the father's place—indeed, if he were, his in-
tent would be no less impious. The father yields to the prayers of both.
The girl is filled with joy; she thanks her father and, poor unhappy
wretch, she deems that success for both sisters which is to prove a woe-
ful happening for them both.

Now Phoebus' toils were almost done and his horses were pacing
down the western sky. A royal feast was spread, wine in cups of gold.

Then they lay them down to peaceful slumber. But although the Thracian king retired, his heart seethes with thoughts of her. Recalling her look, her movement, her hands, he pictures at will what he has not yet seen, and feeds his own fires, his thoughts preventing sleep. Morning came; and Pandion, wringing his son-in-law's hand as he was departing, consigned his daughter to him with many tears and said: "Dear son, since a natural plea has won me, and both my daughters have wished it, my Tereus, I give her to your keeping; and by your honour and the ties that bind us, by the gods, I pray you guard her with a father's love, and as soon as possible—it will seem a long time in any case to me—send back to me this sweet solace of my tedious years. And do you, my Philomela, if you love me, come back to me as soon as possible; it is enough that your sister is so far away." Thus he made his last requests and kissed his child good-bye, and gentle tears fell as he spoke the words; and he asked both their right hands as pledge of their promise, and joined them together and begged that they would remember to greet for him his daughter and her son. His voice broke with sobs, he could hardly say farewell, as he feared the forebodings of his mind.

As soon as Philomela was safely embarked upon the painted ship and the sea was churned beneath the oars and the land was left behind, Tereus exclaimed: "I have won! in my ship I carry the fulfilment of my prayers!" The barbarous fellow triumphs, he can scarce postpone his joys, and never turns his eyes from her, as when the ravenous bird of Jove [the eagle] has dropped in his high eyrie some hare caught in his hooked talons; the captive has no chance to escape, the captor gloats over his prize.

And now they were at the end of their journey, now, leaving the travel-worn ship, they had landed on their own shores; when the king dragged off Pandion's daughter to a hut deep in the ancient woods; and there, pale and trembling and all fear, begging with tears to know where her sister was, he shut her up. Then, openly confessing his horrid purpose, he violated her, just a weak girl and all alone, vainly calling, often on her father, often on her sister, but most of all upon the great gods. She trembled like a frightened lamb, which, torn and cast aside by a grey wolf, cannot yet believe that it is safe; and like a dove which, with its own blood all smeared over its plumage, still palpitates with fright, still fears those greedy claws that have pierced it. Soon, when her senses came back, she dragged at her loosened hair, and like one in mourning, beating and tearing her arms, with outstretched hands she cried: "Oh, what a horrible thing you have done, barbarous, cruel wretch! Do you care nothing for my father's injunctions, his affectionate tears, my sister's love, my own virginity, the bonds of wedlock? You have confused all natural relations: I have become a concubine, my sister's rival; you, a husband to both. Now Procne must be my enemy. Why do you not take my life, that no crime may be left undone, you traitor? Aye, would that you had killed me before you wronged me so. Then would my shade have been innocent and clean. If those who dwell on high see these things, nay, if there are any gods at all, if all things have not perished with me, sooner or later you shall pay dearly for this deed. I will myself cast shame aside and proclaim what you have done. If I should have the chance, I would go where people throng and tell it; if I am kept shut up in these woods, I will fill the woods with my story and move the very rocks to pity. The air of heaven shall hear it, and, if there is any god in heaven, he shall hear it too."

The savage tyrant's wrath was aroused by these words, and his fear no less. Pricked on by both these spurs, he drew his sword, which was hanging by his side in its sheath, caught her by the hair, and twisting her arms behind her back, he bound them fast. At sight of the sword Philomela gladly offered her throat to the stroke, filled with the eager hope of death. But he seized her tongue with pincers, as it protested against the outrage, calling ever on the name of her father and strug-gling to speak, and cut it off with his merciless blade. The mangled root quivers, while the severed tongue lies palpitating on the dark earth, faintly murmuring; and, as the severed tail of a mangled snake is wont to writhe, it twitches convulsively, and with its last dying movement it seeks its mistress's feet. Even after this horrid deed—one would scarce believe it—the monarch is said to have worked his lustful will again and again upon the poor mangled form.

With such crimes upon his soul he had the face to return to Procne's presence. She on seeing him at once asked where her sister was. He groaned in pretended grief and told a made-up story of death; his tears gave credence to the tale. Then Procne tore from her shoulders the robe gleaming with a golden border and put on black weeds; she built also a cenotaph in honour of her sister, brought pious offerings to her imag-ined spirit, and mourned her sister's fate, not meet so to be mourned.

Now through the twelve signs, a whole year's journey, has the sun-god passed. And what shall Philomela do? A guard prevents her flight; stout walls of solid stone fence in the hut; speechless lips can give no token of her wrongs. But grief has sharp wits, and in trouble cunning comes. She hangs a Thracian web on her loom, and skilfully weaving purple signs on a white background, she thus tells the story of her wrongs. This web, when completed, she gives to her one attendant and begs her with gestures to carry it to the queen. The old woman, as she was bid, takes the web to Procne, not knowing what she bears in it. The savage tyrant's wife unrolls the cloth, reads the pitiable tale of her mis-fortune, and (a miracle that she could!) says not a word. Grief chokes the words that rise to her lips, and her questing tongue can find no words strong enough to express her outraged feelings. Here is no room for tears, but she hurries on to confound right and wrong, her whole soul bent on the thought of vengeance.

It was the time when the Thracian matrons were wont to celebrate the biennial festival of Bacchus [god of wine]. Night was in their secret; by night Mount Rhodope would resound with the shrill clash of brazen cymbals; so by night the queen goes forth from her house, equips herself for the rites of the god and dons the array of frenzy; her head was wreathed with trailing vines, a deer-skin hung from her left side, a light spear rested on her shoulder. Swift she goes through the woods with an attendant throng of her companions, and driven on by the madness of grief, Procne, terrific in her rage, mimics thy madness, O Bacchus! She comes to the secluded lodge at last, shrieks aloud and cries "Euhoe!" breaks down the doors, seizes her sister, arrays her in the trappings of a Bacchante, hides her face with ivy-leaves, and, dragging her along in amazement, leads her within her own walls.

When Philomela perceived that she had entered that accursed house the poor girl shook with horror and grew pale as death. Procne found a place, and took off the trappings of the Bacchic rites and, uncovering the shame-blanched face of her wretched sister, folded her in her arms. But Philomela could not lift her eyes to her sister, feeling herself to have wronged her. And, with her face turned to the ground, longing to swear and call all the gods to witness that that shame had been forced upon her, she made her hand serve for voice. But Procne was all on fire, could not contain her own wrath, and chiding her sister's weeping, she said: "This is no time for tears, but for the sword, for something stronger than the sword, if you have such a thing. I am prepared for any crime, my sister; either to fire this palace with a torch, and to cast Tereus, the author of our wrongs, into the flaming ruins, or to cut out his tongue and his eyes, to cut off the parts which brought shame to you, and drive his guilty soul out through a thousand wounds. I am prepared for some great deed; but what it shall be I am still in doubt."

While Procne was thus speaking Itys came into his mother's presence. His coming suggested what she could do, and regarding him with pitiless eyes, she said: "Ah, how like your father your are!" Saying no more, she began to plan out a terrible deed and boiled with inward rage. But when the boy came up to her and greeted his mother, put his little arms around her neck and kissed her in his winsome, boyish way, her mother-heart was touched, her wrath fell away, and her eyes, though all unwilling, were wet with tears that flowed in spite of her. But when she perceived that her purpose was wavering through excess of mother-love, she turned again from her son to her sister; and gazing at both in turn, she said: "Why is one able to make soft, pretty speeches, while her ravished tongue dooms the other to silence? Since he calls me mother, why does she not call me sister? Remember whose wife you are, daughter

of Pandion! Will you be faithless to your husband? But faithfulness to
such a husband as Tereus is a crime." Without more words she dragged
Itys away, as a tigress drags a suckling fawn through the dark woods
on Ganges' banks. And when they reached a remote part of the great
house, while the boy stretched out pleading hands as he saw his fate,
and screamed, "Mother! mother!" and sought to throw his arms around
her neck, Procne smote him with a knife between breast and side—
and with no change of face. This one stroke sufficed to slay the lad; but
Philomela cut the throat also, and they cut up the body still warm and
quivering with life. Part bubbles in brazen kettles, part sputters on spits;
while the whole room drips with gore.

   This is the feast to which the wife invites Tereus, little knowing what
it is. She pretends that it is a sacred feast after their ancestral fashion,
of which only a husband may partake, and removes all attendants and
slaves. So Tereus, sitting alone in his high ancestral banquet-chair, begins the feast and gorges himself with flesh of his own flesh. And in the
utter blindness of his understanding he cries; "Go, call me Itys hither!"
Procne cannot hide her cruel joy, and eager to be the messenger of her
bloody news, she says: "You have, within, him whom you want." He
looks about and asks where the boy is. And then, as he asks and calls
again for his son, just as she was, with streaming hair, and all stained
with her mad deed of blood, Philomela springs forward and hurls the
gory head of Itys straight into his father's face; nor was there ever any
time when she longed more to be able to speak, and to express her joy
in fitting words. Then the Thracian king overturns the table with a great
cry and invokes the snaky sisters from the Stygian pit. Now, if he could,
he would gladly lay open his breast and take thence the horrid feast and
vomit forth the flesh of his son; now he weeps bitterly and calls himself
his son's most wretched tomb; then with drawn sword he pursues the
two daughters of Pandion. As they fly away from him you would think
that the bodies of the two Athenians were poised on wings! One flies to
the woods, the other rises to the roof. And even now their breasts have
not lost the marks of their murderous deed, their feathers are stained
with blood. Tereus, swift in pursuit because of his grief and eager desire
for vengeance, is himself changed into a bird. Upon his head a stiff
crest appears, and a huge beak stands forth instead of his long sword.
He is the hoopoë, with the look of one armed for war.

103 [Jug Jug]: This was a conventional way of representing the nightingale's song,
   as seen in the first four lines of an untitled song which appears in a play by
   John Lyly (1553–1606), *Alexander and Campaspe* (1584), act V, scene i, echoed
   here and at lines 204–206 by Eliot:

   What bird so sings, yet so does wail?
   O 'tis the ravish'd nightingale.

Jug, jug, jug, jug, Tereu! She cries,
And still her woes at midnight rise.

"Tereu" is the vocative form of Tereus, the ravisher of Philomela, whose cry, after she metamorphosed into a nightingale, could be heard as an outcry against Tereus. In contrast, "jug jug" was also a crude reference to sexual intercourse.

118 [The wind under the door]: Eliot's note directs the reader to John Webster's play *The Devil's Law Case*, III.ii.148. Contarino has been stabbed, and while undergoing treatment at the hands of two surgeons is stabbed again by the villain Romelio, unbeknownst to the surgeons, who have left the room. They return, thinking him dead, but he groans, and one surgeon asks the other, "Is the wind in that door still?"

125 [Those are pearls that were his eyes]: See note to line 48.

128–130 [O O O O . . . So intelligent]: A popular song published in 1912 by Joseph W. Stern and Co. and composed for performance at the Ziegfeld Follies, with words by Gene Buck and Herman Ruby, music by David Stamper. An advertisement for the song in *Variety* (19 July 1912) noted: "If you want a song that can be acted as well as sung send for this big surprise hit." The "grizzly bear," used as a verb in the song's lyrics, was a popular dance which loosely mimed a bear's motions. For the song's lyrics and music, see 96–99.

137: Eliot's note refers to the game of chess in Thomas Middleton's *Women Beware Women*; see the note to the title of part II.

139 [demobbed]: A popular contraction of "demobilized," or released from military service. The earliest *OED* citation of the term is from a newspaper, the *Glasgow Herald* of 2 June 1920: "Some young soldiers . . . who had been recently demobbed." According to Valerie Eliot, in her notes to *TWL:AF*, Eliot said that this portion of the poem (lines 137–197) was "pure Ellen Kellond," a maid who worked for them occasionally.

141 [HURRY UP PLEASE IT'S TIME]: A time-honored expression used by bartenders to announce the imminent closing of a pub, or public house, in Britain.

160 [She's had five already]: The size of the British family had shrunk from an average of 5.5 children in the mid-Victorian era to 2.2 between 1924 and 1929. Systematic practice of birth control had started among the middle classes in the 1870s and had spread downward before the First World War. Popular interest in birth control surged after the war; Marie Stopes's book, *Married Love: A New Contribution to the Solution of Sex Difficulties* (London: A. C. Fifield, 1918), sold 400,000 copies between 1918 and 1923.

161 [chemist]: A pharmacist, in American usage.

166 [gammon]: Smoked ham, in American usage.

172 [Good night . . . good night]: The last line of part II quotes from Ophelia's mad scene, where she appears distracted by the news that Hamlet has murdered her father and her sense that he will repudiate his affection for her, *Hamlet* IV.v.72–73. Later Ophelia drowns herself.

GENE BUCK AND HERMAN RUBY

That Shakespearian Rag†

Words by
GENE BUCK and HERMAN RUBY

Music by
DAVID STAMPER

Bill Shakespeare nev-er knew Of rag-time in his days, ___ But the
"As you like it" Bru-tus, We'll play a rag to-day. ___ Then old

high browed rhymes, Of his syn-co-pat-ed lines, You'll ad-mit, sure-ly fit, an-y
Shy-lock danced, And the Moor, O-thel-lo pranced, Feel-ing gay, he would say, as he

song that's now a hit, So this rag, I sub-mit. ___
start-ed in to sway, "Bring the rag, right a-way."

CHORUS. Not fast

That Shakes-pea-ri-an rag, ___ Most in-tel-li-gent, ve-ry

el-e-gant, That old clas-si-cal drag, Has the proper stuff, the line "Lay

on Macduff," Des - de - mon - a was the col - ored pet,

Ro - me - o ____ loved his Ju - li - et ____ And they were some

lov - ers, you can bet, ____ and yet, I know ___

___ if they were here to - day, They'd Grizz -

- ly Bear in a diff - rent way, And you'd hear old

Ham - let say,   "To __ be   or   not to be,"   That __

Shakespea-ri - an   Rag.

The Fire Sermon: The title is taken from a sermon by the great religious teacher
Siddartha Gautama (ca. 563–483 B.C.), called by his followers the Buddha or
the Enlightened One. The text was translated and edited by Henry Clarke
Warren (1854–1899), a Harvard University professor whose *Buddhism in
Translations* (Cambridge: Harvard University Press, 1896) became a standard
text (the Fire Sermon is found at 151–152), though more recent translators
would quarrel with his decision to translate "bhikku" as "priest" rather than
"monk." (All ellipses are Warren's.)

Then the Blessed One, having dwelt in Uruvela as long as he wished,
proceeded on his wanderings in the direction of Gaya Head, accompanied by a great congregation of priests, a thousand in number, who had
all of them aforetime been monks with matted hair. And there in Gaya,
on Gaya Head, the Blessed One dwelt, together with the thousand
priests. And there he addressed the priests:

"All things, O priests, are on fire. And what, O priests, are all these
things which are on fire?

"The eye, O priests, is on fire; forms are on fire; eye-consciousness
is on fire; impressions received by the eye are on fire; and whatever sensation, pleasant, unpleasant, or indifferent, originates in dependence
on impressions received by the eye, that also is on fire.

"And with what are these on fire?

"With the fire of passion, say I, with the fire of hatred, with the fire
of infatuation; with birth, old age, death, sorrow, lamentation, misery,
grief, and despair are they on fire.

"The ear is on fire; sounds are on fire; . . . the nose is on fire; odors are on fire; . . . the tongue is on fire; tastes are on fire; . . . the body is on fire; things tangible are on fire; . . . the mind is on fire; ideas are on fire; . . . mind-consciousness is on fire; impressions received by the mind are on fire; and whatever sensation, pleasant, unpleasant, or indifferent, originates in dependence on impressions received by the mind, that also is on fire.

"And with what are these on fire?

"With the fire of passion, say I, with the fire of hatred, with the fire of infatuation; with old age, death, sorrow, lamentation, misery, grief and despair are they on fire.

"Perceiving this, O priests, the learned and noble disciple conceives an aversion for the eye, conceives an aversion for forms, conceives an aversion for eye-consciousness, conceives an aversion for the impressions received by the eye; and whatever sensation, pleasant, unpleasant, or indifferent, originates in dependence on impressions received by the eye, for that he also conceives an aversion. Conceives an aversion for the ear, conceives an aversion for sounds, . . . conceives an aversion for the nose, conceives an aversion for odors, . . . conceives an aversion for the tongue, conceives an aversion for tastes, . . . conceives an aversion for the body, conceives an aversion for things, tangible, . . . conceives an aversion for the mind, conceives an aversion for ideas, conceives an aversion for mind-consciousness, conceives an aversion for the impressions received by the mind; and whatever sensation, pleasant, unpleasant, or indifferent, originates in dependence on impressions received by the mind, for this also he conceives an aversion. And in conceiving this aversion, he becomes divested of passion, and by the absence of passion he becomes free, and when he is free he becomes aware that he is free; and he knows that rebirth is exhausted, that he has lived the holy life, that he has done what it behooved him to do, and that he is no more for this world."

Now while this exposition was being delivered, the minds of the thousand priests became free from attachment and delivered from the depravities.

176 [Sweet Thames . . . my song]: Eliot's note cites the refrain to the "Pro-thalamion" (1596) by Edmund Spenser (1552–1599), a poem which celebrated the ideal of marriage to commemorate the wedding of the two daughters of the Earl of Worcester. The first two stanzas (of ten in the poem) read:

Calme was the day, and through the trembling ayre,
Sweete breathing *Zephyrus* did softly play
A gentle spirit, that lightly did delay
Hot *Titans* beames, which then did glyster fayre:
When I whom sullein care,

Through discontent of my long fruitlesse stay
In Princes Court, and expectation vayne
Of idle hopes, which still doe fly away,
Like empty shaddowes, did afflict my brayne,
Walkt forth to ease my payne
Along the shoare of siluer streaming *Themmes,*
Whose rutty Bancke, the which his River hemmes
Was paynted all with variable flowers,
And all the meades adorned with daintie gemmes,
Fit to decke maydens bowres,
And crown their Paramours,
Against the Brydale day, which is not long:
    Sweet *Themmes* run softly, till I end my Song.
There in a Meadow, by the Riuers side,
A Flocke of *Nymphes* I chaunced to espy,
All louely Daughters of the Flood thereby,
With goodly greenish locks all loose vntyede,
As each had bene a Bryde,
And each one had a little wicker basket,
Made of fine twigs entrayled curiously,
In which they gathered flowers to fill their flasket:
And with fine Fingers, cropt full feateously
The tender stalks on hye.
Of euery sort, which in that Meadow grew,
They gathered some; the Violet pallid blew,
The little Dazie, that at euening closes,
The virgin Lillie, and the Primrose trew,
With score of vermeil Roses,
To decke their Bridegromes posies,
Against the Brydale day, which was not long:
    Sweet *Themmes* run softly, till I end my Song.

182 [By the waters of Leman . . .]: Eliot is adapting the first verse of Psalm 137:

    1 By the rivers of Babylon, there sat we down, yea, we wept, when we
remembered Zion.
    2 We hanged our harps upon the willows in the midst thereof.
    3 For there they that carried us away captive required of us a song;
and they that wasted us required of us mirth, saying, Sing us one of the
songs of Zion.
    4 How shall we sing the Lord's song in a strange land?

In the Biblical passage, the ancient Hebrews are lamenting their exile in
Babylon and remembering the lost city of Jerusalem. Eliot has substituted
the word "Leman" for Babylon, which is the French name for the Lake of

Geneva, where he spent several weeks from 28 November 1921 to 1 January 1922, ostensibly resting his nerves and also writing parts IV and V of *The Waste Land*. As Eliot was also aware, "leman" is an archaic term, used still by Elizabethan and Jacobean poets, designating an illicit mistress.

185 [But at my back . . .]: An adaptation which virtually reverses the original sense of lines 21–22 of "To His Coy Mistress" by Andrew Marvell (1621–1678):

> Had we but world enough, and time,
> This coyness, lady, were no crime.
> We would sit down, and think which way
> To walk, and pass our long love's day.
> Thou by the Indian Ganges' side
> Shouldst rubies find; I by the tide
> Of Humber would complain. I would
> Love you ten years before the flood.
> And you should, if you please, refuse
> Till the conversion of the Jews.   10
> My vegetable love should grow
> Vaster than empires and more slow;
> An hundred years should go to praise
> Thine eyes, and on thy forehead gaze;
> Two hundred to adore each breast,
> But thirty thousand to the rest;
> An age at least to every part,
> And the last age should show your heart.
> For, lady, you deserve this state,
> Nor would I love at lower rate.   20
>   But at my back I always hear
> Time's wingèd chariot hurrying near;
> And yonder all before us lie
> Deserts of vast eternity.
> Thy beauty shall no more be found;
> Nor, in thy marble vault, shall sound
> My echoing song; then worms shall try
> That long-preserved virginity,
> And your quaint honor turn to dust,
> And into ashes all my lust: 30
> The grave's a fine and private place,
> But none, I think, do there embrace.
>   Not therefore, while the youthful hue
> Sits on thy skin like the morning glow,
> And while thy willing soul transpires
> At every pore with instant fires,
> Now let us sport us while we may,
> And now, like amorous birds of prey,

Rather at once our time devour
Than languish in his slow-chapped power.   40
Let us roll all our strength and all
Our sweetness up into one ball,
And tear our pleasures with rough strife
Thorough the iron gates of life:
Thus, though we cannot make our sun
Stand still, yet we will make him run.

192 [And on the king my father's death]: Eliot's note directs the reader to *The Tempest*, I.ii.388–393; Ferdinand, musing by himself on the shore where he has been shipwrecked, hears a song by one of the spirits of the air and asks:

Where should this music be? I' th' air or th' earth?
It sounds no more; and sure it waits upon
Some god o' th' island. Sitting on a bank,
Weeping again the king my father's wrack
This music crept by me upon the waters,
Allaying both their fury and my passion
With its sweet air.

196 [But at my back . . .]: See note to line 185.

197 [The sound of horns and motors]: Eliot's note directs the reader to a poem by John Day (1574–1640?), *The Parliament of Bees* (1641). Day was a playwright for the theater proprietor and manager Philip Henslowe; he collaborated on plays with Thomas Dekker and Henry Chettle, and also wrote two plays of his own, *The Isle of Gulls* (1606) and *Humour Out of Breath* (1608). *The Parliament of Bees* is a series of pastoral eclogues about "the doings, the births, the wars, the wooings" of bees. It is divided into twelve chapters or "Characters," each dramatizing a bee or insect that represents a human type. Character III is devoted to "Thraso or Polypragmus, the Plush Bee," who is "A mere vainglorious reveller, / Who scorns his equals, grinds the poor." He is perturbed that the sun "strives to outshine us" and proposes to build a hive which will outdo the sun's. The ceiling will be "gilt / And interseamed with pearl," and there will be artificial clouds, and a mechanical sun and moon:

Overhead
A roof of woods and forests I'll have spread,
Trees growing downwards, full of fallow-deer;
When of the sudden, listening, you shall hear
A sound of horns and hunting, which shall bring
Actaeon to Diana in the spring,
Where all shall see her naked skin; and there
Actaeon's hounds shall their own master tear,
An emblem of his folly that will keep
Hounds to devour and eat him up asleep.

All this I'll do that men with praise may crown
My fame for turning the world upside-down.

The text is taken from "The Parliament of Bees," ed. Arthur Symons, in
Nero and Other Plays, ed. Herbert P. Horne, Havelock Ellis, Arthur Symons,
and A. Wilson Verity (London: T. Fisher Unwin; New York: Charles Scribner's Sons, 1904), 227. For the myth of Actaeon and Diana, see the next note.

198 [Sweeney to Mrs. Porter . . .]: Sweeney figures in two earlier poems by Eliot,
"Sweeney Erect" and "Sweeney Among the Nightingales." In the first, the
protagonist disturbs a brothel when he draws out a razor in order to shave
but is thought by others to be planning some act of violence. In the second
he is in a brothel again, the object of ribald teasing by nightingales, and it
has been speculated that his unnamed "host" is Mrs. Porter. Here in *The
Waste Land*, Sweeney is approaching Mrs. Porter just as Actaeon approaches
Diana in the myth recapitulated by John Day (see the preceding note): Actaeon was torn apart by his own hunting dogs for gazing at Diana, goddess
of chastity as well as the hunt, while she was bathing. (Freudian interpretations of this myth see it as expressing a fear of castration.) The most
celebrated version of the Diana and Actaeon myth is given in Ovid's *Metamorphoses*, III, 198–252.

199 [O the moon shone bright]: Contemporary American critics noted that this
line echoes an anonymous, popular ballad known as "Red Wing":

There once lived an Indian maid,
A shy little prairie maid,
Who sang a lay, a love song gay,
As on the plain she'd while away the day;
She loved a warrior bold,
This shy little maid of old,
But brave and gay he rode one day
To the battlefield far away.

CHORUS:
Now the moon shines bright on pretty Red Wing,
The breezes sighing, the night birds crying,
For afar 'neath his star her brave is sleeping
While Red Wing's weeping her heart away.

She watched for him day and night,
She kept all the camp fires bright,
And under the sky each night she would lie
And dream about his coming by and by;
But when all the braves returned
The heart of Red Wing yearned,
For far, far away, her warrior gay
Fell bravely in the fray.

Eliot, in a note to these lines which may not be serious, reports that lines
   199–201 derived from a ballad "reported to me from Sydney, Australia."
   According to one scholar, who cites no evidence for his claim, this soldiers'
   ballad originally had the word "cunts" instead of feet.
201 [soda water]: bicarbonate of soda, or baking soda, used for cleaning.
202 [*Et O ces voix d'enfants* . . .]: The last line of a sonnet by the French poet Paul
   Verlaine (1844–1896), "Parsifal," first published in the *Revue Wagnérienne*
   (6 June 1886).

> Parsifal a vaincu les Filles, leur gentil
> Babil et la luxure amusant—et sa pente
> Vers la Chair de garçon vierge que cela tente
> D'aimer les seins légers et ce gentil babil;
> Il a vaincu la Femme belle, au coeur subtil,
> Étalant ses bras frais et sa gorge excitante;
> Il a vaincu l'Enfer et rentre sous sa tente
> Avec un lourd trophée à son bras puéril,
> Avec la lance qui perça le Flanc suprême!
> Il a guéri le roi, le voici roi lui-même,
> Et prêtre du très saint Trésor essentiel.
> En robe d'or il adore, gloire et symbole,
> Le vase pur où resplendit le Sang réel.
> —Et, O ces voix d'enfants chantant dans la coupole!

The French can be translated as follows:

> Parsifal has overcome the maidens, their pretty
> Babble and alluring lust—and the downward slope
> Toward the Flesh of the virgin youth who tempts him
> To love their swelling breasts and pretty babble.
> He has overcome fair Woman, of subtle heart,
> Holding out her tender arms and thrilling throat;
> He has overcome Hell and returns under his tent
> With a heavy trophy at his youthful arm,
> With the lance which pierced the Savior's side!
> He has healed the King, he himself a king,
> And a priest of the most holy Treasure.
> In a robe of gold he worships the vase,
> Glory and symbol, where the actual Blood shined.
> —And O those voices of children singing under the cupola.

Verlaine's poem refers to Richard Wagner's opera, *Parsifal* (1882), in which
the innocent knight Parsifal overcomes first the temptations of the flower
maidens in Klingsor's magic garden, then the temptations of the beautiful
Kundry, who acts under a spell cast by Klingsor. Parsifal recovers the sacred
spear with which Christ's side had been pierced and returns to the Castle

of Monsalvat, where the Knights of the Holy Grail are waiting, and Anfortas, the Fisher King, will be healed by a touch from the spear. Before he heals Anfortas, Kundry (now free from Klingsor's spell) washes his feet (compare with Mrs. Porter and her daughter), and after Anfortas is healed a choir of young boys sings.

204–206 [Jug . . . Tereu]: See note to line 103.

209 [Mr. Eugenides, the Smyrna merchant]: In both ancient Greek and Latin, *euge* means "well done" or "bravo!" In ancient Greek, *eugeneia* meant "high descent, nobility of birth," and *eugenes* "well-born." The word persists in the modern term "eugenics." Smyrna, modern day Izmir, is on the western coast of modern Turkey, or Asia Minor, and until 1914 was part of the Ottoman Empire. Like other cities on the coast, it had had a heterogeneous population and was divided into Turkish, Jewish, Armenian, Greek, and Frankish quarters. During World War I, the Ottoman Empire had supported the Central Powers (Germany and the Austro-Hungarian Empire), while Greece had allied itself to the Entente (France, Britain, Russia). With the end of the war, obtaining Smyrna became Greece's primary goal. In May 1919 a Greek occupation force, protected by allied warships, disembarked in the city. Meanwhile, the collapse of the Ottoman Empire and allied occupation of Constantinople had begun to produce support for the Turkish nationalist movement headed by Mustafa Kemal (Atatürk), which had declared itself the successor to the Ottoman Empire. In February 1921 an international conference was held in London to resolve the problem of Asia Minor, but no agreement was reached. The Greeks launched a major offensive in March and by the end of the summer were only forty miles from Ankara. But in August, Mustafa Kemal launched a counteroffensive which completely routed the Greeks. On 8 September the Greek army evacuated Smyrna; the next day the Turks entered it and engaged in a full-scale massacre of the city's Christian inhabitants, killing some thirty thousand. The conflict was not resolved until July 1923, with the signing of the Treaty of Lausanne, in which Greece ceded all territories in Asia Minor to the newly created Republic of Turkey. In short, Greece and Smyrna were much in the news throughout the period that Eliot was writing *The Waste Land.*

212 [demotic]: As spoken by ordinary people, versus correct or learned speech.

213 [Cannon Street Hotel]: Cannon Street runs westward from King William Street (see notes to lines 66, 67). The Cannon Street Station was designed by John Hawkshaw, the South Eastern Railway's consulting engineer, and built between 1863 and 1866; it became a terminus for suburban commuters and businessmen traveling to and from the Continent. The massive, glass-roofed shed yawned over the north bank of the Thames. Though the station was remodeled in 1926 and badly damaged by bombs in World War II, its two distinctive towers, a familiar City landmark, were reconstructed as part of a redevelopment in 1969. Attached to the station was the City Terminus Hotel, later renamed the Cannon Street Hotel (see Fig. 10), designed by Edward Middleton Barry (1830–1880) and opened in May 1867. The building pre-

sented an uneasy mixture of Italianate and French Renaissance styles. The
Cannon Street facade had its east and west corners, each crowned with a
mansard roof and spirelet brought forward from the main building line.
The hotel closed in 1931, due to a decline in business; its public rooms were
kept open for meetings and banquets, but the remainder were converted to
offices, and the building was renamed Southern House. It was demolished
in 1963 and replaced with a fifteen-story office block of sterile appearance.
The architect, Edward Middleton Barry, is best known for having designed
several notable buildings in London, including the railway hotel at Charing
Cross, and Floral Hall in Covent Garden, Royal Opera House.

214 [a weekend at the Metropole]: The Metropole is a hotel in Brighton (see Fig.
11), a holiday resort on the southern coast of England. Designed by Alfred
Waterhouse (1830–1905) and opened in July 1890, it was the largest in Britain outside London, with 328 rooms of various sizes. The seven-story building, erected in red brick and terra-cotta, was also the first to break with the
traditional cream color of buildings on the seafront; at the time it was called
the ugliest building in Brighton. Today it is rather plain, adorned largely by
ironwork balconies, since alterations made in 1959 included removing the
distinctive bronze spire and several turrets, cupolas, and pinnacles.

218 [I Tiresias . . . two lives]: A legendary blind seer from Thebes. One day, when
he saw snakes coupling and struck them with his stick, he was instantly
transformed into a woman; seven years later the same thing happened again
and he was turned back into a man. Since he had experienced the body in
both sexes, he was asked by Jove and Juno to settle a dispute concerning
whether men or women had greater pleasure in making love. Tiresias took
the side of Jove and answered that women had more pleasure. Juno, an-
gered, blinded him. In compensation, Jove gave him the gift of prophecy
and long life. The story is told in Ovid's *Metamorphoses*, III, 316–338 (Eliot,
in his notes, gives the original Latin for lines 320–338), given here in
Rolfe Humphries's translation:

So, while these things were happening on earth
And Bacchus, Semele's son, was twice delivered,
Safe in his cradle, Jove, they say, was happy
And feeling pretty good (with wine) forgetting
Anxiety and care, and killing time
Joking with Juno. "I maintain," he told her,
"You females get more pleasure out of loving
Than we poor males do, ever." She denied it,
So they decided to refer the question
To wise Tiresias' judgment: he should know
What love was like, from either point of view.
Once he had come upon two serpents mating
In the green woods, and struck them from each other,
And thereupon, from man was turned to woman,

And was a woman seven years, and saw
The serpents once again, and once more stuck them
Apart, remarking: "If there is such magic
In giving you blows, that man is turned to woman,
It may be that woman is turned to man. Worth trying."
And so he was a man again; as umpire,
He took the side of Jove. And Juno
Was a bad loser, and she said that umpires
Were nearly always blind, and made him so forever.
No god can over-rule another's action,
But the Almighty Father, out of pity,
In compensation, gave Tiresias power
To know the future, so there was some honor
Along with punishment.

Tiresias also figures prominently in Sophocles' play *Oedipus Rex*, in which
he recognizes that the curse on Thebes has come about because Oedipus has
unknowingly committed incest with his mother Jocasta and killed his father.
Thebes has been turned into a waste land, its land and people infertile.

221 [Homeward . . . the sailor home from sea]: Eliot's note refers to Fragment 149
by Sappho, a Greek poet of the seventh century B.C.: "Hesperus, you bring
home all the bright dawn disperses, / bring home the sheep, / bring home
the goat, bring the child home its mother." For many readers the entire passage on "the violet hour" (lines 215–223) recalls Dante, *Purgatorio* VIII, 1–6:

Era già l'ora che volge il disio
ai navicanti e 'ntenerisce il core
lo dí c'han detto ai dolci amici addio;
e che lo novo peregrin d'amore
punge s'e' ode squilla di lontano
che paia il giorno pianger che si more.

The passage can be translated as follows:

It was now the hour that turns back the desire
of sailors and melts their heart
the day that they have bidden dear friends farewell,
and pierces the new traveler with love
if he hears in the distance
the bell that seems to mourn the dying day.

222 [The typist . . .]: It is difficult today to appreciate just how innovative Eliot
was in making a typist a protagonist in a serious poem. Prior to *The Waste
Land* typists had appeared almost exclusively in light verse, humorous or
satirical in nature. Their ever increasing presence in offices after 1885 was
registered instead in fiction and early film. While they were sometimes inte-

grated into genre fiction (the thriller, detective fiction), often they were
shown being tempted by unscrupulous bosses or fellow workers. Early novels about typists, from 1893 to 1908, were often melodramatic and lurid (see,
for example, Clara Del Rio, *Confessions of a Type-Writer* [Chicago: Rio, 1893]),
but these vanished after 1910. Instead, typists became a subject increasingly
explored by writers working in the tradition of realism. American writers
who did this were David Graham Phillips (mentioned by Eliot in the London
Letter, March 1921, 137), *The Grain of Dust* (New York: D. Appleton, 1911);
Sinclair Lewis, *The Job* (New York: Harcourt, Brace, 1917); and Winston
Churchill, *The Dwelling Place of Light* (New York: Macmillan, 1917). In Great
Britain authors who did this were Ivy Low, *The Questing Beast* (London:
Secker, 1914); Arnold Bennett, *Lilian* (London: Cassell, 1922); and Rebecca
West, *The Judge* (London: Hutchinson, 1922). In four of these novels the
heroine engages in what would now be termed consensual premarital sex.

225 [Her drying combinations]: A "combination" was the popular term for a
"combination garment," so-called because it combined a chemise with draw-
ers or panties in a single undergarment. Combinations were introduced in
the 1880s and vanished after World War II.

234 [a Bradford millionaire]: Bradford is located in the western part of Yorkshire,
a county in the northeast of England; it has always been a woolen and textile
center, and during the nineteenth century it experienced fantastic growth, its
population rising from 13,000 in 1801 to 280,000 by 1901. In Eliot's era the
town was still known for its textile industries, which employed more than
33 percent of the city's workers. Its mills prospered during World War I by
manufacturing serge, khaki uniforms, and blankets for the armed forces.
After the war there were charges of wartime profiteering.

246 [And walked among . . . the dead]: See Homer, *Odyssey*, book XI, which
recounts Odysseus's journey to the underworld, where he consults Tiresias.

253 [When lovely woman . . .]: Eliot's note directs the reader to a novel by Oliver
Goldsmith (1730?–1774), *The Vicar of Wakefield* (1762), chapter 24. The chapter begins with the song of Livia, which is introduced thus:

> The next morning the sun rose with peculiar warmth for the season;
> so that we agreed to breakfast together on the honey-suckle bank: where,
> wile we sate, my yongest daughter, at my request, joined her voice to the
> concert of the trees about us. It was in this place my poor Olivia first
> met her seducer, and every object served to recall her sadness. But that
> melancholy, which is excited by objects of pleasure, or inspired by
> sounds of harmony, soothes the heart instead of corroding it. Her
> mother too, upon this occasion, felt a pleasing distress, and wept, and
> loved her daughter as before. "Do, my pretty Olivia," she cried, "let us
> have that little melancholy air your pappa was so fond of, your sister
> Sophy has already obliged us. Do child, it will please your old father."
> She complied in a manner so exquisitely pathetic as moved me.

When Lovely woman stoops to folly,
And finds too late that men betray,
What charm can sooth her melancholy,
What art can wash her guilt away?
The only art her guilt to cover,
    To hide her shame from every eye,
To give repentance to her lover,
    And wring his bosom—is to die.

257 ["This music . . . upon the waters"]: See note to line 192.

258: The Strand, three-fourths of a mile long, is one of the busiest and most congested streets in London. It runs northeast from Trafalgar Square parallel to the Thames. Together with its prolongation, Fleet Street, it connects the City (or financial district) with Westminster (the political district). The street contains many restaurants, theaters, pubs, and hotels. Queen Victoria Street runs from Bank Junction, the very heart of the City, southwest and then west to Blackfriars Bridge (see Fig. 9).

260 [Lower Thames Street]: This street runs eastward from London Bridge along the north bank of the Thames (see Figs. 9, 12, 13). At this time the eastern end of it still housed Billingsgate Market, and "fishmen" were laborers who carried or wheeled the fish from docks to the market. At its western end still stands the church of St. Magnus Martyr (see below, line 263). In Eliot's time the area was still lively with colorful fishmen and local tradespeople (see Fig. 13).

264 [St. Magnus Martyr]: Built between 1671 and 1676 by Sir Christopher Wren, it is one of fifty-one churches which Wren built in the wake of the fire of London of 1666. Wren is best known as the architect of St. Paul's Cathedral. Eliot refers to the slender Ionic columns which grace the church's interior (see Figs. 12–14).

266 [The river sweats . . .]: Eliot's note states that "the song of the (three) Thames-daughters begins here" and continues to line 306, and compares their song with that of the Rhine-daughters in Wagner's opera, *Götterdämmerung (The Twilight of the Gods)* (1876), the fourth and final part of *Der Ring der Nibelungen (The Ring Cycle)*. The Rhine-daughters first appear in Wagner's *Das Rheingold* (1869), part one of the cycle. They are nymphs who guard a lump of gold in the river, and their ecstatic joy is expressed in their repeated cry, "Weialala leia wallala leialala." At the start of the opera Alberich, the leader of the Nibelung dwarfs, interrupts their play and wants them to satisfy his lust. But he is made to flounder in the waters as they mock him with these cries. Only someone who has overcome the lusts of the flesh, they tell him, can hope to possess the Rhine gold. Alberich curses love, then steals the gold. In *Götterdämmerung* the three Rhine-daughters reappear to sing of the Rhine gold they have lost. Even here their song is not mournful, but joyously praises the gold and looks forward to the hero who will return it to them. When Siegfried returns with the ring and refuses to give it to

them, they prophesy his death. Siegfried is then murdered. His beloved
Brünnhilde orders a vast funeral pyre to be built, which she lights and then
mounts. The flames destroy the hall and engulf all of Valhalla, destroying all
the gods (whence the opera's title). The Rhine overflows its banks, and the
Rhine-daughters take back their gold. It should be noted that the two-beat
measure which typifies much of this passage is adapted from Wagner's
nymphs, who use this measure whenever they sing.

275–276 [Greenwich reach . . . the Isle of Dogs]: The Isle of Dogs is a peninsula
created by a loop in the River Thames. Past the Isle of Dogs the Thames is
called Greenwich Reach.

279 [Elizabeth and Leicester]: Eliot's note refers the reader to James Anthony
Froude (1818–1894), *History of England from the Fall of Wolsey to the Death of
Elizabeth*, 12 vols. (London: Longman, Green, 1856–1870); vol. 7, *Reign of
Elizabeth: Volume 1* [1863]). Froude was Regius professor of history at Oxford
and a friend of Thomas Carlyle. His history draws heavily on the reports sent
by Alvarez de Quadra (bishop of Aquila), the Spanish ambassador at Queen
Elizabeth's court, to his master Philip II, King of Spain. Since Elizabeth was
only twenty-five years old when she ascended the throne on 17 November
1558, the question of whom she might marry loomed large. One perennial
candidate was Lord Robert Dudley, whose fortunes she encouraged from the
moment she became queen, naming him her master of the horse, a high-
ranking position. But when Dudley's wife was found dead on 8 September
1560, it was widely speculated that he had had some hand in her death. He
was banished from the court until a coroner's jury had found him innocent,
then returned. Throughout the early months of 1561 de Quadra reported his
growing conviction that Elizabeth would marry Robert, and that together
they would return England to the Catholic faith. But when a papal nuncio
applied to come to Elizabeth's court in June that year, the Council of State
(headed by William Cecil, who opposed Robert Dudley) rejected his applica-
tion, leaving de Quadra enraged. It was in this context that de Quadra wrote
to Philip on 30 June, a letter which Froude reports in translation, 347–349:

London, June 30
    Five or six clergy have been exposed on the pillory as conjurors and
necromancers. These were found making nativities of the Queen and
Lord Robert, with I know not what other strange things—trifles all of
them, had they not fallen into the hands of men who were glad to make
priests ridiculous.
    The Queen invited me to a party given by Lord Robert on St. John's
day [24 June]. I asked her whether she thought her ministers had done
good to their country by making a laughing-stock of Catholics in this
way. She assured me the secretary was not to blame. In speaking of your
Majesty, she said that as long as you were in England, you had been a
general benefactor, and had never injured a creature.

I professed myself shocked at the doings of the Council. I told her she should look better to them, and not allow these headstrong violent men to guide her in so serious a matter as religion.

She listened patiently and thanked me for my advice. In the afternoon we were in a barge, watching the games on the river. She was alone with the Lord Robert and myself on the poop, when they began to talk nonsense, and went so far that Lord Robert at last said, as I was on the spot there was no reason why they should not be married if the Queen pleased. She said that perhaps I did not understand sufficient English. I let them trifle in this way for a time, and then I said gravely to them both, that if they would be guided by me they would shake off the tyranny of those men who were oppressing the realm and them; they would restore religion and good order; and they could then marry when they pleased—and gladly would I be the priest to unite them. Let the heretics complain if they dared. With your Majesty at her side, the Queen might defy danger. At present it seemed she could marry no one who displeased Cecil and his companions.

I enlarged on this point, because I see that unless I can detach her and Lord Robert from the pestilential heresy with which they are surrounded, there will be no change. If I can once create a schism, things will go as we desire. This therefore appears to me the wisest course to follow. If I keep aloof from the Queen, I leave the field open to the heretics. If I keep her in good humour with your Majesty, there is always hope—especially if the heretics can be provoked into some act of extravagance. They are irritated to the last degree to see me so much about the Queen's person.

Your Majesty need not fear that I shall alienate the Catholics. Not three days ago, those persons whom your Majesty knows of, sent to me to say that their party was never so strong as at this moment, nor the Queen and Council so universally abhorred.

That the poem seems to link the historical Elizabeth with the legendary Cleopatra, or with Mrs. Porter, has troubled many critics. And unlike the Thames-daughters who appear in the following passages, Elizabeth did not become a victim of her lover (if Dudley was indeed her lover).

293–294 [Highbury bore me. Richmond and Kew / Undid me]: Eliot's note directs the reader to Dante, *Purgatorio* V, 130–136. In canto V, Dante encounters three spirits who have died violent deaths and repented only at the last moment. Their speeches have a terse, tormented quality commensurate with their fate, and they ask Dante to remember them when he returns to the world in order to speed their progress through Purgatory. The third, in particular, has a special poignancy which has always been admired:

"Deh, quando tu sarai tornato al mondo,
    e riposato della lunga via,"

seguitò il terzo spirito al secondo,
"ricorditi di me che son la Pia:
    Siena mi fe'; disfecemi Maremma:
    salsi colui che 'nnanellata pria
disposando m'avea con la sua gemma."

This can be translated as follows:

"Please, when you've returned to the world
    and rested from your long journey,"
    the third spirit said, following on the second,
"remember me, who am La Pia:
    Sienna bore me; the Maremma undid me:
    He knows of it who, first being engaged to me,
Married me with his gem."

Medieval commentators agreed in identifying the enigmatic speaker as the wife of Nello d'Inghiramo dei Pannocchieschi, a ruler in the Maremma, an area in southern Tuscany. She was murdered by him, according to some so that he could marry another woman, according to others because of her infidelity. These historical details, however, matter less than the mood evoked by her speech, one which Eliot captures perfectly and transposes in a modern key. Highbury was a drab, middle-class suburb in the north of London which had been developed in the late Victorian and Edwardian eras. Kew Gardens (officially, the Royal Botanic Gardens) is situated on the Banks of the River Thames between Richmond and Kew in southwest London. The Gardens comprise 132 hectares (288 acres), containing an extensive arboretum, water features, flower beddings, botanical glass houses, and historic buildings. Formerly estates of George III and his father, they were donated to the state in 1840, and are still a popular excursion site for city dwellers.

296 [Moorgate]: Moorgate was a gate in the London wall, built in 1415 and pulled down in 1761. The street that led to it runs north from the southwest corner of the Bank of England (see Fig. 9).

300 [Margate Sands]: Margate Sands (see Fig. 15) is the principal beach in Margate, a seaside resort in the county of Kent, some seventy miles east of London. Like many resorts, it expanded enormously with the growth of large-scale tourism in the late nineteenth century. The majority of its tourists were from the lower middle classes, shopkeepers and typists. Eliot himself stayed at the Albemarle Hotel, in Cliftonville, Margate, for three weeks in late October and early November 1921, the first part of a three-month leave from work to rest his nerves (see Introduction). Lines 259–311 were drafted while he was there.

307 [To Carthage then I came]: Eliot cites a passage that begins book III of *The Confessions of Saint Augustine*, trans. Edward B. Pusey (London: Dent, 1907),

31–32. A more extended transcription of the passage follows, which includes the last lines of book II:

I sank away from Thee, and I wandered, O my God, too much astray from Thee my stay, in these days of my youth, and I became to myself a barren land.

Book III

To Carthage I came, where there sang all around me in my ears a cauldron of unholy loves. I loved not yet, yet I loved to love, and out of deep-seated want, I hated myself for wanting not. I sought what I might love, in love with loving, and safety I hated, and a way without snares. For within me was a famine of that inward food, Thyself, my God; yet, through that famine I was not hungered; but was without all longing for incorruptible sustenance, not because filled therewith, but the more empty, the more I loathed it. For this cause my soul was sickly and full of sores, it miserably cast itself forth, desiring to be scraped by the touch of objects of sense. Yet if these had not a soul, they would not be objects of love. To love then, and to be loved, was sweet to me; but more, when I obtained to enjoy the person I loved. I defiled, therefore, the spring of friendship with the filth of concupiscence, and I beclouded its brightness with the hell of lustfulness; and thus foul and unseemly, I would fain, through exceeding vanity, be fine and courtly. I fell headlong into the love, wherein I longed to be ensnared. My God, my Mercy, with how much gall didst thou of thy great goodness besprinkle for me that sweetness? For I was both beloved, and secretly arrived at the bond of enjoying; and was with joy fettered with sorrow-bringing bonds, that I might be scoured with the iron burning rods of jealousy, and suspicions, and fears, and angers, and quarrels.

308 [Burning burning burning burning]: Eliot cites "The Fire Sermon" by the Buddha; for the text, see the note to the title of part III of *The Waste Land.* Another passage from book III of *The Confessions of Saint Augustine* is also pertinent. Augustine describes how he was converted to faith in God by reading Cicero's "Hortensius," then comments (36): "How I did burn then, my God, how did I burn to re-mount from earthly things to thee."

309–310 [O Lord Thou . . . pluckest]: Compare this passage from book X of *The Confessions of Saint Augustine,* 237–238:

But I, my God and my Glory, do hence also sing a hymn to Thee, and do consecrate praise to Him who consecrateth me, because those beautiful patterns which through men's souls are conveyed into their cunning hands, come from that Beauty, which is above our souls, which my soul day and night sigheth after. But the framers and followers of the out-ward beauties derive thence the rule of judging of them, but not of us-ing them. And He is there, though they perceive Him not, that so they might not wander, but keep their strength for Thee, and not scatter it

abroad upon pleasurable wearinesses. And I, though I speak and see
this, entangle my steps with these beauties; but Thou pluckest me out,
O Lord, Thou pluckest me out; because Thy loving-kindness is before
my eyes.

Death by Water: The title replicates a part of Madame Sosostris's warning to an
unnamed client in part I, line 55: "Fear death by water." Earlier critics often
associated this title with Jessie Weston's comments on the worship of Adonis
that was spread by traders from Phoenicia (an ancient kingdom on the eastern shores of the Mediterranean which included the coasts of modern-day
Lebanon and Syria). According to Weston, the spring festival of Adonis in
Alexandria "began with the solemn and joyous celebration of the nuptials of
Adonis and Aphrodite, at the conclusion of which a Head, of papyrus, representing the god, was with every show of mourning, committed to the waves,
and borne within seven days by a current (always to be counted upon at that
season of the year) to Byblos [in ancient Phoenicia], where it was received
and welcomed with popular rejoicing. The duration of the feast varied from
two days, as at Alexandria, to seven or eight" (*From Ritual to Romance*, 47).
More recent critics have questioned the significance or usefulness of part IV,
noting that it is a translation of poem written by Eliot in 1916–1917 (see next
note) and hence not originally related in any way to Weston's theses. Eliot
himself had doubts about part IV and briefly jettisoned it, but then restored
it at the insistence of Ezra Pound (see Introduction, 25).

312 [Phlebas the Phoenician]: This section is a close adaptation of the last seven
lines of a poem written by Eliot in French in 1916–1917, "Dans le Restaurant" (In the restaurant):

Plebas, le Phénicien, pendant quinze jours noyé,
Oubliait les cris des mouettes et le houle de Cornouaille,
Et les profits ets pertes, et la cargaison d'étain:
Un courant de sous-mer l'emporta très loin,
Le repassant aux étapes de sa vie antérieure.
Figurez-vous donc, c'était un sort pénible;
Cependant, ce fut jadis un bel homme, de haute taille.

Phlebas the Phoenician, a fortnight drowned,
Forgot the cries of the gulls, and swell of the Cornish sea,
And the profits and losses, and the cargo of tin.
An undercurrent carried him far away,
Taking him back through the stages of his former life.
Imagine it—a terrible fate;
Yet he was once so handsome and tall.

The name Phlebas may be derived from the Latin adjective *flebilis*, meaning
"lamentable, to be wept over."

319 [Gentile or Jew]: Compare Romans 3:9–12:

9 What then? are we no better than they? No, in no wise: for we have before proved both Jews and Gentiles, that they are all under sin;

10 As it is written, There is none righteous, no, not one:

11 There is none that understandeth, there is none that seeketh after God.

12 They are all gone out of the way, they are together become unprofitable; there is none that does good, no, not one.

What the Thunder Said: On the title, see note to lines 399–401.

322 [torchlight]: While the verse paragraph from line 322 to 330 draws on images associated with the betrayal and arrest of Christ in the garden of Gethsemane, these are highly stylized and remote from biblical particulars. Compare John 18:3: "Judas then, having received a band of men and officers from the chief priests and Pharisees, cometh thither with lanterns and torches and weapons."

324 [After the agony in stony places]: In the garden of Gethsemane, Jesus withdraws to pray, according to Luke 22:44: "And being in an agony he prayed more earnestly: and his sweat was as it were great drops of blood falling down o the ground." The phrase "stony places" is also biblical. It occurs in Psalm 141:6: "When their judges are overthrown in stony places, they shall hear my words; for they are sweet." It occurs again in Matthew 3:5, in the parable of the sower whose seeds are cast in various places: "Some fell upon stony places, where they had not much earth: and forthwith they sprung up, because they had no deepness of earth." And it occurs a third time in Matthew 13:20, when the meaning of the parable is expounded: "But he that received the seed into stony places, the same is he that heareth the word, and anon with joy receiveth it."

357: Eliot's factitious note directs the reader to a book by the Canadian author Frank M. Chapman (1864–1945) titled *Handbook of Birds of Eastern North America* (New York: D. Appleton, 1895). But the reader who follows up this lead will discover that the quotation Eliot cites is actually taken by Chapman from the American naturalist Eugene Pintard Bicknell (1859–1925), *A Study of the Singing of Our Birds* (Boston, 1885).

359 [Who is the third . . .]: Eliot's note at the beginning of part V outlining "three themes" to appear in the first part of part V, refers to the story of the journey to Emmaus. The story, recounted in Luke 24:13–32, takes place immediately after the disciples of Jesus return to his grave on Easter Sunday and discover that his body is no longer there, leaving them bewildered "at that which was come to pass."

13 And, behold, two of them went that same day to a village called Emmaus, which was from Jerusalem about threescore furlongs.

14 And they talked together of all these things which had happened.

15 And it came to pass, that, while they communed together and reasoned, Jesus himself drew near, and went with them.

16 But their eyes were holden that they should not know him.

17 And he said unto them, What manner of communications are these that ye have one to another, as ye walk and are sad?

18 And one of them, whose name was Cleopas, answering said unto him, Art thou only a stranger in Jerusalem, and hast not known the things which are come to pass there in these days?

19 And he said unto them, What things? And they said unto him, Concerning Jesus of Nazareth, which was a prophet mighty in deed and word before God and all the people:

20 And how the chief priests and our rulers delivered him to be condemned to death, and have crucified him.

21 But we trusted that it had been he which should have redeemed Israel: and beside all this, to-day is the third day since these things were done.

22 Yea, and certain women also of our company have made us astonished, which were early at the sepulchre;

23 And when they found not his body, they came, saying, that they had also seen a vision of angels, which said that he was alive.

24 And certain of them which were with us went to the sepulchre, and found it even so as the women had said: but him they saw not.

25 Then he said unto them, O fools, and slow of heart to believe all that the prophets have spoken:

26 Ought not Christ to have suffered these things, and to enter into his glory?

27 And beginning at Moses and all the prophets, he expounded unto them in all the Scriptures the things concerning himself.

28 And they drew nigh unto the village, whither they went: and he made as though he would have gone further.

29 But they constrained him, saying, Abide with us; for it is toward evening, and the day is far spent. And he went in to tarry with them.

30 And it came to pass, as he sat at meat with them, he took bread, and blessed it, and brake, and gave to them.

31 And their eyes were opened, and they knew him; and he vanished out of their sight.

32 And they said one to another, Did not our heart burn within us, while he talked with us by the way, and while he opened to us the Scriptures?

360 [When I count]: Eliot's note directs the reader to "the account of the one of the Antarctic expeditions (I forget which, but think one of Shackleton's)." Sir Ernest Shackleton (1874–1922) made three journeys to the Antarctic, each beset with problems. His third one attempted to cross the entire Antarctic ice cap on foot, a journey of 1,500 miles. The expedition set sail on the *Endurance* from the island of South Georgia in December 1914, but their ship became trapped in ice and was eventually crushed. To return they

made an almost two-year journey. Three years later Shackleton published his account of the trip, *South: The Story of Shackleton's Last Expedition, 1914–1917* (London: W. Heinemann, 1919), which includes the following passage (209):

When I look back at those days I have no doubt that Providence guided us, not only across those snow-fields, but across the storm-white sea that separated Elephant Island from our landing-place on South Georgia. I know that during that long and racking march of thirty-six hours over the unnamed mountains and glaciers of South Georgia it seemed to me often that we were four, not three. I said nothing to my companions on the point, but afterwards Worsely said to me, "Boss, I had a curious feeling on the march that there was another person with us." Crean confessed to the same idea. One feels "the dearth of human words, the roughness of mortal speech" in trying to describe things intangible, but a record of our journeys would be incomplete without a reference to a subject very near to our hearts.

The phrase "O dearth / Of human words! roughness of mortal speech!" is from John Keats (1795–1821), *Endymion* (1818), book II, lines 819–820.

366–367 [What is that sound . . . lamentation]: Eliot's note directs the reader to a book by the German author Hermann Hesse (1872–1962), *Blick ins Chaos: Drei Aufsätze (A Look into the Chaos: Three Essays)* (Berne: Verlag Seldwyla, 1920), from which Eliot quotes a passage in the original German, one that refers to the Russian Revolution and the collapse of the German and Austro-Hungarian empires: "Already half of Europe, and at the least half of Eastern Europe, is on the way toward chaos; it is drunkenly driving forward in a holy frenzy toward the abyss, drunkenly singing, as if singing hymns, the way Dmitri Karamazov sang. The offended bourgeois laughs over these songs; the holy seer hears them with tears." Dmitri Karamazov is a character in the novel *The Brothers Karamazov* by Feodor Dostoevsky (1821–1881). Eliot was so taken with Hesse's book that he urged his friend Sydney Schiff (1868–1948) to translate it into English. His translation, titled *In Sight of Chaos*, appeared a year later under Schiff's nom de plume, Stephen Hudson (Zurich: Verlag Seldwyla, 1923). Schiff was a well-to-do man who financed the quarterly journal *Art and Letters* (1917–1920), to which Eliot contributed two poems and four essays and reviews in 1919 and 1920.

377–384 [A woman . . . exhausted wells]: Conrad Aiken (1890–1972), who had been a friend of Eliot's since their student days at Harvard, later recalled that when he first read *The Waste Land* in 1922, he "had long been familiar with such passages as 'A woman drew her long black hair out tight,' which I had seen as poems, or part-poems, in themselves. And now saw inserted into *The Waste Land* as into a mosaic." See his Prefatory Note (1958) in Charles Brian Cox and Arnold P. Hinchliffe, eds., *T. S. Eliot, The Waste Land: A Casebook* (London: Macmillan, 1978), 91.

385–394 [In this decayed hole . . . rain]: Eliot's note at the beginning of part V
states that "the approach to the Chapel Perilous" is one of "three themes"
employed in this part's opening section (322–394), and he tells the reader to
"see Miss Weston's book." Weston's *From Ritual to Romance* devotes a chapter
(chapter 13, 175–188) to "The Perilous Chapel," a motif which she summarizes in her opening paragraph:

> Students of the Grail romances will remember that in many of the ver-
> sions the hero—sometimes it is a heroine—meets with a strange and
> terrifying adventure in a mysterious Chapel, an adventure which, we
> are given to understand, is fraught with extreme peril to life. The details
> vary: sometimes there is a Dead Body laid on the altar; sometimes a
> Black Hand extinguishes the tapers; there are strange and threatening
> voices, and the general impression is that this is an adventure in which
> supernatural, and evil, forces are engaged.

392 [Co co rico]: In French and Italian, "cocorico" is the onomatopoeic word
which represents the sound of a rooster, like the English "cock-a-doodle-do."

395 [Ganga]: A colloquial version of the Ganges, the sacred river of India.

397 [Himavant]: A Sanskrit adjective meaning "snowy," applied to one or more
mountains in the Himalayas.

399 [Then spoke the thunder]: Eliot's note to line 402 directs the reader to
"the fable of the meaning of the Thunder," recounted in the *Brihadaranyaka
Upanishad* 5. The Upanishads are sacred texts written in Sanskrit, the earliest of which belong to the eighth and seventh centuries B.C., a group including the *Brihadaranyaka Upanishad*. Their number exceeds two hundred,
though Indian tradition put it at one hundred and eight. The Indian philosopher Shankara, who flourished around A.D. 800, commented on eleven
Upanishads, including the *Brihadaranyaka Upanishad,* and these with two
or three others are considered the principal Upanishads. Upanishads were
first translated into English in 1817–1818 by Rammohun Roy (1772–1832),
a Bengali scholar, and other translations followed throughout the nineteenth
century. The German translation cited by Eliot, Paul Deussen's *Sechzig Upanishads des Veda* (Leipzig: F. A. Brockhaus, 1897), comprised sixty Upanishads.

   Eliot studied Sanskrit at Harvard in 1911–1913. In the fable of the Thunder which he cites, the Lord of Creation, Prajapati, thunders three times, the
sound being represented by the Sanskrit word "da." The text of the fable is
from *The Upanishads,* ed. and trans. Swami Nikhilananda (London: George
Allen and Unwin, 1963), 239–240:

> Prajāpati had three kinds of offspring: gods, men, and demons. They
> lived with Prajāpati, practicing the vows of brahmachārins. After finish-
> ing their term, the gods said to him: "Please instruct us, Sir." To them
> he uttered the syllable *da,* and asked: "Have you understood?" They
> replied: "We have. You said to us, 'Control yourselves (dāmyata).'"
> He said: "Yes, you have understood."

Then the men said to him: "Please instruct us, Sir." To them he uttered the same syllable *da,* and asked: "Have you understood?" They replied: "We have. You said to us, 'Give (datta).'" He said: "Yes, you have understood."

Then the demons said to him: "Please instruct us, Sir." To them he uttered the same syllable *da,* and asked: "Have you understood?" They replied: "We have. You said to us: 'Be compassionate (dayadhvam).'" He said: "Yes, you have understood."

This very thing is repeated even today by the heavenly voice, in the form of thunder, as "Da," "Da," "Da," which means: "Control your-selves," "Give," and "Have compassion." Therefore one should learn these three: self-control, giving, and mercy.

In one tradition of commentary, it was said that self-control was demanded of the gods because they were naturally unruly, charity of men because they were naturally greedy, and compassion of the demons because they were naturally cruel. But it was also suggested that there were no gods or demons other than men. Men who lack self-control, while endowed with other good qualities, are gods. Men who are particularly greedy are men. And those who are cruel are demons.

407: Eliot's note directs the reader to John Webster's play *The White Devil,* V.vi.154–158. Flamineo, a villain who has prostituted his sister, murdered his brother-in-law, and slaughtered his own brother, discovers that his sister Vittoria has betrayed him:

> O men
> That lie upon your death-beds, and are haunted
> With howling wives, ne'er trust them: they'll re-marry
> Ere the worm pierce your winding-sheet, ere the spider
> Make a thin curtain for your epigraphs.

411 [I have heard the key]: Eliot's note refers the reader to Dante's *Inferno,* XXXIII, 46–47. In the previous canto Dante has come upon Ugolino della Gherardesca, who is forever devouring the head of Archbishop Ruggieri of Pisa. Ugolino now explains that Ruggieri had locked up him and his four children in a tower, leaving them to starve. His four children had died first, and Ugolino had eaten their corpses. Ugolino had "heard the key / Turn in the door once and turn once only" because the guards were leaving him and his children to starve. Eliot's adaptation of these lines is based on a minor mistake. Because the word for "key" in modern Italian is *chiave,* he assumes that the verb *chiavar* in the passage by Dante must mean "to lock" or "to turn the key." But the word *chiavi* in medieval Italian meant "a nail," and what Ugolino heard, in the English translation of John Sinclair, was "the door of the terrible tower nailed up."

Eliot also quotes from *Appearance and Reality: A Metaphysical Essay* (London: Swan Sonnenschein, 1893), a book by the philosopher Francis Herbert Bradley (1846–1924). Bradley attended University College, Oxford, and graduated in 1869. In 1870 he was elected to a fellowship at Merton College, Oxford, tenable for life, with no teaching duties. He published *Ethical Studies* (1876), *The Principles of Logic* (1883), and then *Appearance and Reality*. During his lifetime he published only one other book, *Essays on Truth and Reality* (1914). He was the first philosopher to receive an Order of Merit, from King George V in 1924, three months before his death. Eliot wrote his Ph.D. thesis on Bradley for Harvard University, begun in 1911 and completed in 1916 (though never formally submitted). He lived in Merton College from October to December 1914 and again in the spring term of 1915. His thesis, *Knowledge and Experience in the Philosophy of F. H. Bradley*, was published in 1964.

416 [a broken Coriolanus]: the protagonist of Shakespeare's play *Coriolanus* (1607–1608) is a Roman general who despises the fickle mob. Driven by pride and his desire to punish an ungrateful Roman populace, he joins the Volscian forces against Rome. Though victorious, he is persuaded by his mother, wife, and son to spare Rome from sacking. To punish this new treachery, the Volscians hack him to death.

424 [Fishing . . . behind me]: Eliot's note refers the reader to chapter 9, "The Fisher King" (112–136), in Jessie Weston's *From Ritual to Romance*. Weston sums up her arguments to this point in the chapter when she declares: "We have already seen that the personality of the King, the nature of the disability under which he is suffering, and the reflex effect exercised upon his folk and his land, correspond, in a most striking manner, to the intimate relation at one time held to exist between the ruler and his land; a relation mainly dependent upon the identification of the King with the Divine principle of Life and Fertility" (114). She goes on to argue that the Fisher King's name in no way derived from early Christian use of the fish as a symbol, nor from any Celtic myth or legend. Instead, fish played "an important part in Mystery Cults, as being the 'holy' food" (129), partly because of "the belief . . . that all life comes from the water" (133) and partly because "the Fish was considered a potent factor in ensuring fruitfulness" among certain prehistoric peoples (135), a belief that had persisted and helped shape the figure of the Fisher King.

425 [Shall I . . . in order]: Compare Isaiah 38:1: "Thus saieth the Lord, Set thine house in order: for thou shalt die, and not live."

426 [London Bridge . . . falling down]: A nursery rhyme.

427 [Poi s'ascose . . . affina]: "Then he vanished into the fire that refines them" (Italian). Eliot's note cites Dante, *Purgatorio* XXVI, 145–148:

"Now I beseech you, by that virtue
which conducts you to the summit of the steps [in Purgatory],
at times bethink yourself of my suffering."
Then he vanished into the fire that refines them.

Dante hears these words from the Provençal poet Arnaut Daniel, whom he has met in the seventh circle of Purgatory, reserved for the lustful.

428 [Quando fiam . . . swallow]: Eliot's note refers the reader to the anonymous
Latin poem the *Pervigilium Veneris* (The vigil of Venus). The poem is now
thought to have been written in the early fourth century, most likely by
Tiberianus. But in Eliot's day both the date and authorship of the poem were
uncertain. We do not know which edition of the poem Eliot used, nor why
his memory introduced a small variant ("ceu" instead of the more common
"uti") into the text. (See Note on the Text.) Eliot quotes from line 90, three
lines before the poem ends, set within a passage which shifts from religious
hymn to a deeply personal note:

> Iam loquaces ore rauco stagna cygni perstrepunt;   85
> adsonat Terei puella subter umbram populi,
> ut putes motus amore ore dici musico,
> et neges queri sororem de marito barbaro,
> illa cantat, nos tacemus. quand ver venit meum?
> quando fiam uti chelidon, ut tacere desinam?   90
> perdidi Musam tacendo, nec me Apollo respicit:
> sic Amyclas, cum tacerent, perdidit silentium.
> cras amet qui numquam amavit, quique amavait cras amet.

This can be translated:

> The swans, with hoarse voice, are trumpeting over the pools;
> The young wife of Tereus sings under the poplar shade,
> Making you think her melodious mouth was moved by love,
> And not a sister's complaint of her barbarous husband.
> She is singing, I am mute. When will my springtime come?
> When shall I become like the swallow, that I cease being silent?
> I have lost my Muse through being silent, and Phoebus does not
>   regard me;
> So did Amyclae, through being voiceless, perish by its very silence.
> Tomorrow let him love who has never loved, and let him who has
>   tomorrow love.

The town of Amyclae was proverbially silent. The legend ran that it had several times suffered false alarms over spurious reports of an enemy's approach and so had passed a law which forbade the spreading of such news;
when eventually the enemy did come, no one was prepared to violate the law,
and thus did the city "perish by its very silence."

Some critics are convinced Eliot is also referring in this line to "O Swallow, Swallow," a poem by Alfred Tennyson:

> O Swallow, Swallow, flying, flying South,
> Fly to her and fall upon her gilded eaves,
> And tell her, tell her, what I tell to thee.

> O tell her, Swallow, if I could follow, and light

Upon her lattice, I would pipe and trill,
And cheep and twitter twenty million loves.

O were I thou that she might take me in,
And lay me on her bosom, and her heart
Would rock the snowy cradle till I did.

Why lingereth she to clothe her heart with love,
Delaying as the tender ash delays
To cloth herself, when all the woods are green?

O tell her, Swallow, that thy brood is flown:
Say to her, I do but wanton in the South,
But in the North long since my nest is made.

O tell her, brief is life but love is long,
And brief the sun of summer in the North,
And brief the moon of beauty in the South.

O Swallow, flying from the golden woods,
Fly to her, and pipe and woo her, and make her mine,
And tell her, tell her, that I follow thee.

429 [Le Prince . . . tour abolie]: Eliot's note directs the reader to "El Desdichado"
(1853), a celebrated but cryptic sonnet by the French poet Gerard de Nerval
(1808–1855):

Je suis le ténébreux, —la veuf, —l'inconsolé,
Le Prince d'Aquitaine à la tour abolie:
Ma seule *étoile* est morte, —et mon luth constellé
Porte le *Soleil noir* de la *Mélancholie*.
Dans la nuit du tombeau, toi qui m'as consolé,
Rends-moi le Pausilipe et la mer d'Italie,
La *fleur* qui plaisait tant à mon coeur désolé,
Et la treille où le pampre à la rose s'allie.
Suis-je Amour ou Phoebus? . . . Lusignan ou Biron?
Mon front est rouge encor du baiser de la reine;
J'ai rêvé dans la grotte où nage la syrène . . .
Et j'ai deux foix vainquer traversé l'Achéron:
Modulant tour à tour sur la lyre d'Orphée
Les soupirs de la sainte et les cries de la fée.

This can be translated:

I am the man of gloom, —the widower, —the unconsoled,
The Prince of Aquitania, his tower in ruins:
My only *star* is dead, and my constellated lute
Bears the *Black Sun* of *Melancholia*.
In the night of the tomb, you who've consoled me,

Give me back Posillipo and the Italian sea,
The *flower* that so pleased my desolate heart,
And the arbor where the vine and rose are intertwined.
Am I Amor or Phoebus? . . . Lusignan or Biron?
My brow still burns from the kiss of the queen;
I have dreamed in the grotto where the siren swims . . .
And twice I have crossed Acheron victorious:
Modulating on the lyre of Orpheus
Now the sighs of the saint, now the cry of the fairy.

Mount Posillipo in Naples is celebrated for its grottoes and is the site of
Virgil's grave. Guy de Lusignan (1129–1194) was king of Jerusalem and
Cyprus and supposedly a descendant of the fairy Melusina; Charles de
Gontaut, duke of Biron (1561–1602), was famous as a lover and adventurer.

431 [Why then . . . mad againe]: Eliot's note refers to *The Spanish Tragedy* (1592)
by Thomas Kyd (1557?–1595), subtitled *Hieronymo Is Mad Againe*. Hieronymo has been driven mad by the murder of his son. He is asked to write
a court entertainment or play, and he persuades the murderers to act in it.
Crucially, he also persuades them to speak their parts in different languages,
much as in the *The Waste Land*. *The Spanish Tragedy*, IV.i.59–106:

BALTHAZAR: It pleasèd you
At the entertainment of the ambassador
To grace the King so much as with a show.
Now, were your study so well furnishèd
As for the passing of the first night's sport
To entertain my father with the like,
Or any such-like pleasing motion,
Assume yourself it would content them well.

HIERONIMO: Is this all?

BALTHAZAR: Ay, this is all.

HIERONIMO: Whey then I'll fit you, say no more.
When I was young, I gave my mind
And plied myself to fruitless poetry;
Which, though it profit the professor naught,
Yet is it passing pleasing to the world.

LORENZO: And how for that?

HIERONIMO: Marry, my good lord, thus—
And yet methinks you are too quick with us—
When in Toledo there I studied,
It was my chance to write a tragedy—
See here, my lords—

                    He shows them a book.

Which, long forgot, I found this other day.
Now would your lordships favor me so much
As but to grace me with your acting it—
I mean each one of you to play a part—
Assure you it will prove most passing strange
And wondrous plausible to that assembly.

BALTHAZAR: What, would you have us play a tragedy?

HIERONIMO: Why, Nero thought it no disparagement,
And kings and emperors have ta'en delight
To make experience of their wits in plays!

LORENZO: Nay, be not angry, good Hieronimo;
The prince but asked a question.

BALTHAZAR: In faith, Hieronimo, and you be in earnest,
I'll make one.

LORENZO: And I another.

HIERONIMO: Now, my good lord, could you entreat
Your sister Bel-imperia to make one?
For what's a play without a woman in it?

BEL-IMPERIA: Little entreaty shall serve me, Hieronimo,
For I must needs be employèd in your play.

HIERONIMO: Why, this is well; I tell you, lordlings,
It was determined to have been acted
By gentlemen and scholars too,
Such as could tell what to speak.

BALTHAZAR: And now it shall be played by princes and courtiers,
Such as can tell how to speak,
If, as it is our country manner,
You will but let us know the argument.

IV.ii.169–192:

HIERONIMO: There's one thing more that rests for us to do.

BALTHAZAR: What's that, Hieronimo? Forget not anything.

HIERONIMO: Each one of us must act his part
In unknown languages,
That it may breed the more variety.
As you, my lord, in Latin, I in Greek,
You in Italian, and for because I know
That Bel-imperia hath practisèd the French,
In courtly French shall all her phrases be.

BEL-IMPERIA: You mean to try my cunning then, Hieronimo.

BALTHAZAR: But this will be a mere confusion,
And hardly shall we all be understood.

HIERONIMO: It must be so, for the conclusion
Shall prove the invention and all was good:
And I myself, in an oration,
And with a strange and wondrous show besides,
That I will have there behind a curtain,
Assure yourself shall make the matter known.
And all shall be concluded in one scene,
For there's no pleasure in tediousness.

BALTHAZAR: [*Aside to Lorenzo*] How like you this?

LORENZO: Why thus, my lord,
We must resolve to soothe his humors up.

BALTHAZAR: On then, Hieronimo, farewell till soon.

433 [Shantih Shantih Shantih]: Eliot's note explains that the repetition of this
word marks the ending of an Upanishad and is a loose counterpart to
the phrase "The Peace which passeth understanding." That phrase, in turn,
comes from Saint Paul's letter to the Philippians 4:7: "And the peace of God,
which passeth all understanding, shall keep your hearts and minds through
Christ Jesus."

Historical Collation

THE FIRST READING GIVEN HERE IS ALWAYS THAT OF THE
PRESENT EDITION, WHICH IS ALSO THAT OF *B* (OR THE BONI
AND LIVERIGHT EDITION OF THE POEM), EXCEPT IN THE
INSTANCES SPECIFIED IN A NOTE ON THE TEXT. OTHER
VERSIONS COLLATED ARE THE *CRITERION* (*C*), THE *DIAL* (*D*),
AND THE HOGARTH EDITION OF 1923 (*H*). VARIANTS FROM
POEMS, 1909–1925 (*F*) ARE RECORDED ONLY WHEN THEY
DIFFER FROM *B* AND *H*. VARIANTS FROM ELIOT'S *COLLECTED
POEMS, 1909–1935* (*1936*) ARE RECORDED ONLY IN THE
CASE OF LINE 427.

[Epigraph] *D, H; C* omits
"Nam] Nam *D, H*
dicerent:] *D;* dicerent, *H*
illa:] *D;* illa, *H*
θέλω."] θέλω. *D, H*
[Dedication] *F;* not in *C, D, H*
1 cruellest] *C, H;* cruelest *D*
10 in sunlight] *D, H;* in the sunlight *C*
11 Bin . . . deutsch] *C, H; Bin . . . deutsch D*
15 Marie] *D, H;* "Marie *C*
16 tight.] *D, H;* tight." *C*
26 red rock),] *C, H;* red rock) *D*
31–34 *Frisch . . . du?*] *D;* Frisch . . . du? *C, H*
37 —Yet] *D, H;* Yet *C*
37 Hyacinth] *C, H;* hyacinth *D*
41–42 silence. | Öd' . . . Meer.] silence. | Öd' . . . *Meer. D;* silence. | Od' . . .
    Meer. *B, H;* silence. | [blank line] | Od' . . . Meer. *C*

42–43 Meer. | [blank line] | Madame] C; *Meer.* | Madame D; Meer. |
   Madame H
46 Here,] D, H; "Here," C
47 Is] D, H; "Is C
57 Mrs.] C, H; Mrs D
59 these days.] D, H; in these days." C
76 hypocrite lecteur! . . . frère!"] H; *hypocrite lecteur! . . . frère!"* D; hypocrite
   lecteur, . . . frère!" C
77 Chair] D, H; chair C
77 throne,] H; throne C, D
80 From which] D, H; Wherefrom C
82 sevenbranched] D; seven-branched C, H
87 perfumes,] H; perfumes C, D
96 carvèd] C, D; coloured H
100 forced] C, D; forc'd H
101 voice] D; voice, C, H
102 cried,] D; cried C; cries H
102 and . . . pursues] D; (and . . . pursues), C; *(and . . . pursues)* H
111 to-night] C, D, H; tonight B
112 "Speak] Speak C, D, H
112 never speak?] C, D, H; never speak. B
113 "What] What C, D, H
114 "I] I C, D, H
115 rats'] C, D; rat's H
123 "Nothing] Nothing C, D, H
125 [indented] Those] C, D, H; [flush left] Those B
128–129 Rag— | It's] D, H; Rag | [blank line] | It's C
131 do?] C, D; do?" B, H
132 "I] H; I C, D
133 "With] With C, D, H
134 "What] H; What C, D
139 said—] H; said, C, D
141 it's] C, H; its B, D
141 TIME] D, H; TIME. C
148 good time,] C, D; good time. H
149 don't] C, D, H; dont B
150 Oh] D, H; Hoh C

152 IT's] *C, H;* ITS *B, D*

152 TIME] *D, H;* TIME. *C*

153 don't] *C, D, H;* dont *B*

155 won't] *C, D, H;* wont *B*

156 antique.] *C, D;* antique, *H*

158 said] *D, H;* says *C*

159 said] *D, H;* says *C*

161 all right] *C, D;* alright *B, H*

163 Well,] *C, H;* Well *D*

163 won't] *C, D, H;* wont *B*

164 don't] *C, D, H;* dont *B*

165 IT's] *C, H;* ITS *B, D*

165 TIME] *D, H;* TIME. *C*

166 Well,] *D, H;* Well *C*

168 IT's] *C, H;* ITS *B, D*

168 TIME] *D, H;* TIME. *C*

169 IT's] *C, H;* ITS *B, D*

169 TIME] *D, H;* TIME. *C*

170 Goonight Bill. Goonight Lou. Goonight May.] *D, H;* Goonight, Bill.
 Goonight, Lou. Goonight, May. *C*

171 Goonight. Goonight.] *D, H;* Goonight, goonight. *C*

180 directors;] *D;* directors, *C, H*

182 wept . . .] *D, H;* wept. . . . *C*

183 song,] *D, H;* song; *C*

187 vegetation] *D, H;* vegetation, *C*

188 bank] *D, H;* bank, *C*

190 gashouse] *D, H;* gas-house *C*

192 him.] *D, H;* him; *C*

198 Mrs.] *C, H;* Mrs *D*

198–199 spring. | O] *D, H;* spring | [blank line] | O *C*

199 Mrs.] *C, H;* Mrs *D*

200 daughter] *D, H;* daughter, *C*

202 *Et . . . coupole!*] *D;* Et . . . coupole! *C, H*

203 Twit twit twit] *D, H;* Twit, twit, twit, *C*

205 forc'd.] *D, H;* forced, *C*

207 City] *D, H;* City, *C*

209 Mr.] *C;* Mr *D, H*

211 C.i.f.] C. i. f. *D*, *H*; C.I.F. *C*

211 London:] *D*, *H*; London, *C*

213 Hotel] *D*, *H*; Hotel, *C*

214 weekend] *H*; week-end *C*, *D*

216 upward] *D*, *H*; upwards *C*

217 throbbing] *D*, *H*; throbbing, *C*

218 I Tiresias] *D*; I, *Tiresias C*, *H*

218 blind,] *C*, *D*; blind *H*

222 teatime] *H*; tea-time *C*, *D*

228 I Tiresias] *D*; I, Tiresias *C*, *H*

228 dugs] *D*, *H*; dugs, *C*

229 rest—] *D*, *H*; rest; *C*

242 indifference.] *D*, *H*; indifference *C*

243 And I Tiresias] *D*, *H*; and I, Tiresias, *C*

245 below] *D*, *H*; beneath *C*

246 dead.) *D*, *H*; dead); *C*

248 unlit . . .] *D*, *H*; unlit. . . . *C*

252 now] *D*, *H*; now, *C*

255 smoothes] *D*, *H*; smooths *C*

257 waters] *D*, *H*; waters, *C*

259 O City City] *D*, *H*; O City city *B*; O City, City *C*

260 Lower] *D*, *H*; Upper *C*

273 wash] *H*; wash, *C*, *D*

278–279 leialala | Elizabeth] *D*, *H*; leialala | [blank line] | Elizabeth *C*

286 Southwest] *H*; South-west *C*, *D*

287 down stream] *D*, *H*; down-stream *C*

300 Sands.] *D*, *H*; Sands, *C*

313 swell] *D*, *H*; swell, *C*

319 Jew] *D*, *H*; Jew, *C*

322 torchlight] *D*, *H*; torch-light

335 water we should stop and drink] *C*, *H*; water amongst the rock *D*

339 mountain] *C*, *D*, *H*; mount in *B*

345 mudcracked] *H*; mud-cracked *C*, *D*

345–346 houses | If] *D*, *H*; houses | [blank line] | If *C*

356 pine trees] *D*, *H*; pine-trees *C*

358 no water] *D*, *H*; no water. *C*

363 wrapt] *C*, *D*; wrapped *H*

365 —But] *D, H;* But *C*

366 air] *D, H;* air,

370–371 only | What] *D, H;* only | [blank line] | What *C*

388 home,] *D, H;* home *C;* home. *B*

391 rooftree] roof-tree *C, D, H*

401 *Datta:*] *D, H; Datta:* C

411 *Dayadhvam:*] *D, H; Dayadhvam:* C

415 aethereal] *C, F;* aetherial *B, D, H*

418 *Damyata:*] *D, H; Damyata:* C

419 oar] *D, H;* oar. *C*

420 calm,] *D, H;* calm; *C*

426–427 down | *Poi s'ascose nel foco che gli affina | Quando fiam ceu cheli-don*] *H;* down | [blank line] | Poi s'ascose nel foco che gli affina | Quando fiam ceu chelidon *C;* down | [blank line] | *Poi s'ascose nel foco che gli affina | Quando fiam ceu chelidon D;* down | *Poi s'ascose nel foco che gli affina | Quando fiam uti chelidon* 1936

429–430 *Le Prince . . . à la tour abolie* | These] *D; Le Prince . . . à la tour abolie* | [blank line] | These *H;* Le Prince . . . de la tour abolie | These *C*

432 Datta . . . Damyata.] *C, H; Datta . . . Damyata. D*

433 Shantih   shantih   shantih] *D, H;* shantih shantih shantih *C*

Notes

Notes are omitted from *C, D.*

[Introductory note] Cambridge *F;* Macmillan *B, H*

[Introductory note] will immediately recognise] will immediately recognize *H*

[Introductory note] *Adonis, Attis, Osiris] Atthis Adonis Osiris B, H*

23. Cf. Ecclesiastes XII, v.] *H* omits

31. V. *Tristan und Isolde] ed.;* 31. Tristan und Isolde *B, H*

60. Cf. Baudelaire: | "Fourmillante . . . | "Où . . . passant."] 60. Cf Baudelaire: | Fourmillante . . . | Où . . . passant. *H*

63. Cf. *Inferno] ed.;* 63. Cf. Inferno *B, H*

[Note to l. 63] "di . . . | "che] di . . . | che *B, H*

64. Cf. *Inferno* IV, 25–] *ed.;* 64. Cf. Inferno 25– *B* 64. Cf. Inferno IV, 2v– *H*

[Note to l. 64] "Quivi . . . | "non . . . | "che . . . tremare"] Quivi . . . | non . . . | che . . . tremare] *H*

[Note to l. 64] pianto, ma'] pianto ma] *H*

[Note to l. 92] "dependent . . . vincunt."] *ed.;* dependent . . . vincunt *B, H*

[Note to l. 100] III, l.] *ed.;* III l. *B, H*

[Note to l. 115] III, l.] *ed.;* III l. *B, H*

126. Cf. Part I, ll. 37, 48.] *ed.;* 126. Cf. Part I l. 37, 48. *B; H* omits

138. Cf. the game . . . *Women Beware Women*] *ed.;* 138. Cf. the game . . . *Women
beware Women B, H*

196. Cf. Marvell . . . | 197. Cf. Day . . .] 196. Cf. Day . . . | 197. Cf. Marvell . . . *B, H*

[Note to l. 197 (final ellipsis is Eliot's)] "When . . . | "A . . . | "Actaeon . . . | "Where
. . . skin . . ."] When . . . | A . . . | Actaeon . . . | Where . . . skin . . . *H*

[Note to l. 196] "To His Coy Mistress"] *To His Coy Mistress B, H*

[Note to l. 202] "Parsifal"] *ed.; Parsifal B, H*

[Note to l. 218 (opening ellipsis is Eliot's)] " . . . Cum . . . | . . . maribus," dixisse,
"voluptas."] *ed.;* ' . . . Cum . . . | . . . maribus', dixisse, 'voluptas.' *B, H*

[Note to line 218] "est . . . plagae," | . . . "ut . . . | . . . feriam!"] *ed.;* 'est . . . plagae,' |
. . . 'ut . . . | . . . feriam!' *B, H*

[Note to l. 264] *Churches*] *Churches:* B, H

[Note to l. 266] *Götterdämmerung*] Götterdämmerung *H*

[Note to l. 266] Rhine-daughters] *ed.;* Rhinedaughters *B, H*

[Note to l. 276] *Elizabeth,*] *Elizabeth B, H*

[Note to l. 357] unequaled] unequalled *H*

[Note to l. 401] sympathise] sympathize *H*

[Note to l. 401] *Brihadaranyaka-Upanishad*] *H; Brihadaranyaka—Upanishad B*

[Note to l. 407] "Ere . . . | "Make . . .] *ed.;* Ere . . . | Make . . . *B, H*

[Note to l. 411] "all'orribile] *ed.;* all'orribile *B, H*

[Note to l. 429] "El Desdichado"] *ed.; El Desdichado B, H*

ELIOT'S CONTEMPORARY PROSE

The Two Stupidities

I take up this task of writing a London letter with an overwhelming sense of difficulty. As I first proposed it to myself, there was no difficulty at all: it was to mention any work, or any momentary appearance of intellect or feeling, which seemed to deserve mention, to use any opportunity to consider the writing of living authors whom I respect, and to construct such a portrait of the time as might be in my power. Then I reflected that there is in contemporary English literature a very great deal which I cordially detest; and that I could not make an honest portrait without calling attention to these things. Yet I recognized that by so doing I might arouse the glee, and draw upon myself the approval, of exactly that part of American opinion which I abominate. One must face the fact that the imbeciles on either side of the water are very glad and quite able to perceive, by that sort of hostile sympathy which exists only among members of the same family, the imbecilities of the great fraternity on the other side; and that this perception only confirms them in their own variety of stupidity. I can claim no great originality in diagnosing either of the two stupidities; the only possible originality is in their collocation. There is Mr. Mencken, a brilliant specialist in American depravity, whose last book I have read with strong admiration.[2] And only recently, when I mentioned, rather gently as I thought, a very conspicuous feature of English stupidity, I was gaped

at by one of the smaller English reviewers, for my words of "elegant anguish."[3] It pleased me to reflect that a critic of the same stripe had once
referred to Matthew Arnold as an "elegant Jeremiah"; although this coinci-
dence merely proved the immortality of the English reviewer, and not any
similarity between Matthew Arnold and myself.[4] However, if these letters
succeed in being written with any competence, I am almost certain to become an object of international execration; a disaster in which I pray very
vigorously that *The Dial* may not share.

Prolegomena to Poetry

Mr. Harold Monro has just produced a book entitled *Some Contemporary
Poets: 1920*, which is a particularly useful book for my horrid purpose.[5] It
is, I hope, no injustice to Mr. Monro to say that his book has every appearance of having been written to order. We have all written books to order,
or we have conceived the desire, at times of penury, of being asked to write
a book to order, and some moralists tell us that desire is as sinful as com-
mission. But the peculiar effect of Mr. Monro's labours appears to be, that
everything in contemporary poetry (1920) is reduced to a precise level of
flatness. Our judgement is thus left free, if unguided. It is to be wondered
that the "general reading public," to whom its publishers say it should appeal, and who can hardly be other than a small section of what Arnold
called the Philistines, will make of it.[6] Some of the poets whom Mr. Monro
chats about are dull, some are immature, some are slight, some are down-
right bad: Mr. Monro's effect is to make them all seem dull, immature,
slight, and bad. And some are good, but we do not get that impression
from the book.

The first suggestion which this book gives me is that what I may call
the centre of gravity of dulness lies, in America and England, at different
points. Nearly the whole body of the Established Church of contemporary
literature in America must appear a little ridiculous, if no worse, to even
the most latitudinarian *littérateurs* of Established contemporary literature
in England. I cannot conceive Mr. Edmund Gosse, for example, really being taken in by the effusions of Miss Repplier or the Reverend Mr. Crothers,
although I can conceive of his commending them with a kindly Olympian
patronage which might take in the recipients.[7] The Polite Essay is, in fact,
done rather better in England, and this truth is not reserved for a few profound minds. Nevertheless the Established Church of literature does occa-

sionally patronize, with the semblance of enthusiasm, American literature which happens to amuse it. It is creditable that *Spoon River* should for a time have aroused interest here; unfortunately, its success has been more lately duplicated by the poetry of Mr. Vachel Lindsay.[8] His apparent "Americanism" and vigorous freedom from shame about his simple tastes amuse the orthodox, while his Y.M.C.A. morality represents something more remote than a massacre in Armenia.[9] His verses have appeared in an English periodical.[10] But I cannot believe that he is treated with more respect than that with which Clemenceau and Lloyd George bonified President Wilson.[11]

One must therefore reject the belief that there is any near equivalent in England for the Reverend Mr. Crothers, or Lindsay, or Mr. Mabie, or that there is any exact parallel anywhere between English life and American life (though there are constant curious resemblances when one has ceased to expect them).[12] And the standards by which one disposes of American bad writing and English bad writing will not be the same. The conventional literature of America is either wretchedly imitative of European culture, or ignorant of it, or both; and by this standard one easily expels either the Reverend Mr. Crothers, with his parish tea-party wit, his dreadful Nonconformity, or Mr. David Graham Phillips, with his exploitation of the Noble Fallen Woman who, in England, has vanished into the underworld of romance.[13] But there is no simple international comparison of cultures by which to deal so easily with, let us say, Mr. John Drinkwater.[14] I cannot point to any existing society which produces finer average specimens than Mr. Drinkwater; I can only point to a few individuals in England; and it is always open to Mr. Drinkwater's admirers to protest that my few individuals are impostors. The most obvious thing to say, the thing which makes it difficult for the critic to say more, is that the work of Mr. Drinkwater is dull, supremely dull. But when one turns to view the work of a numerous host of Drinkwaters, incipient Drinkwaters, decayed Drinkwaters, cross-bred Drinkwaters, this adjective ceases to satisfy the intelligence. Any social phenomenon of such dimensions must present more interest than that.

I do not make the mistake of supposing that Keats, or Shelley, or Wordsworth, or Tennyson can be incriminated in the production of the Georgian Anthology.[15] Good poets may usually have a bad influence, but their influence is usually much more restricted. I cannot see in the Georgian Anthology any such influence as Wordsworth, Keats, and Shelley had upon Arnold, Tennyson, and Browning. The dulness of the Georgian Anthology is original, unique; we shall find its cause in something much more profound than the influence of a few predecessors. The subtle spirit inspiring the ouija-board of Mr. J. C. Squire's patient prestidigitators is not the shattered Keats but the solid and eternal Podsnap himself.[16] This party represents, in fact, the insurgent middle class, Mr. Monro's General Reading Public. At the very moment when the middle class appears to be on the point of perdition—beleaguered by a Coalition Government, the Three Trades-Unions, and the Income Tax—at this very moment it enjoys the triumph, in intellectual matters, of being able to respect no other standards than its own.[17] And indeed, while its citadels appear to topple, it is busy strengthening its foundations. Year by year, royal birth-day by royal birth-day, it gains more seats in the House of Lords; and on the other hand, if it rejects with contumely the independent man, the free man, all the individuals who do not conform to a world of mass-production, the Middle Class finds itself on one side more and more approaching identity with what used to be called the Lower Class. Both middle class and lower class are finding safety in Regular Hours, Regular Wages, Regular Pensions, and Regular Ideas. In other words, there will soon be only one class, and the second Flood is here.

This social evolution is not, of course, peculiarly British, and I am ready to admit that it may have more revolting forms elsewhere. I have no wish to dwell upon the subject; I only introduced it as a background to the Georgian Anthology. I do not wish either to dwell upon the dulness of this book; that the writers cannot help. What I wish to comment on is the extreme lack of culture on the part of a number of writers in prose and verse; and when I say this I hear already the repeated epithets of "elegant anguish," and "dusty face," and "*précieux ridicule*" with which my efficient clipping-bureau has lately refreshed me.[18] I am prepared to be accused, so unconscious is the humour of the multitude, of self-advertisement. But it is certain that culture does not reside solely in a university education, or in extensive reading; and it is doubtful whether culture is perceptibly developed by a busy life of journalism. A literature without any critical sense; a poetry which takes not the faintest notice of the development of French verse from Baudelaire to the present day, and which has perused English literature with only a wandering antiquarian passion, a taste for which everything is either too hot or too cold; there is no culture here. Culture is traditional, and loves novelty; the General Reading Public knows no tradition, and loves staleness. And it must not be supposed that this great middle class public which consumes Georgian poetry corresponds to the public of Mrs. Ella Wheeler Wilcox.[19] I intend no disrespect to that lady, whose verse I have read with ease and some pleasure. The Georgian public is a smallish but important public, it is that offensive part of the middle class which believes itself superior to the rest of the middle class; and superior for precisely this reason that it believes itself to possess culture.

Returning to Mr. Monro's book, we find a number of poets, a very small number, who cannot simply be described as purveyors to the General Reading Public. There is Mr. Nichols, who is too nimble to be dull, and who is very immature; if he could free himself from the circumambient vulgarity and in several ways forget himself, he might rise to a superior place.[20] Then there is the curious spectacle of Mr. Huxley, one of the very few who have experienced the influence of Laforgue, and who writes (I believe it is no secret) one of the brightest pages in the *Athenaeum;* before he has thoroughly worked out Laforgue into a perfect language of his own, he skews off into "Leda," which, although the work of a much more sophisticated temperament than Mr. Squire's, is really a concession to the creamy top of the General Reading Public.[21] There is Miss Sitwell.[22] She is tediously given to repeating herself, but this repetition is perhaps her consciousness of the fact that she has a genuine little vision of the age, quite her own. This peculiar way of seeing things, which is not capable of much development, is what is interesting; not her technique, which is insufficient. And individually, there are poems by Mr. Herbert Read and Mr. Aldington which endure.[23] But what is good (on looking over for the last time Mr. Monro's list of names) is very scattered, and the bad poetry is very compact. I have avoided mentioning the Elder Poets, such as Mr. Bridges, or Mr. Yeats, or Mr. Pound.[24] One becomes old very quickly in these days.

What I propose to myself, in continuation of this tentative essay, is to compare the use of the English language in contemporary English and American verse, a comparison which will probably show a balance in favour of London (or Dublin); and further to institute a comparison of English and American verse with French. There are pitfalls too in the question of the Revival of Criticism in England; I should rightly have discussed the revival of criticism in this letter, as it may be dead before I write again.[25] Again, the Palladium has at this moment an excellent bill, including Marie

Lloyd, Little Tich, George Mozart, and Ernie Lotinga;[26] and that provokes an important chapter on the Extinction of the Music Hall, the corruption of the Theatre Public, and the incapacity of the British public to appreciate Miss Ethel Levey.[27] Next week the admirable Phoenix Society will perform *Volpone or the Fox* and this requires a word on Shakesperian acting in England.[28] All of these problems are integral to my plan, and I hope can be included before the next visit of M. Diaghileff's Ballet.[29] A small but varied exhibition by Picasso is the most interesting event of London at this moment—but that lies outside my province.[30]

THE ROMANTIC ENGLISHMAN, THE COMIC SPIRIT, AND THE FUNCTION OF CRITICISM[1]

SIR TUNBELLY CLUMSY, Sir Giles Overreach, Squire Western, and Sir Sampson Legend, who was lately so competently revived by Mr. Byford at the Phoenix, are different contributions by distinguished mythmakers to the chief myth which the Englishman has built about himself.[2] The myth that a man makes has transformations according as he sees himself as hero or villain, as young or old, but it is essentially the same myth; Tom Jones is not the same person, but he is the same myth, as Squire Western; Midshipman Easy is part of the same myth; Falstaff is elevated above the myth to dwell on Olympus, more than a national character.[3] Tennyson's broad-shouldered genial Englishman is a cousin of Tunbelly Clumsy; and Mr. Chesterton, when he drinks a glass of beer (if he does drink beer), and Mr. Squire, when he plays a game of cricket (if he does play cricket), contribute their little bit.[4] This myth has seldom been opposed or emulated; Byron, a great mythmaker, did, it is true, set up the Giaour, a myth for the whole of Europe.[5] But in our time, barren of myths—when in France there is no successor to the *honnête homme qui ne se pique de rien*, and René, and the dandy, but only a deliberate school of mythopoeic nihilism—in our time the English myth is pitiably diminished.[6] There is that degenerate descendent, the modern John Bull, the John Bull who usually alternates with Britannia in the cartoons of *Punch*, a John Bull composed of Podsnap and Bottomley.[7] And John Bull becomes less and less a force, even in a purely political role.

The theatre, naturally the best platform for the myth, affords in our time singularly little relief. What a poor showing, the military and nautical V.C.'s, the Spy, the Girl who sank the Submarine![8] The Englishman with a craving for the ideal (there are, we believe, a good many) famishes in the stalls of the modern theatre. The exotic spectacle, the sunshine of *Chu Chin Chow,* is an opiate rather than a food.[9] Man desires to see himself on the stage, more admirable, more forceful, more villainous, more comical, more despicable—and more much else—than he actually is. He has only the opportunity of seeing himself, sometimes, a little better dressed. The romantic Englishman is in a bad way.

It is perhaps in the music hall, and sometimes in the cinema, that we have an opportunity for partial realization. Charlie Chaplin is not English, or American, but a universal figure, feeding the idealism of hungry millions in Czecho-Slovakia and Peru. But the English comedian supplies in part, and unconsciously, the defect: Little Tich, Robey, Nellie Wallace, Marie Lloyd, Mozart, Lupino Lane, George Graves, Robert Hale, and others, provide fragments of a possible English myth.[10] They effect the Comic Purgation. The romantic Englishman, feeling in himself the possibility of being as funny as these people, is purged of unsatisfied desire, transcends himself, and unconsciously lives the myth, seeing life in the light of imagination. What is sometimes called "vulgarity" is therefore one thing that has not been vulgarised.

Only unconsciously, however, is the Englishman willing to accept his own ideal. If he were aware that the fun of the comedian was more than fun he would be unable to accept it; just as, in all probability, if the comedian were aware that his fun was more than fun he might be unable to perform it. The audience do not realize that the performance of Little Tich is a compliment, and a criticism, of themselves. Neither could they appreciate the compliment, or swallow the criticism, implied by the unpleasant persons whom Jonson put upon the stage.[11] The character of the serious stage, when he is not simply a dull ordinary person, is confected of abstract qualities, as loyalty, greed, and so on, to which we are supposed to respond with the proper abstract emotions. But the myth is not composed of abstract qualities; it is a point of view, transmuted to importance; it is made by the transformation of the actual by imaginative genius.

   The modern dramatist, and probably the modern audience, is terrified of the myth. The myth is imagination and it is also criticism, and the two are one. The Seventeenth Century had its own machinery of virtues and vices, as we have, but its drama is a criticism of humanity far more serious than its conscious moral judgements. *Volpone* does not merely show that wickedness is punished; it criticises humanity by intensifying wickedness. How we are reassured about ourselves when we make the acquaintance of such a person on the stage! I do not for a moment suggest that anyone is affected by *Volpone* or any of the colossal Seventeenth Century figures as the newspapers say little boys are by cinema desperados. The myth is degraded by the child who points a loaded revolver at another, or ties his sister to a post, or rifles a sweet-shop; the Seventeenth Century populace was not appreciably modified by its theatre; and a great theatre in our own time would not transform the retired colonel from Maida Vale into a Miles Gloriosus.[12] The myth is based upon reality, but does not alter it. The material was never very fine, or the Seventeenth Century men essentially superior to ourselves, more intelligent or more passionate. They were surrounded, indeed, by fewer prohibitions, freer than the millhand, or the petrified product which the public school pours into our illimitable suburbs.

THE LESSON OF BAUDELAIRE[1]

WITH REGARD TO CERTAIN intellectual activities across the Channel, which at the moment appear to take the place of poetry in the life of Paris, some effort ought to be made to arrive at an intelligent point of view on this side. It is probable that this French performance is of value almost exclusively for the local audience; I do not here assert that it has any value at all, only that its pertinence, if it has any, is to a small public formidably well instructed in its own literary history, erudite and stuffed with tradition to the point of bursting. Undoubtedly the French man of letters is much better read in French literature than the English man of letters is in any literature; and the educated English poet of our day must be too conscious, by his singularity in that respect, of what he knows, to form a parallel to the Frenchman. If French culture is too uniform, monotonous,[2] English culture, when it is found, is too freakish and odd. Dadaism is a diagnosis of a disease of the French mind; whatever lesson we extract from it will not be directly applicable in London.[3]

Whatever value there may be in Dada depends upon the extent to which it is a moral criticism of French literature and French life. All first-rate poetry is occupied with morality: this is the lesson of Baudelaire.[4] More than any poet of his time, Baudelaire was aware of what most mattered: the problem of good and evil. What gives the French Seventeenth

Century literature its solidity is the fact that it had its Morals, that it had a coherent point of view. Romanticism endeavoured to form another Morals—Rousseau, Byron, Goethe, Poe were moralists. But they have not sufficient coherence; not only was the foundation of Rousseau rotten, his structure was chaotic and inconsistent. Baudelaire, a deformed Dante (somewhat after the intelligent Barbey d'Aurevilly's phrase), aimed, with more intellect *plus* intensity, and without much help from his predecessors, to arrive at a point of view toward good and evil.[5]

English poetry, all the while, either evaded the responsibility, or assumed it with too little seriousness. The Englishman had too much fear, or too much respect, for morality to dream that possibly or necessarily he should be concerned with it, *vom Haus aus,* in poetry.[6] This it is that makes some of the most distinguished English poets so trifling. Is anyone seriously interested in Milton's view of good and evil? Tennyson decorated the morality he found in vogue; Browning really approached the problem, but with too little seriousness, with too much complacency; thus *The Ring and the Book* just misses greatness—as the revised version of *Hyperion* almost, or just, touches it.[7] As for the verse of the present time, the lack of curiosity in technical matters, of the academic poets of to-day (Georgian et caetera) is only an indication of their lack of curiosity in moral matters. On the other hand, the poets who consider themselves most opposed to Georgianism, and who know a little French, are mostly such as could imagine the Last Judgement only as a lavish display of Bengal lights, Roman candles, catherine-wheels, and inflammable fire-balloons.[8] *Vous, hypocrite lecteur . . .*[9]

ANDREW MARVELL[1]

THE TERCENTENARY OF THE former member for Hull deserves not only the celebration proposed by that favoured borough, but a little serious reflection upon his writing.[2] That is an act of piety, which is very different from the resurrection of a deceased reputation. Marvell has stood high for some years; his best poems are not very many, and not only must be well known, from the *Golden Treasury* and the *Oxford Book of English Verse*, but must also have been enjoyed by numerous readers.[3] His grave needs neither rose nor rue nor laurel; there is no imaginary justice to be done; we may think about him, if there be need for thinking, for our own benefit, not his. To bring the poet back to life—the great, the perennial, task of criticism—is in this case to squeeze the drops of the essence of two or three poems; even confining ourselves to these, we may find some precious liquor unknown to the present age. Not to determine rank, but to isolate this quality, is the critical labour. The fact that of all Marvell's verse, which is itself not a great quantity, the really valuable part consists of a very few poems indicates that the unknown quality of which we speak is probably a literary rather than a personal quality; or, more truly, that it is a quality of a civilization, of a traditional habit of life. A poet like Donne, or like Baudelaire or Laforgue, may also be considered the inventor of an attitude, a system of feeling or of morals.[4] Donne is difficult to analyse: what appears at one time a curious personal point of view may at another time appear rather the precise concentration of a kind of feeling diffused in the air about him. Donne and his shroud, the shroud and his motive for wearing it, are inseparable, but they are not the same thing. The seventeenth century sometimes seems for more than a moment to gather up and to digest into its art all the experience of the human mind which (from the same point of view) the later centuries seem to have been partly engaged in repudiating. But Donne would have been an individual at any time and place; Marvell's best verse is the product of European, that is to say Latin, culture.

Out of that high style developed from Marlowe through Jonson (for Shakespeare does not lend himself to these genealogies) the seventeenth century separated two qualities: wit and magniloquence.[5] Neither is as simple or as apprehensible as its name seems to imply, and the two are not in practice antithetical; both are conscious and cultivated, and the mind which cultivates one may cultivate the other. The actual poetry, of Marvell, of Cowley, of Milton and of others, is a blend in varying proportions.[6] And we must be on guard not to employ the terms with too wide a comprehension; for like the other fluid terms with which literary criticism deals, the meaning alters with the age, and for precision we must rely to some degree upon the literacy and good taste of the reader. The wit of the Caroline poets is not the wit of Shakespeare, and it is not the wit of Dryden, the great master of contempt, or of Pope, the great master of hatred, or of Swift, the great master of disgust.[7] What is meant is something which is a common quality to the songs in Comus and Cowley's Anacreontics and Marvell's "Horatian Ode."[8] It is more than a technical accomplishment, or the vocabulary and syntax of an epoch; it is, what we have designated tentatively as wit, a tough reasonableness beneath the slight lyric grace. You cannot find it in Shelley or Keats or Wordsworth; you cannot find more than an echo of it in Landor; still less in Tennyson or Browning; and among contemporaries Mr. Yeats is an Irishman and Mr. Hardy is a modern Englishman—that is to say, Mr. Hardy is without it and Mr. Yeats is outside of the tradition altogether.[9] On the other hand, as it certainly exists in Lafontaine, there is a large part of it in Gautier.[10] And of the magniloquence, the deliberate exploitation of the possibilities of magnificence in language which Milton used and abused, there is also use and even abuse in the poetry of Baudelaire.

Wit is not a quality that we are accustomed to associate with "Puritan" literature, with Milton or with Marvell. But if so, we are at fault partly in our conception of wit and partly in our generalizations about the Puritans. And if the wit of Dryden or of Pope is not the only kind of wit in the language, the rest is not merely a little merriment or a little levity or a little impropriety or a little epigram. And, on the other hand, the sense in which a man like Marvell is a "Puritan" is restricted. The persons who opposed Charles I and the persons who supported the Commonwealth were not all of the flock of Rabbi Zeal-of-the-land Busy or the United Grand Junction Ebenezer Temperance Association.[11] Many of them were gentlemen of the time who merely believed, with considerable show of reason, that government by a Parliament of gentlemen was better than government by a Stuart; though they were, to that extent, Liberal Practitioners, they could hardly foresee the tea-meeting and the Dissidence of Dissent. Being men of education and culture, even of travel, some of them were exposed to that spirit of the age which was coming to be the French spirit of the age. This spirit, curiously enough, was quite opposed to the tendencies latent or the forces active in Puritanism; the contest does great damage to the poetry of Milton; Marvell, an active servant of the public, but a lukewarm partisan, and a poet on a smaller scale, is far less injured by it. His line on the statue of Charles II, "It is such a King as no chisel can mend," may be set off against his criticism of the Great Rebellion: "Men . . . ought and might have trusted the King."[12] Marvell, therefore, more a man of the century than a Puritan, speaks more clearly and unequivocally with the voice of his literary age than does Milton.

This voice speaks out uncommonly strong in the "Coy Mistress." The theme is one of the great traditional commonplaces of European literature. It is the theme of "O mistress mine," of "Gather ye rosebuds," of "Go, lovely rose";[13] it is in the savage austerity of Lucretius and the intense levity of Catullus.[14] Where the wit of Marvell renews the theme is in the variety and order of the images. In the first of the three paragraphs Marvell plays with a fancy which begins by pleasing and leads to astonishment.

> Had we but world enough and time,
> This coyness, lady, were no crime.
>   . . . I would
> Love you ten years before the Flood,
> And you should, if you please, refuse

> Till the conversion of the Jews;
> My vegetable love should grow
> Vaster than empires and more slow. . . .

We notice the high speed, the succession of concentrated images, each magnifying the original fancy. When this process has been carried to the end and summed up, the poem turns suddenly with that surprise which has been one of the most important means of poetic effect since Homer:

> But at my back I always hear
> Time's wingèd chariot hurrying near,
> And yonder all before us lie
> Deserts of vast eternity.[15]

A whole civilization resides in these lines:

> Pallida Mors aequa pulsat pede pauperum tabernas
> Regumque turris. . . .
>
> Eheu fugaces, Postume, Postume,
> Labuntur anni. . . .
>
> Post equitem sedet atra Cura.[16]

And not only Horace, but Catullus himself:

> Nobis, cum semel occidit brevis lux,
> Nox est perpetua una dormienda.[17]

The verse of Marvell has not the grand reverberation of Catullus's Latin; but the image of Marvell is certainly more comprehensive and penetrates greater depths than any of those quoted from Horace.

A modern poet, had he reached the height, would very likely have closed on this moral reflection. But the three strophes of Marvell's poem have something like a syllogistic relation to each other. After a close approach to the mood of Donne,

> then worms shall try
> That long-preserved virginity . . .
> The grave's a fine and private place,
> But none, I think, do there embrace,

the conclusion,

> Let us roll all our strength and all
> Our sweetness up into one ball,
> And tear our pleasures with rough strife,
> Thorough the iron gates of life.

It will hardly be denied that this poem contains wit; but it may not be evident that this wit forms the crescendo and diminuendo of a scale of great imaginative power. The wit is not only combined with, but fused into, the imagination. We can easily recognize a witty fancy in the successive images ("my *vegetable* love," "till the conversion of the Jews"), but this fancy is not indulged, as it sometimes is by Cowley or Cleveland, for its own sake.[18] It is structural decoration of a serious idea. In this it is superior to the fancy of "L'Allegro," "Il Penseroso," or the lighter and less successful poems of Keats.[19] In fact, this alliance of levity and seriousness (by which the seriousness is intensified) is a characteristic of the sort of wit we are trying to identify. It is found in

> Le squelette était invisible
> Aux temps heureux de l'art païen![20]

of Gautier, and in the *dandyisme* of Baudelaire and Laforgue. It is in the poem of Catullus which has been quoted, and in the variation by Ben Jonson:

> Cannot we deceive the eyes
> Of a few poor household spies?
> 'Tis no sin love's fruits to steal,
> But that sweet sin to reveal,
> To be taken, to be seen,
> These have sins accounted been.[21]

It is in Propertius and Ovid.[22] It is a quality of a sophisticated literature; a quality which expands in English literature just at the moment before the English mind altered; it is not a quality which we should expect Puritanism to encourage. When we come to Gray and Collins, the sophistication remains only in the language, and has disappeared from the feeling.[23] Gray and Collins were masters, but they had lost that hold on human values, that firm grasp of human experience, which is a formidable achievement of the Elizabethan and Jacobean poets. This wisdom, cynical perhaps but untired (in Shakespeare, a terrifying clairvoyance), leads toward, and is only completed by, the religious comprehension; it leads to the point of the *Ainsi tout leur a craqué dans la main* of Bouvard and Pécuchet.[24]

The difference between imagination and fancy, in view of this poetry of wit, is a very narrow one.[25] Obviously, an image which is immediately and unintentionally ridiculous is merely a fancy. In the poem "Upon Appleton House," Marvell falls in with one of these undesirable images, describing the attitude of the house toward its master:

> Yet thus the laden house does sweat,
> And scarce endures the master great;
> But, where he comes, the swelling hall
> Stirs, and the square grows spherical;

which, whatever its intention, is more absurd than it was intended to be. Marvell also falls into the even commoner error of images which are over-developed or distracting; which support nothing but their own misshapen bodies:

> And now the salmon-fishers moist
> Their leathern boats begin to hoist;
> And, like Antipodes in shoes,
> Have shod their heads in their canoes.[26]

Of this sort of image a choice collection may be found in Johnson's "Life of Cowley."[27] But the images in the "Coy Mistress" are not only witty, but satisfy the elucidation of Imagination given by Coleridge:

> This power . . . reveals itself in the balance or reconcilement of
> opposite or discordant qualities: of sameness, with difference;
> of the general, with the concrete; the idea with the image; the
> individual with the representative; the sense of novelty and
> freshness with old and familiar objects; a more than usual state
> of emotion with more than usual order; judgement ever awake
> and steady self-possession with enthusiasm and feeling pro-
> found or vehement . . .[28]

Coleridge's statement applies also to the following verses, which are selected because of their similarity, and because they illustrate the marked caesura which Marvell often introduces in a short line:

The tawny mowers enter next,
Who seem like Israelites to be
Walking on foot through a green sea.

And now the meadows fresher dyed,
Whose grass, with moister colour dashed,
Seems as green silks but newly washed.[29]

He hangs in shades the orange bright,
Like golden lamps in a green night.[30]

Annihilating all that's made
To a green thought in a green shade.[31]

Had it lived long, it would have been
Lilies without, roses within.[32]

The whole poem, from which the last of these quotations is drawn ("The Nymph and the Fawn"), is built upon a very slight foundation, and we can imagine what some of our modern practitioners of slight themes would have made of it. But we need not descend to an invidious contemporaneity to point the difference. Here are six lines from "The Nymph and the Fawn":

I have a garden of my own,
But so with roses overgrown
And lilies, that you would it guess
To be a little wilderness;
And all the spring-time of the year
It only lovèd to be there.[33]

And here are five lines from "The Nymph's Song to Hylas" in the *Life and Death of Jason*, by William Morris:

I know a little garden close
Set thick with lily and red rose,
Where I would wander if I might
From dewy dawn to dewy night,
And have one with me wandering.[34]

So far the resemblance is more striking than the difference, although we might just notice the vagueness of allusion in the last line to some indefinite person, form, or phantom, compared with the more explicit reference of emotion to object which we should expect from Marvell. But in the latter part of the poem Morris divaricates widely:

> Yet tottering as I am, and weak,
> Still have I left a little breath
> To seek within the jaws of death
> An entrance to that happy place;
> To seek the unforgotten face
> Once seen, once kissed, once reft from me
> Anigh the murmuring of the sea.[35]

Here the resemblance, if there is any, is to the latter part of "The Coy Mistress." As for the difference, it could not be more pronounced. The effect of Morris's charming poem depends upon the mistiness of the feeling and the vagueness of its object; the effect of Marvell's upon its bright, hard precision. And this precision is not due to the fact that Marvell is concerned with cruder or simpler or more carnal emotions. The emotion of Morris is not more refined or more spiritual; it is merely more vague; if anyone doubts whether the more refined or spiritual emotion can be precise, he should study the treatment of the varieties of discarnate emotion in the *Paradiso*. A curious result of the comparison of Morris's poem with Marvell's is that the former, though it appears to be more serious, is found to be the slighter; and Marvell's "Nymph and Fawn," appearing more slight, is the more serious.

> So weeps the wounded balsam; so
> The holy frankincense doth flow;
> The brotherless Heliades
> Melt in such amber tears as these.[36]

These verses have the suggestiveness of true poetry; and the verses of Morris, which are nothing if not an attempt to suggest, really suggest nothing; and we are inclined to infer that the suggestiveness is the aura around a bright clear centre, that you cannot have the aura alone. The daydreamy feeling of Morris is essentially a slight thing; Marvell takes a slight affair, the feeling of a girl for her pet, and gives it a connexion with that inexhaustible and terrible nebula of emotion which surrounds all our exact and practical passions and mingles with them. Again, Marvel does this in a poem which, because of its formal pastoral machinery, may appear a trifling object:

CLORINDA: Near this, a fountain's liquid bell
　　Tinkles within the concave shell.
DAMON: Might a soul bathe there and be clean,
　　Or slake its drought?[37]

where we find that a metaphor has suddenly rapt us to the image of spiritual purgation. There is here the element of *surprise,* as when Villon says:

　　Nécessité faict gens mesprendre
　　Et faim sailler le loup des boys,[38]

the surprise which Poe considered of the highest importance, and also the restraint and quietness of tone which make the surprise possible.[39] And in the verses of Marvell which have been quoted there is the making the familiar strange, and the strange familiar, which Coleridge attributed to good poetry.

The effort to construct a dream-world, which alters English poetry so greatly in the nineteenth century, a dream-world utterly different from the visionary realities of the *Vita Nuova* or of the poetry of Dante's contemporaries, is a problem of which various explanations may no doubt be found; in any case, the result makes a poet of the nineteenth century, of the same size as Marvell, a more trivial and less serious figure. Marvell is no greater personality than William Morris, but he had something much more solid behind him: he had the vast and penetrating influence of Ben Jonson. Jonson never wrote anything so pure as Marvell's "Horation Ode"; but this ode has that same quality of wit which was diffused over the whole Elizabethan product and concentrated in the work of Jonson. And, as was said before, this wit which pervades the poetry of Marvell is more Latin, more refined, than anything that succeeded it. The great danger, as well as the great interest and excitement, of English prose and verse, compared with French, is that it permits and justifies an exaggeration of particular qualities to the exclusion of others. Dryden was great in wit, as Milton in magniloquence; but the former, by isolating this quality and making it by itself into great poetry, and the latter, by coming to dispense with it altogether, may perhaps have injured the language. In Dryden wit becomes almost fun, and thereby loses some contact with reality; becomes pure fun, which French wit almost never is.

> The midwife placed her hand on his thick skull,
> With this prophetic blessing: *Be thou dull.*

> A numerous host of dreaming saints succeed,
> Of the true old enthusiastic breed.[40]

This is audacious and splendid; it belongs to satire, besides which Marvell's "Satires" are random babbling; but it is perhaps as exaggerated as:

> Oft he seems to hide his face,
> But unexpectedly returns,
> And to his faithful champion hath in place
> Bore witness gloriously; whence Gaza mourns,
> And all that band them to resist
> His uncontrollable intent.[41]

How oddly the sharp Dantesque phrase "whence Gaza mourns" springs out from the brilliant but ridiculous contortions of Milton's sentence!

> Who from his private gardens, where
> He lived reservèd and austere,
>   (As if his highest plot
>   To plant the bergamot)
> Could by industrious valour climb
> To ruin the great work of Time,
>   And cast the kingdoms old
>   Into another mold;

> The Pict no shelter now shall find
> Within his parti-coloured mind,
> But, from this valour sad,
> Shrink underneath the plaid.[42]

There is here an equipoise, a balance and proportion of tones, which, while it cannot raise Marvell to the level of Dryden or Milton, extorts an approval which these poets do not receive from us, and bestows a pleasure at least different in kind from any they can often give. It is what makes Marvell, in the best sense, a classic: classic in a sense in which Gray and Collins are not; for the latter, with all their accredited purity, are comparatively poor in shades of feeling to contrast and unite.

We are baffled in the attempt to translate the quality indicated by the dim and antiquated term wit into the equally unsatisfactory nomenclature of our own time. Even Cowley is only able to define it by negatives:

> Comely in thousand shapes appears;
> Yonder we saw it plain; and here 'tis now,
> Like spirits in a place, we know not how.[43]

It has passed out of our critical coinage altogether, and no new term has been struck to replace it; the quality seldom exists, and is never recognized.

> In a true piece of Wit all things must be
>   Yet all things there agree;
> As in the Ark, join'd without force or strife,
> All creatures dwelt, all creatures that had life.
>   Or as the primitive forms of all
>   (If we compare great things with small)
> Which, without discord or confusion, lie
> In that strange mirror of the Deity.[44]

So far Cowley has spoken well. But if we are to attempt even no more than Cowley, we, placed in a retrospective attitude, must risk much more anxious generalizations. With our eye still on Marvell, we can say that wit is not erudition; it is sometimes stifled by erudition, as in much of Milton. It is not cynicism, though it has a kind of toughness which may be confused with cynicism by the tender-minded. It is confused with erudition because it belongs to an educated mind, rich in generations of experience; and it is confused with cynicism because it implies a constant inspection and criticism of experience. It involves, probably, a recognition, implicit in the expression of every experience, of other kinds of experience which are possible, which we find as clearly in the greatest as in poets like Marvell. Such a general statement may seem to take us a long way from "The Nymph and the Fawn," or even from the "Horatian Ode"; but it is perhaps justified by the desire to account for that precise taste of Marvell's which finds for him the proper degree of seriousness for every subject which he treats. His errors of taste, when he trespasses, are not sins against this virtue; they are conceits, distended metaphors and similes, but they never consist in taking a subject too seriously or too lightly. This virtue of wit is not a peculiar quality of minor poets, or of the minor poets of one age or of one school; it is an intellectual quality which perhaps only becomes noticeable by itself, in the work of lesser poets. Furthermore, it is absent from the work of Wordsworth, Shelley, and Keats, on whose poetry nineteenth-century criticism has unconsciously been based. To the best of their poetry wit is irrelevant:

> Art thou pale for weariness
> Of climbing heaven and gazing on the earth,
> Wandering companionless
> Amongst the stars that have a different birth,
> And ever changing, like a joyless eye,
> That finds no object worth its constancy?[45]

We should find it difficult to draw any useful comparison between these lines of Shelley and anything by Marvell. But later poets, who would have been the better for Marvell's quality, were without it; even Browning seems oddly immature, in some way, beside Marvell. And nowadays we find occasionally good irony, or satire, which lacks wit's internal equilibrium, because their voices are essentially protests against some outside sentimentality or stupidity; or we find serious poets who are afraid of acquiring wit, lest they lose intensity. The quality which Marvell had, this modest and certainly impersonal virtue—whether we call it wit or reason, or even urbanity—we have patently failed to define. By whatever name we call it, and however we define that name, it is something precious and needed and apparently extinct; it is what should preserve the reputation of Marvell. *C'était une belle âme, comme on ne fait plus à Londres.*[46]

PROSE AND VERSE[1]

ON THE SUBJECT OF prose-poetry I have no theory to expound; but as I find I cannot state my position merely by denying the existence of the subject-matter, I may be excused for explaining it at greater length than a simple denial requires. I have found it convenient to put my remarks in the form of disconnected paragraphs. The present condition of English literature is so lifeless that there surely needs no extenuation of any research into past or possible forms of speech; the chief benefit of such a symposium as the present is not the verdict but the enquiry: an enquiry which might help to stimulate the worn nerves and release the arthritic limbs of our diction.

The Definition.—I have not yet been given any definition of the prose poem, which appears to be more than a tautology or a contradiction. Mr. Aldington, for example, has provided me with the following: "The prose poem is poetic content expressed in prose form."[2] Poetic content must be either the sort of thing that *is usually,* or the sort of thing that *ought to be,* expressed in verse. But if you say the latter, the prose poem is ruled out; if you say the former, you have said only that certain things can be said in either prose or verse, or that anything can be said either in prose or verse. I am not disposed to contest either of these conclusions, as they stand, but they do not appear to bring us any nearer to a definition of the prose poem. I do not assume the identification of poetry with verse; good poetry is obviously something else besides good verse; and good verse may be very indifferent poetry. I quite appreciate the meaning of anyone who says that passages of Sir Thomas Browne are "poetry," or that Denham's "Cooper's Hill" is not poetry.[3] Also, the former may be good prose, and the latter is certainly good verse; and Sir Thomas is justified for writing in prose, and Sir John Denham for writing in verse. Mr. Aldington would say that there are two kinds of prose— that of Voltaire or Gibbon, on the one hand, and that of "Gaspard de la Nuit" or "Suspiria de Profundis" on the other.[4] Perhaps he will admit, what seems to me equally likely, that there are two kinds of verse: we may contrast Poe and Dryden, Baudelaire and Boileau.[5] He might fairly say that we need a fourth term: we have the term "verse" and the term "poetry," and only the one term "prose" to express their opposites. The distinction between "verse" and "prose" is clear; the distinction between "poetry" and "prose" is very obscure. I do not wish to quibble over "content"; I know that it is not a question of "subject-matter" so much as of the way in which this subject-matter is treated, apart from its expression in metrical form.

The Value of Verse and Prose.—I take it for granted that prose is allowed to be, potentially or actually, as important a medium as verse, and that it may cost quite as much pains to write. Also that any enjoyment that can be communicated by verse may be communicated by prose, with the exception of the pleasure of metrical form. And there is an equivalent pleasure in the movement of the finest prose, which is peculiar to prose and cannot be compensated by verse. It may, for all that we have yet decided, be proper to call this prose poetry; but if we deny that *all* of the best prose is poetry, we have got no farther; and we have still to find two qualities or sets of qualities, and divide the best literature, verse and prose, into two parts which shall exemplify these two qualities. Each group of works of literature will comprehend both verse and prose.

Intensity.—This is sometimes held, implicitly or explicitly, to be a character of poetry and not of prose. It must not be confused with concentration, which is stating or implying much in proportion to the space occupied, or with length, which is a different matter from either. The feeling communicated by a long piece of prose may be more intense than that of a short poem: Newman's *Apology* is thus more intense than a poem of Anacreon, but this intensity of feeling cannot be extracted from select passages; you must read the whole book to get it.[6] I should not care to deny intensity to

Gibbon's history; but this intensity is slowly cumulative, and required seven volumes for its communication.

Length.—While the preceding paragraph has pointed to what I believe a valued and useful qualification, it has also come near to juggling with the term. No long work can maintain the same high tension throughout, and although Gibbon's history, or Newman's *Apology,* leave a single intense feeling behind, they have in their progress a movement of tension and relaxation. This leads us to Poe's law: that no poem should be more than one hundred lines.[7] Poe demands the static poem; that in which there shall be no movement of tension or relaxation, only the capture of a single unit of intense feeling. We are, most of us, inclined to agree with him: we do not like long poems. This dislike is due, I believe, partly to the taste of the day, which will pass, and partly to the abuse of the long poem in the hands of distinguished persons who did not know how to employ it. No one who is willing to take some trouble about his pleasures complains of the *length* of the *Divine Comedy,* the *Odyssey,* or even the *Aeneid.* Any long poem will contain certain matter of ephemeral interest, like some of Dante's divine processions, but this does not imply that the long poem should not have been written—that, in other words, it should have been composed as a number of short poems. The poems I have just mentioned have, in different degrees, the movement toward and from intensity which is life itself. Milton and Wordsworth, on the other hand, lack this unity, and therefore lack life; and the general criticism on most of the long poems of the nineteenth century is simply that they are not good enough.

Verse and Prose Again.—It might be suggested that the proper form would be one which combined verse and prose in waves of intense or relaxed feeling. We have not, however, committed ourselves to the statement that intensity of feeling should be expressed in verse, or that verse should always be intense. And such a mixture of prose and verse would sin against a different kind of unity. A single work must have some metrical unity. This may vary widely in practice: I see no reason why a considerable variety of verse forms may not be employed within the limits of a single poem; or why a prose writer should not vary his cadences almost indefinitely; that is question for discretion, taste and genius to settle. We seem to see clearly enough that prose is allowed to be "poetic"; we appear to have overlooked the right of poetry to be "prosaic." On the other hand, if we admit the long poem, we surely ought to admit the short "prose" (we cannot speak conveniently in English, as we can in French, of "Proses" in the plural). And the short prose is, I believe, what most people have in mind when they speak of "poems in prose." (But shortness is evidently not a sufficient characterisation, else we should have to denominate the writings of Mr. Pearsall Smith as "poems" in prose.)[8]

Another Sense of "Poetic" and "Prosaic."—I have spoken only of verse in which there is a more or less periodic movement between intensity and relaxation, but there is another kind of verse which is disparaged. Is *Absalom and Achitophel,* is the "Letter to Arbuthnot," poetry?[9] These are great literature; and I cannot see that it matters much whether we call them poetry or prose. In any case, they do something that great poetry does: they capture and put into literature an emotion: we may say, in Dryden's case, the emotion of contempt, and in Pope's case, the emotion of hatred or spite. In this sort of verse also there is movement between greater and less intensity.

One Kind of "Poetic" Prose.—A number of prose works, especially several of the seventeenth century, are spoken of as "poetic." Namely, the writings of Sir Thomas Browne and Jeremy Taylor.[10] We agree with Remy de Gourmont's assertion that it is only the style that preserves literature; but we must emphasise the "preservation," and ask what is preserved.[11] Possibly by some prejudice or narrowness of taste, I have always held these writers to be of a mediocrity of mind which forbade my taking any keen pleasure in their style. I find them diffuse, and precisely lacking in that intensity which raises the history of Newman's religious doubts to the highest importance even for the otherwise alien reader. But let us examine a passage of one of these authors, which is not unjustly celebrated as a piece of poetic prose:

> Now since these dead bones have already out-lasted the living
> ones of Methuselah, and in a yard underground, and thin walls
> of clay, out-worn all the strong and spacious buildings above
> it; and quietly rested under the drums and tramplings of three
> conquests: what prince can promise such diuturnity unto
> his relics, or might not gladly say, *"Sic ego componi versus in
> ossa velim?"* Time, which antiquates antiquities, and hath
> an art to make dust of all things, hath yet spared these minor
> monuments.[12]

I recognise the beauty of the cadence, the felicity and Latin sonority of the phrase; and I am hard put to it to justify my affirmation that the substance of this passage is but a pinch of dust, and therefore there is not really great style. Even if it be "poetry," it is not great poetry like such sepulchral things as the Grave Digger Scene in *Hamlet* (which is prose, besides), or certain poems of Donne, or Bishop King's "Exequy" for his dead wife.[13] I believe that in each of these a human emotion is concentrated and fixed, and that in the prose of Sir Thomas Browne only a commonplace sententiousness is decorated by reverberating language.

We have to face the puzzling fact that in English literature there are a number of writers—Milton, Tennyson, Sir Thomas Browne, and others —whose style, far from "preserving" the content, appears to survive and to seduce quite apart from the content. It is "style" in this restricted sense, that it is not the incorporation of any interesting personality; it is the sort of style which is a dangerous temptation to any student who is anxious to write good English. It is language dissociated from things, assuming an independent existence. And unless Milton and Tennyson are the authors of the most "poetical" verse in English, how can we say that Sir Thomas Browne's is the most "poetical" prose?

The conclusion is, that we shall not find the prose poem in the "purple patch." Launcelot Andrewes is, I think, a great prose writer, but you cannot really get at the poetry in his prose unless you are willing to read at least one of his sermons entire; his style preserves the content, yes, but you cannot get the pleasure of the style unless you interest yourself in something more than the words.[14] Donne also is a great prose writer, but even the passages which Mr. Pearsal Smith has judiciously selected remain only selections.[15] There is no question of separating wheat and chaff, digging jewels out of mud; they serve as a sample, a taste.

If there is such a thing as prose poetry it is not a poetry of verbal beauty merely. "Verbal beauty" is probably never, in literature, a beauty of *pure* sound; I doubt whether there is a beauty of pure sound. What Pater tries to do in prose is much like what Swinburne often does in verse: to arouse indefinite evocation, depending as much upon literary association as upon the beauty of the rhythm.[16] "This is the head upon which all the ends of the world have come, and the eyelids are a little weary."[17] Compare this whole passage about *La Gioconda* with the last chapter of Ecclesiastes, and see the difference between direct suggestiveness by precise reference, and the meretricious suggestiveness of vague literary association. There is more essential poetry in Turgenev's *Sportsman's Sketches,* even in translation, than in the whole of Sir Thomas Browne and Walter Pater.[18]

De Quincey and Poe.—Here are two prose writers who seem to me to deserve a very different distinction. They were both men of very great intellectual power, of much greater intelligence than Browne, or Pater, or even Ruskin.[19] What is remarkable is their range: in other words, their courage and adventurousness in tackling anything that had to be expressed. The difference between De Quincey's "Dream Fugue" and Browne's *Urn Burial* is that De Quincey aims to express a content of some intensity, and that he is not diverted into verbal suggestiveness.[20]

"If, as a musician, as the leader of a mighty orchestra," he said to Lamb, "you had this theme offered you—'Belshazzar the King gave a great feast to a thousand of his lords,'—or this, 'And on a certain day Marcus Cicero stood up, and in a set speech rendered thanks to Caius Caesar for Quintus Ligarius pardoned and Marcus Marcellus restored'—surely no man would deny that in such a case simplicity, though in a passive sense not lawfully absent, must stand aside as totally insufficient for the *positive* part."[21]

The Image.—But the wide range of subject and treatment of Poe and De Quincey makes it difficult to draw any line between what is prose, in their writings, and what is "prose poetry." I suppose that the "Murders in the Rue Morgue" would be called prose, "Shadow" prose poetry, and "The Assignation" perhaps something between the two.[22] This suggests the suspicion that the distinction between prose and poetry upon which the term "prose poetry" is based, is probably the old assertion that poetry is the language of emotion and imagination—proceeding by concrete images— and that prose is the language of thought and ratiocination—proceeding by argument, by definition, by inference, by the use of abstract terms.

Logic and Imagination.—It proves impossible, however, to draw any line between thinking and feeling, or between those works the chief aim or effect of which is aesthetic pleasure, and those which give aesthetic pleasure in the production of some other effect. The work of poetry is often said to be performed by the use of images; by a cumulative succession of images each fusing with the next; or by the rapid and unexpected combination of images apparently unrelated, which have their relationship enforced upon them by the mind of the author. This appears to be true, but it does not follow that there are two distinct faculties, one of imagination and one of reason, one of poetry and one of prose, or that "feeling," in a work of art, is any less an intellectual product than is "thought."

To attempt to construct a theory with the terms I have been using would be a futile building with straw; my remarks are only valid, if valid they be, so far as they are destructive of false distinctions. I object to the term "prose-poetry" because it seems to imply a sharp distinction between "poetry" and "prose" which I do not admit, and if it does not imply this distinction, the term is meaningless and otiose, as there can be no combination of what is not distinguished. If the writing of prose can be an art just as the writing of verse can be an art, we do not seem to require any other admission. Versification, in any of the systems known to European and other cultures, brings in something which is not present in prose, because it is from any other point of view than that of art, a superfluity, a definite concession to the desire for "play." But we must remember, on the one hand, that verse is always struggling, while remaining verse, to take up to itself more and more of what is prose, to take something more from life and turn it into "play." Seen from this angle, the labour of Mallarmé with the French language becomes something very important; every battle he fought with syntax represents the effort to transmute lead into gold, ordinary language into poetry; and the real failure of the mass of contemporary verse is its failure to draw anything new from life into art.[23] And, on the other hand, prose, not being cut off by the barrier of verse which must at the same time be affirmed and diminished, can transmute life in its own way by raising it to the condition of "play," precisely because it is not verse.

The real decadence in literature occurs when both verse and prose cease their effort: Alexandrianism, or more truly Georgianism, is present when verse becomes a language, a set of feelings, a style quite remote from life, and when prose becomes a mere practical vehicle.[24] The attempt to impart motion to this lifeless condition may result in such writing as is now pretty current in America: verse which is simply *prosaic,* and prose which is simply *artificial,* and verse again which mimics the artificiality of the artificial prose.

Practical Conclusion.—We must be very tolerant of any attempt in verse that appears to trespass upon prose, or of any attempt in prose that appears to strive toward the condition of "poetry." And there is no reason why prose should be confined to any of the recognised forms, the Novel, the Essay, or whatever else there may be in English. I have heard Mr. James Joyce's *Ulysses* condemned on the ground that it is "poetry" and therefore should have been written in verse; whereas it seems to me to be the most vital development of prose that has taken place in this generation.[25] I only wish to take the precaution of looking upon the Monna Lisas of prose, the drums and tramplings of three conquests, the eloquent just and mightie deaths, with a suspicious and interrogating eye, and making quite certain what, if any, solid and genuine bit of life they have pounced upon and raised to the dignity of poetry.[26]

LONDON LETTER, MAY 1921[1]

The Phoenix Society

In my last letter I mentioned an approaching performance by the Phoenix Society of Ben Jonson's *Volpone;* the performance proved to be the most important theatrical event of the year in London.[2] The play was superbly carried out; the performance gave evidence of Jonson's consummate skill in stage technique, proceeding without a moment of tedium from end to end; it was well acted and both acted and received with great appreciation.

Almost the only opportunity for seeing a good play is that given by a few private societies, which by reason of their "private" character are allowed to give performances (for subscribers) on Sunday evenings. These are not commercial enterprises, but depend upon the enthusiasm of a few patrons and the devotion of a few actors, most of whom have other engagements during the week. The Phoenix, which restricts itself to Elizabethan and Restoration drama, is an off-shoot of the Incorporated Stage Society, which produces modern and contemporary plays of the better sort —the better sort usually being translations.[3] At the beginning of its venture, last year, the Phoenix was obliged to suffer a good deal of abuse in the daily press, especially from the *Daily News* and the *Star.* These two journals are, to my mind, the least objectionable of the London newspapers in their political views, but their Manchester-School politics gives a strong aroma of the Ebenezer Temperance Association to their views on art.[4] The bloodiness of Elizabethan tragedy, and the practice of the Society in presenting the complete text of the plays, were the points of attack. The *Daily News* reviewed the performance of *The Duchess of Malfi* under the heading, "Funnier than Farce!" Mr. William Archer mumbled "this farrago of horrors . . . shambling and ill-composed . . . funereal affectation . . . I am far from calling *The Duchess of Malfi* garbage, but . . ."[5] Still droller was a certain Sir Leo Money: "I agree with Mr. Robert Lynd that 'there are perhaps a dozen Elizabethan plays apart from Shakespeare's that are as great as his third-best work,' but I should not include *The Duchess of Malfi* in the dozen. . . . I did not see the Phoenix production, but I hope that some fumigation took place."[6] Sir Leo writes frequently about the Tariff, the income tax, and kindred topics. For my part, I am more and more convinced that the Phoenix is wholly justified in its refusal to admit any expurgation whatever. The sense of relief, in hearing the indecencies of Elizabethan and Restoration drama, leaves one a better and a stronger man.

I do not suggest that Jonson is comparable to Shakespeare. But we do not know Shakespeare; we only know Sir J. Forbes-Robertson's Hamlet and Irving's Shylock, and so on.[7] The performance of *Volpone* had a significance for us which no contemporary performance of Shakespeare has had; it brought the great English drama to life as no contemporary performance of Shakespeare has done. Shakespeare (that is to say, such of his plays as are produced at all), strained through the nineteenth century, has been dwarfed to the dimensions of a part for Sir Johnston Forbes-Robertson, Sir Frank Benson, or other histrionic nonentities: Shakespeare is the avenue to knighthood.[8] But the continued popularity of Shakespeare perhaps has this meaning, that the appetite for poetic drama, and for a peculiarly English comedy or farce, has never disappeared; and that a native popular drama, if it existed, would be nearer to Shakespeare than to Ibsen or Chekhov. It is curious that the popular desire for Shakespeare, and for the operas of Gilbert and Sullivan, should be insatiable, although no attempt is ever made to create anything similar; and that on the other hand the crudest American laughter-and-tears plays, such as *Romance* or *Peg o' My Heart,* should be constantly imported.[9] Curious, again, that with so much comic talent in England—more than any other country—no intelligent attempt has been made to use it to advantage in a good comic opera or revue.

Music-Hall and Revue

This is an age of transition between the music-hall and the revue. The music-hall is older, more popular, and is sanctified by the admiration of the Nineties.[10] It has flourished most vigorously in the North; many of its most famous stars are of Lancashire origin. (Marie Lloyd, if I am not mistaken, has a bit of a Manchester accent.) Lancashire wit is mordant, ferocious, and personal; the Lancashire music-hall is excessively *intime;* success depends upon the relation established by a comedian of strong personality with an audience quick to respond with approval or contempt. The fierce talent of Nellie Wallace (who also has a Lancashire accent) holds the most boisterous music-hall in complete subjection.[11] Little Tich and George Robey (though the latter has adapted himself in recent years to some inferior revues) belong to this type and generation.[12] The Lancashire comedian is at his best when unsupported and making a direct set, pitting himself, against a suitable audience; he is seen to best advantage at the smaller and more turbulent halls. As the smaller provincial or suburban hall disappears, supplanted by the more lucrative Cinema, this type of comedian disappears with it.

The music-hall comedian, however, can still be seen to perfection, whereas the revue comedian never is, because the revue is never good enough. Our best revue comedienne, Miss Ethel Levey, has seldom had the revue, and never the appreciation, that she deserves.[13] Her type is quite different from that of Marie Lloyd or Nellie Wallace. She is the most aloof and impersonal of personalities; indifferent, rather than contemptuous, towards the audience; her appearance and movement are of an extremely modern type of beauty. Hers is not broad farce, but a fascinating inhuman grotesquerie; she plays for herself rather than for the audience. Her art requires a setting which (in this country at least) it has never had. It is not a comedy of mirth.

An element of *bizarrerie* is present in most of the comedians whom we should designate as of the revue stage rather than the music-hall stage: in Lupino Lane, in Robert Hale and George Graves; a *bizarrerie* more mature, perhaps more cosmopolitan, than that of Little Tich.[14] But the revue itself is still lacking.

Caricature

Baudelaire, in his essay on "Le Rire" (*qui vaut bien celui de Bergson*), re-marks of English caricature:

> *Pour trouver du comique féroce et très-féroce, il faut passer la*
> *Manche et visiter les royaumes brumeux du spleen . . . le signe*
> *distinctif de ce genre de comique était la violence.*[15]

Perhaps the best of the English caricaturists of journalism is H. M. Bate-man. He has lately held a very interesting exhibition at the Leicester Gal-leries.[16] It is curious to remark that some of his drawings descend to the pure and insignificant funniness without seriousness which appeals to the readers of *Punch;* while others continue the best tradition from Rowland-son and Cruikshank.[17] They have some of the old English ferocity. Bate-man is, I imagine, unconscious of the two distinct strains in his work; Mr. Wyndham Lewis, in his exhibition now on show at the same gallery, is wholly conscious and deliberate in his attempt to restore this peculiarly English caricature and to unite it with serious work in paint. Mr. Lewis is the most English of English painters, a student of Hogarth and Rowland-son; his fantastic imagination produces something essentially different from anything across the Channel.[18] I have always thought his design at its greatest when it approached the border of satire and caricature; and his Tyros may be expected to breed a most interesting and energetic race.

The State of Criticism

The disappearance of the *Athenaeum* as an independent organ, and its gradual suffocation under the ponderous mass of the *Nation,* are greatly to be deplored. It leaves the *Times Literary Supplement* and the *London Mer-cury* as the only literary papers.[19] The former is a useful bibliographer; it fills, and always will fill, an important place of its own. This place it can only hold by maintaining the anonymity of its contributions; but this ano-nymity, and the large number of its contributors, prevents it from uphold-ing any definite standard of criticism. Nevertheless it possesses more au-thority than the *Mercury,* which is homogeneous enough, but suffers from the mediocrity of the minds most consistently employed upon it. Mr. Murry, as editor of the *Athenaeum,* was genuinely studious to maintain a serious criticism. With his particular tastes, as well as his general statements,

I find myself frequently at variance: the former seem to me often perverse or exaggerated, the latter tainted by some unintelligible Platonism. But there is no doubt that he had much higher standards and greater ambitions for literary journalism than any other editor in London. When he is not deceived by some aberration of enthusiasm or dislike, and when he is not deluded by philosophy, he is the only one of the accredited critics whom I can read at all. There is Mr. Clutton-Brock, whose attention is not focussed upon literature but upon a very mild type of philosophic humanitarian religion; he is like a very intelligent archdeacon.[20] There is Mr. Robert Lynd, who has successfully cultivated the typical vices of daily journalism and has risen to the top of his profession; and there is Mr. Squire, whose solemn trifling fascinates multitudes; and there are several writers, like Mr. Edmund Gosse and Sir Sidney Colvin, whom I have never read and so cannot judge.[21]

I cannot find, after this muster, that there is any ground for the rumour current in the chatty paragraphs of the newsprint several months ago, that the younger generation has decided to revive criticism.[22] There has been a brisk business in centenaries. Keats and Marvell have just been celebrated in this way.[23] The former has been particularly fortunate. All the approved critics, each in a different paper, blew a blast of glory enough to lay Keats' ghost for twenty years. I have never read such unanimous rubbish, and yet Keats was a poet. Possibly, after the chatty columns of the newsprint have ceased to cheer the "revival" of criticism, they will get a tip to lament its decay. Yet the "revival" of criticism as a "form" is not the essential thing; if we are intelligent enough, and really interested in the arts, both criticism and "creation" will in some form flourish.

The True Church and the Nineteen Churches

While the poetry lovers have been subscribing to purchase for the nation the Keats house in Hampstead as a museum, the Church of England has apparently persisted in its design to sell for demolition nineteen religious edifices in the City of London.[24] Probably few American visitors, and certainly few natives, ever inspect these disconsolate fanes; but they give to the business quarter of London a beauty which its hideous banks and commercial houses have not quite defaced. Some are by Christopher Wren himself, others by his school; the least precious redeems some vulgar street, like the plain little church of All Hallows at the end of London Wall.

Some, like St. Michael Paternoster Royal, are of great beauty.[25] As the prosperity of London has increased, the City churches have fallen into desuetude; for their destruction the lack of congregation is the ecclesiastical excuse, and the need of money the ecclesiastical reason. The fact that the erection of these churches was apparently paid for out of a public coal tax and their decoration probably by the parishioners, does not seem to invalidate the right of the True Church to bring them to the ground. To one who, like the present writer, passes his days in this City of London (*quand'io sentii chiavar l'uscio di sotto*) the loss of these towers, to meet the eye down a grimy lane, and of these empty naves, to receive the solitary visitor at noon from the dust and tumult of Lombard Street, will be irreparable and unforgotten.[26] A small pamphlet issued for the London County Council (*Proposed Demolition of Nineteen City Churches:* P. S. King & Son, Ltd., 2–4 Gt. Smith Street, Westminster, S.W.I, 3s.6d. net) should be enough to persuade of what I have said.[27]

JOHN DRYDEN[1]

IF THE PROSPECT OF delight be wanting (which alone justifies the pe-
rusal of poetry) we may let the reputation of Dryden sleep in the manu-
als of literature.[2] To those who are genuinely insensible of his genius (and
these are probably the majority of living readers of poetry) we can only
oppose illustrations of the following proposition: that their insensibility
does not merely signify indifference to satire and wit, but lack of perception of qualities not confined to satire and wit and present in the work of
other poets whom these persons feel that they understand. To those whose
taste in poetry is formed entirely upon the English poetry of the nineteenth century—to the majority—it is difficult to explain or excuse Dryden: the twentieth century is still the nineteenth, although it may in time
acquire its own character. The nineteenth century had, like every other,
limited tastes and peculiar fashions; and, like every other, it was unaware
of its own limitations. Its tastes and fashions had no place for Dryden; yet
Dryden is one of the tests of a catholic appreciation of poetry.

He is a successor of Jonson, and therefore the descendant of Marlowe;
he is the ancestor of nearly all that is best in the poetry of the eighteenth
century. Once we have mastered Dryden—and by mastery is meant a full
and essential enjoyment, not the enjoyment of a private whimsical fashion—we can extract whatever enjoyment and edification there is in his

contemporaries—Oldham, Denham, or the less remunerative Waller;[3] and still more his successors—not only Pope, but Phillips, Churchill, Gray, Johnson, Cowper, Goldsmith.[4] His inspiration is prolonged in Crabbe and Byron; it even extends, as Mr. Van Doren cleverly points out, to Poe.[5] Even the poets responsible for the revolt were well acquainted with him: Wordsworth knew his work, and Keats invoked his aid. We cannot fully enjoy or rightly estimate a hundred years of English poetry unless we fully enjoy Dryden; and to enjoy Dryden means to pass beyond the limitations of the nineteenth century into a new freedom.

> All, all of a piece throughout:
> Thy Chase had a Beast in View;
> Thy Wars brought nothing about;
> Thy Lovers were all untrue.
> 'Tis well an Old Age is out,
> And time to begin a new.[6]

> The world's great age begins anew,
> The golden years return,
> The earth doth like a snake renew
> Her winter weeds outworn:
> Heaven smiles, and faiths and empires gleam
> Like wrecks of a dissolving dream.[7]

The first of these passages is by Dryden, the second by Shelley; the second is found in the *Oxford Book of English Verse,* the first is not; yet we might defy anyone to show that the second is superior on intrinsically poetic merit.[8] It is easy to see why the second should appeal more readily to the nineteenth, and what is left of the nineteenth under the name of the twentieth, century. It is not so easy to see propriety in an image which divests a snake of "winter weeds"; and this is a sort of blemish which would have been noticed more quickly by a contemporary of Dryden than by a contemporary of Shelley.

These reflections are occasioned by an admirable book on Dryden which has appeared at this very turn of time, when taste is becoming perhaps more fluid and ready for a new mould.[9] It is a book which every practitioner of English verse should study. The consideration is so thorough, the matter so compact, the appreciation so just, temperate, and enthusiastic, and supplied with such copious and well-chosen extracts from the poetry, the suggestion of astutely placed facts leads our thought so far, that there only remain to mention, as defects which do not detract from its value, two omissions: the prose is not dealt with, and the plays are somewhat slighted. What is especially impressive is the exhibition of the very wide range of Dryden's work, shown by the quotations of every species. Everyone knows *MacFlecknoe,* and parts of *Absalom and Achitophel;*[10] in consequence, Dryden has sunk by the persons he has elevated to distinction—Shadwell and Settle, Shaftesbury and Buckingham.[11] Dryden was much more than a satirist: to dispose of him as a satirist is to place an obstacle in the way of our understanding. At all events, we must satisfy ourselves of our definition of the term satire; we must not allow our familiarity with the word to blind us to differences and refinements; we must not assume that satire is a fixed type, and fixed to the prosaic, suited only to prose; we must acknowledge that satire is not the same thing in the hands of two different writers of genius. The connotations of "satire" and of "wit," in short, may be only prejudices of nineteenth-century taste. Perhaps, we think, after reading Mr. Van Doren's book, a juster view of Dryden may be given by beginning with some other portion of his work than his celebrated satires; but even here there is much more present, and much more that is poetry, than is usually supposed.

The piece of Dryden's which is the most fun, which is the most sustained display of surprise after surprise of wit from line to line, is *MacFlecknoe.* Dryden's method here is something very near to parody; he applies vocabulary, images, and ceremony which arouse epic associations of grandeur, to make an enemy helplessly ridiculous. But the effect, though disastrous for the enemy, is very different from that of the humour which merely belittles, such as the satire of Mark Twain. Dryden continually enhances: he makes his object great, in a way contrary to expectation; and the total effect is due to the transformation of the ridiculous into poetry. As an example may be taken a fine passage plagiarized from Cowley, from lines which Dryden must have marked well, for he quotes them directly in one of his prefaces.[12] Here is Cowley:

Where their vast courts the mother-waters keep
And undisturbed by moons in silence sleep . . .

Beneath the dens where unfledged tempests lie,
And infant winds their tender voices try.[13]

In *MacFlecknoe* this becomes:

Where their vast courts the mother-strumpets keep,
And undisturbed by watch, in silence sleep.
Near these, a nursery erects its head,
Where queens are formed, and future heroes bred;
Where unfledged actors learn to laugh and cry,
Where infant punks their tender voices try,
And little Maximins the gods defy.[14]

The passage from Cowley is by no means despicable verse. But it is a commonplace description of commonly poetic objects; it has not the element of *surprise* so essential to poetry, and this Dryden provides. A clever versifier might have written Cowley's lines; only a poet could have made what Dryden made of them. It is impossible to dismiss his verses as "prosaic"; turn them into prose and they are transmuted, the fragrance is gone. The reproach of the prosaic, levelled at Dryden, rests upon a confusion between the emotions considered to be poetic, which is a matter allowing considerable latitude of fashion, and the result of personal emotion in poetry; and, in the third place, there is the emotion depicted by the poet in some kinds of poetry, of which the "Testament" of Villon is an example.[15] Again, there is the intellect, the originality and independence and clarity of what we vaguely call the poet's "point of view." Our valuation of poetry, in short, depends upon several considerations, upon the permanent and upon the mutable and upon the transitory. When we try to isolate the essentially poetic, we bring our pursuit in the end to something insignificant; our standards vary with every poet whom we consider. All we can hope to do, in the attempt to introduce some order into our preferences, is to clarify our reasons for finding pleasure in the poetry that we like.

With regard to Dryden, therefore, we can say this much. Our taste in English poetry has been largely founded upon a partial perception of the value of Shakespeare and Milton, a perception which dwells upon sublimity of theme and action. Shakespeare had a great deal more; he had nearly everything to satisfy our various desires for poetry. The point is that the depreciation or neglect of Dryden is not due to the fact that his work is not poetry, but to a prejudice that the material, the feelings out of which he built it, is not poetic. Thus Matthew Arnold observes, in mentioning Dryden and Pope together, that "their poetry is conceived and composed in their wits, genuine poetry is conceived in the soul."[16] Arnold was, perhaps, not altogether the detached critic when he wrote this line: he may have been stirred to a defence of his own poetry, conceived and composed in the soul of a mid-century Oxford graduate. Pater remarks that Dryden

> . . . loved to emphasize the distinction between poetry and prose, the protest against their confusion coming with some-what diminished effect from one whose poetry was so prosaic.[17]

But Dryden was right, and the sentence of Pater is cheap journalism. Hazlitt, who had perhaps the most uninteresting mind of all our distinguished critics, says:

> Dryden and Pope are the great masters of the artificial style of poetry in our language, as the poets whom I have already treated—Chaucer, Spenser, Shakespeare, and Milton—were of the natural.[18]

In one sentence Hazlitt has committed at least four crimes against taste. It is bad enough to lump Chaucer, Spenser, Shakespeare, and Milton together under the denomination of "natural"; it is bad to commit Shakespeare to one style only; it is bad to join Dryden and Pope together; but the last absurdity is the contrast of Milton, our greatest master of the *artificial* style, with Dryden, whose *style* (vocabulary, syntax, and order of thought) is in a high degree natural. And what all these objections come to, we repeat, is a repugnance for the material out of which Dryden's poetry is built.

It would be truer to say, indeed, even in the form of the unpersuasive paradox, that Dryden is distinguished principally by his *poetic* ability. We prize him, as we do Mallarmé, for what he made of his material.[19] Our estimate is only in part the appreciation of ingenuity: in the end the result *is* poetry. Much of Dryden's unique merit consists in his ability to make the small into the great, the prosaic into the poetic, the trivial into the magnificent. In this he differs not only from Milton, who required a canvas of the largest size, but from Pope, who required one of the smallest. If you compare any satiric "character" of Pope with one of Dryden, you will see that the method and intention are widely divergent. When Pope alters, he diminishes; he is a master of miniature. The singular skill of his portrait of Addison, for example, in the "Epistle to Arbuthnot," depends upon the justice and reserve, the apparent determination not to exaggerate.[20] The genius of Pope is not for caricature. But the effect of the portraits of Dryden is to turn the object into something greater, as were transformed the verses of Cowley quoted above.

> A fiery soul, which working out its way,
>   Fretted the pigmy body to decay;
> And o'er informed the tenement of clay.[21]

These lines are not merely a magnificent tribute. They create the object which they contemplate; the poetry is purer than anything in Pope except the last lines of the "Dunciad." Dryden is in fact much nearer to the master of comic creation than to Pope. As in Jonson, the effect is far from laughter; the comic is the material, the result is poetry. The Civic Guards of Rhodes:

> The country rings around with loud alarms,
> And raw in fields the rude militia swarms;
> Mouths without hands; maintained at vast expense,
> In peace a charge, in war a weak defence;
> Stout once a month they march, a blust'ring band,
> And ever, but in times of need, at hand;
> This was the morn, when issuing on the guard,
> Drawn up in rank and file they stood prepared
> Of seeming arms to make a short essay,
> Then hasten to be drunk, the business of the day.[22]

Sometimes the wit appears as a delicate flavour to the magnificence, as in "Alexander's Feast":

> Sooth'd with the sound the king grew vain;
> Fought all his battles o'er again;
> And thrice he routed all his foes, and thrice he slew the slain.[23]

The great advantage of Dryden over Milton is that while the former is always in control of his ascent, and can rise or fall at will (and how masterfully, like his own Timotheus, he directs the transitions!), the latter has elected a perch from which he cannot afford to fall, and from which he is in danger of slipping.

> food alike those pure
> Intelligential substances require
> As doth your Rational; and both contain
> Within them every lower faculty
> Of sense, whereby they hear, see, smell, touch, taste,
> Tasting concoct, digest, assimilate,
> And corporeal to incorporeal turn.[24]

Dryden might have made poetry out of that; his translation from Lucretius is poetry. But we have an ingenious example, on which to test our contrast of Dryden and Milton: it is Dryden's "opera," called *The State of Innocence and Fall of Man* of which Nathaniel Lee neatly says in his preface:

> For Milton did the wealthy mine disclose,
> And rudely cast what you could well dispose:
> He roughly drew, on an old-fashioned ground,
> A chaos, for no perfect world were found,
> Till through the heap, your mighty genius shined.[25]

In the author's preface Dryden acknowledges his debt generously enough:

> The original being undoubtedly one of the greatest, most
> noble, and most sublime poems, which either this age or
> nation has produced.[26]

The poem begins auspiciously:

> *Lucifer:* Is this the seat our conqueror has given?
> And this the climate we must change for Heaven?
> These regions and this realm my wars have got;
> This mournful empire is the loser's lot:
> In liquid burnings, or on dry to dwell,
> Is all the sad variety of hell.

It is an early work; it is on the whole a feeble work; it is not deserving of sustained comparison with *Paradise Lost*. But "all the sad variety of Hell"! Dryden is already stirring; he has assimilated what he could from Milton; and he has shown himself capable of producing as splendid verse.

The capacity for assimilation, and the consequent extent of range, are conspicuous qualities of Dryden. He advanced and exhibited his variety by constant translation; and his translations of Horace, of Ovid, of Lucretius, are admirable.[27] His gravest defects are supposed to be displayed in his dramas, but if these were more read they might be more praised. From the point of view of either the Elizabethan or the French drama they are obviously inferior; but the charge of inferiority loses part of its force if we admit that Dryden was not quite trying to compete with either, but was pursuing a direction of his own. He created no character; and although his arrangements of plot manifest exceptional ingenuity, it is the pure magnificence of diction, of poetic diction, that keeps his plays alive:

How I loved
Witness ye days and nights, and all ye hours,
That danced away with down upon your feet,
As all your business were to count my passion.
One day passed by, and nothing saw but love;
Another came, and still 'twas only love:
The suns were wearied out with looking on,
And I untired with loving.
I saw you every day and all the day;
And every day was still but as the first:
So eager was I still to see you more . . .

While within your arms I lay
The world fell mould'ring from my hands each hour.[28]

Such language is pure Dryden: it sounds, in Mr. Van Doren's phrase, "like a gong."[29] *All for Love,* from which the lines are taken, is Dryden's best play, and this is perhaps the highest reach. In general, he is best in his plays when dealing with situations which do not demand great emotional concentration; when his situation is more trivial, and he can practise his art of making the small great. The back-talk between the Emperor and his Empress Nourmahal, in *Aurungzebe,* is admirable purple comedy.

Emperor: Such virtue is the plague of human life:
A virtuous woman, but a cursèd wife.
In vain of pompous chastity y' are proud:
Virtue's adultery of the tongue, when loud.

> I, with less pain, a prostitute could bear,
> Than the shrill sound of virtue, virtue hear,
> In unchaste wives—
> There's yet a kind of recompensing ease:
> Vice keeps 'em humble, gives 'em care to please:
> But against clamorous virtue, what defence?
> It stops our mouths, and gives your noise pretence . . .
>
> What can be sweeter than our native home?
> Thither for ease, and soft repose, we come;
> Home is the sacred refuge of our life:
> Secure from all approaches but a wife.
> If thence we fly, the cause admits no doubt:
> None but an inmate foe could force us out.
> Clamours, our privacies uneasy make:
> Birds leave their nests undisturbed, and beasts their haunts
>   forsake.[30]

But drama is a mixed form; pure magnificence will not carry it through. The poet who attempts to achieve a play by the single force of the word provokes comparison, however strictly he confine himself to his capacity, with poets of other gifts. Corneille and Racine do not attain their triumphs by magnificence of this sort; they have concentration also, and, in the midst of their phrases, an undisturbed attention to the human soul as they knew it.[31]

Nor is Dryden unchallenged in his supreme ability to make the ridiculous, or the trivial, great:

> Avez-vous observé que maints cercueils de vieilles
> Sont presque aussi petits que celui d'un enfant?[32]

These lines are the work of a man whose verse is as magnificent as Dryden's, and who could see profounder possibilities in wit, and in violently joined images, than ever were in Dryden's mind. For Dryden, with all his intellect, had a commonplace mind. His powers were, we believe, wider, but no greater, than Milton's; he was confined by boundaries as impassable, though less strait. He bears a curious antithetical resemblance to Swinburne. Swinburne was also a master of words, but Swinburne's words are all suggestions and no denotation; if they suggest nothing, it is because they suggest too much. Dryden's words, on the other hand, are precise, they state immensely, but their suggestiveness is almost nothing.

> That short dark passage to a future state;
> That melancholy riddle of a breath,
> That something, or that nothing, after death.[33]

is a riddle, but not melancholy enough, in Dryden's splendid verse. The question, which has certainly been waiting, may justly be asked: whether without this which Dryden lacks, poetry can exist? What is man to decide what poetry is? Dryden's use of language is not, like that of Swinburne, weakening and demoralizing. Let us take as a final test his elegy upon Oldham, which deserves not to be mutilated:

> Farewell, too little and too lately known,
> Whom I began to think and call my own;
> For sure our souls were near allied, and thine
> Cast in the same poetic mould with mine.
> One common note on either lyre did strike,
> And knaves and fools we both abhorred alike.
> To the same goal did both our studies drive;
> The last set out the soonest did arrive.
> Thus Nisus fell upon the slippery place,
> Whilst his young friend performed and won the race.
> O early ripe! to thy abundant store
> What could advancing age have added more?
> It might (what nature never gives the young)
> Have taught the numbers of thy native tongue.
> But satire needs not those, and wit will shine
> Through the harsh cadence of a rugged line.
> A noble error, and but seldom made,
> When poets are by too much force betrayed.
> Thy generous fruits, though gathered ere their prime,
> Still showed a quickness; and maturing time
> But mellows what we write to the dull sweets of rhyme.
> Once more, hail, and farewell; farewell, thou young,

> But ah! too short, Marcellus of our tongue.
> Thy brows with ivy and with laurels bound;
> But fate and gloomy night encompass thee around.[34]

From the perfection of such an elegy we cannot detract; the lack of nebula is compensated by the satisfying completeness of the statement. Dryden lacked what his master Jonson possessed, a large and unique view of life; he lacked insight, he lacked profundity. But where Dryden fails to satisfy, the nineteenth century does not satisfy us either; and where that century has condemned him, it is itself condemned. In the next revolution of taste it is possible that poets may turn to the study of Dryden. He remains one of those who have set standards for English verse which it is desperate to ignore.

LONDON LETTER, JULY 1921[1]

THE VACANT TERM OF wit set in early this year with a fine hot rainless spring; the crop of murders and divorces has been poor compared with that of last autumn; Justice Darling (comic magistrate) has been silent, and has only raised his voice to declare that he does not know the difference between Epstein and Einstein (laughter).[2] Einstein the Great has visited England, and delivered lectures to uncomprehending audiences, and been photographed for the newspapers smiling at Lord Haldane. We wonder how much that smile implies; but Einstein has not confided its meaning to the press. He has met Mr. Bernard Shaw, but made no public comment on that subject.[3] Einstein has taken his place in the newspapers with the comet, the sun-spots, the poisonous jelly-fish and octopus at Margate, and other natural phenomena.[4] Mr. Robert Lynd has announced that only two living men have given their names to a school of poetry: King George V and Mr. J. C. Squire.[5] A new form of influenza has been discovered, which leaves extreme dryness and a bitter taste in the mouth.[6]

The fine weather and the coal strike have turned a blazing glare on London, discovering for the first time towers and steeples of an uncontaminated white.[7] The smile is without gaiety. What is spring without the Opera? Drury Lane and Covent Garden mourn; the singers have flocked, we are told, to New York, where such luxuries can be maintained. They have forgotten thee, O Sion.[8] Opera was one of the last reminders of a former excellence of life, a sustaining symbol even for those who seldom went. England sits in her weeds: eleven theatres are on the point of closing, as the public will no longer pay the prices required by the cost.[9] Considering the present state of the stage, there is little direct cause for regret. An optimist might even affirm that when everything that is bad and expensive is removed, its place may be supplied by something good and cheap; on the other hand it is more likely to be supplied by what is called, in the language of the day, the "super-cinema." Yet the Everyman Theatre at Hampstead, formed on a similar ideal to that of the Théâtre du Vieux Colombier in Paris, has, I hear, done well with a season of Shaw plays, though the performance has been criticized.[10] And M. Diaghileff, who has lately arrived with his Ballet and Stravinsky, has crowded houses.[11] Massine is not there, but Lopokova is perfection.[12] Not yet having had the opportunity of going, I can say nothing about either of the two new ballets, *Chout* or *Cuadro Flamenco*.[13] Two years ago M. Diaghileff's ballet arrived, the first Russian dancers since the war: we greeted the *Good-humoured Ladies*, and the *Boutique Fantasque*, and the *Three-Cornered Hat*, as the dawn of an art of the theatre.[14] And although there has been nothing since that could be called a further development, the ballet will probably be one of the influences forming a new drama, if a new drama ever comes. I mean of course the later ballet which has just been mentioned; for the earlier ballet, if it had greater dancers—Nijinsky or Pavlowa—had far less significance or substantiality.[15] The later ballet is more sophisticated, but also more simplified, and simplifies more; and what is needed of art is a simplification of current life into something rich and strange. This simplification neither Congreve nor Mr. Shaw attained; and however brilliant their comedies, they are a divagation from art.[16]

In this connection, it may be observed that Mr. Gordon Craig has incurred abuse by an essay which fills the February number of the *Chapbook*, entitled "Puppets and Poets."[17] Mr. Craig's style of writing, from what one can judge of it in this essay or series of notes, is certainly deplorable; but his essay contains a great deal of interest and some sense. He was rebuked for pointing out that the Puppet is not intended to deceive us into thinking that it is human, and afterwards praising one of the Japanese figures illustrated by saying that "this . . . hand almost seems prepared to shake another hand." Why, says the critic, this is a contradiction: is the puppet intended to resemble a human being or not? If it is, then it is merely a substitute for a human being, only tolerable on account of the high price of actors; if it is not, why should the proximity of the resemblance be a merit? But Mr. Craig has merely implied what is a necessary condition of all art: the counter-thrust of strict limitations of form and the expression of life. Ordinary social drama acknowledges no limitations, except some tricks of the stage. A form, when it is merely tolerated, becomes an abuse. Tolerate the stage aside and the soliloquy, and they are intolerable; make them a strict rule of the game, and they are a support. A new form, like that of the modern ballet, is as strict as any old one, perhaps stricter. Artists are constantly impelled to invent new difficulties for themselves; cubism is not licence, but an attempt to establish order. These reflections provoked by the ballet suggest at any rate a theory that might be maintained throughout an evening's conversation.

Mr. Strachey's Book

Mr. Lytton Strachey's *Queen Victoria* has succeeded and far surpassed Mrs. Asquith's book in popularity: it is found at every level; it is discussed by *everyone* and is discharged into the suburbs by every lending-library.[18] It would be absurd to say that the vogue of the book is not deserved; equally absurd to say that it is deserved, since vogue and the merits of a book have nothing in common. Its popularity is not due to faults, but rather to merits, though partly to the qualities which are not the most important. The notices which it has had, long and enthusiastic, from every paper, have been of great interest as an index to the simple and unsuspecting mind of the reviewer. What is of most interest in the book is Mr. Strachey's mind, in his motives for choosing his material, in his method in dealing with it, in his style, in his peculiar combination of biography and history. It was evident from *Eminent Victorians,* and it is equally evident from *Queen Victoria,* that Mr. Strachey has a romantic mind—that he deals, too, with his personages, not in a spirit of "detachment," but by attaching himself to them, *tout entier à sa proie attaché.*[19] He has his favourites, and they are chosen by his emotion rather than design, by his feeling for what can be made of them with his great ability to turn the commonplace into something immense and grotesque. But it must be a peculiar commonplace, although Mr. Strachey is limited only by the degree of interest he takes in his personage. There must be a touch of the fantastic, of a fantastic that lies hidden for Mr. Strachey to discover. Gladstone appears to be without it; Disraeli appears to be too consciously playing a *rôle* for Mr. Strachey to extract much fantasy from him.[20] What is especially charming is the fusion of irony with romance, of private with public, of trivial and serious. The fusion is reflected in the style, which, although Mr. Strachey's, may be formulated as a mixture of Gibbon with Macaulay—Gibbon in the irony, and Macaulay in the romance.[21] Mr. Strachey, without your being aware of it, places his sitter in just this light, and with a phrase —"Lord Melbourne, an autumn rose"—"Mr. Creevey, grown old now," imposes his point of view.[22] The innocent accept this under the impression that they are acquiring information. If it were not under the spell of Mr. Strachey's mind, if we examined the letters of the Queen, or Balmoral, or the Albert Memorial, or the Crystal Palace, without Mr. Strachey's directions, we might see them very differently, and quite as justly. Mr. Strachey never seems to impose himself, he never drives towards a theory, but he never relaxes his influence.

Mr. Strachey is a part of history rather than a critic of it; he has invented new sensations from history, as Bergson has invented new sensations from metaphysics.[23] No other historian has so deliberately cultivated the feelings which the inspection of an historical character can arouse. The strange, the surprising, is of course essential to art; but art has to create a new world, and a new world must have a new structure. Mr. Joyce has succeeded, because he has very great constructive ability; and it is the structure which gives his later work its unique and solitary value. There are several other writers—among the very best that we have—who can explore feeling—even Mr. Ronald Firbank, who has a sense of beauty in a very degraded form.[24] The craving for the fantastic, for the strange, is legitimate and perpetual; everyone with a sense of beauty has it. The strongest, like Mr. Joyce, make their feeling into an articulate external world; what might crudely be called a more feminine type, when it is also a very sophisticated type, makes its art by feeling and by contemplating the feeling, rather than the object which has excited it or the object into which the feeling might be made. Of this type of writing the recent book of sketches by Mrs. Woolf, *Monday or Tuesday,* is the most extreme example.[25] A good deal of the secret of the charm of Mrs. Woolf's shorter pieces consists in the immense disparity between the object and the train of feeling which it has set in motion. Mrs. Woolf gives you the minutest datum, and leads you on to explore, quite consciously, the sequence of images and feelings which float away from it. The result is something which makes Walter Pater appear an unsophisticated rationalist, and the writing is often remarkable.[26] The book is one of the most curious and interesting examples of a process of dissociation which in that direction, it would seem, cannot be exceeded.

LONDON LETTER, SEPTEMBER 1921[1]

LOOKING BACK UPON THE past season in London—for no new season has yet begun—it remains certain Strawinsky was our two months' lion. He has been the greatest success since Picasso.[2] In London all the stars obey their seasons, though these seasons no more conform to the almanac than those which concern the weather. A mysterious law of appearance and disappearance governs everybody—or at least everybody who is wise enough to obey it. Who is Mr. Rubinstein? The brilliant pianist.[3] This summer he was everywhere; at every dinner, every party, every week-end; in the evening crisp and curled in a box; sometimes apparently in several boxes at once. He was prominent enough to have several doubles; numbers of men vaguely resembled him. Why this should have happened this year rather than last year, perhaps rather than next year, I for one cannot tell. Even very insignificant people feel the occult influence; one knows, oneself, that there are times when it is desirable to be seen and times when it is felicitous to vanish.

But Strawinsky, Lucifer of the season, brightest in the firmament, took the call many times, small and correctly neat in pince-nez. His advent was well prepared by Mr. Eugene Goossens—also rather conspicuous this year—who conducted two *Sacre du Printemps* concerts, and other Strawinsky concerts were given before his arrival.[4] The music was certainly too new and strange to please very many people; it is true that on the first night it was received with wild applause, and it is to be regretted that only three performances were given. If the ballet was not perfect, the fault does not lie either in the music, or in the choreography—which was admirable, or in the dancing—where Madame Sokolova distinguished herself. To me the music seemed very remarkable—but at all events struck me as possessing a quality of modernity which I missed from the ballet which accompanied it. The effect was like *Ulysses* with illustrations by the best contemporary illustrator.

Strawinsky, that is to say, had done his job in the music. But music that is to be taken like operatic music, music accompanying and explained by an action, must have a drama which has been put through the same process of development as the music itself. The spirit of the music was modern, and the spirit of the ballet was primitive ceremony. The Vegetation Rite upon which the ballet is founded remained, in spite of the music, a pageant of primitive culture. It was interesting to any one who had read *The Golden Bough* and similar works, but hardly more than interesting.[5] In art there should be interpenetration and metamorphosis. Even *The Golden Bough* can be read in two ways: as a collection of entertaining myths, or as a revelation of that vanished mind of which our mind is a continuation. In everything in the *Sacre du Printemps*, except in the music, one missed the sense of the present. Whether Strawinsky's music be permanent or ephemeral I do not know; but it did seem to transform the rhythm of the steppes into the scream of the motor horn, the rattle of machinery, the grind of wheels, the beating of iron and steel, the roar of the underground railway, and the other barbaric cries of modern life; and to transform these despairing noises into music.

Mr. Bernard Shaw

It is not within my province to discuss *Back to Methuselah*, but the appearance of the book may make some observations on Mr. Shaw not impertinent, and it is an advantage for my purpose that the book is as well known in America as it is here.[6] A valedictory tone in this book (already noticed by Mr. Seldes) is not inapposite to a successful season of his plays by Mr. Macdermott's company.[7] *Blanco Posnet* is now running at the Court Theatre.[8] The recognition indicated by this success implies perhaps that Mr. Shaw has attained, in the most eulogistic sense of his own term, the position of an Ancient.[9]

Seven years ago, in 1914, when Mr. Shaw came out with his thoughts about the War, the situation was very different.[10] It might have been predicted that what he said then would not seem subversive or blasphemous now. The public has accepted Mr. Shaw, not by recognizing the intelligence of what he said then, but by forgetting it; but we must not forget that at one time Mr. Shaw was a very unpopular man. He is no longer the gadfly of the commonwealth; but even if he has never been appreciated, it is something that he should be respected. To-day he is perhaps an important elder man of letters in a sense in which Mr. Hardy is not. Hardy represents to us a still earlier generation not by his date of birth but by his type of mind.[11] He is of the day before yesterday, whilst Shaw is of a to-day that is only this evening. Hardy is Victorian, Shaw is Edwardian. Shaw is therefore more interesting to us, for by reflecting on his mind we may form some plausible conjecture about the mind of the next age—about what, in retrospect, the "present" generation will be found to have been. Shaw belongs to a fluid world, he is an insular Diderot, but more serious.[12] I should say—for it is amusing, if unsafe, to prophesy—that we shall demand from our next leaders a purer intellect, more scientific, more logical, more rigorous. Shaw's mind is a free and easy mind: every idea, no matter how irrelevant, is welcome. Twenty years ago, even ten years ago, the "Preface" to *Methuselah* would have seemed a cogent synthesis of thought instead of a delightful farrago of Mr. Shaw's conversation about economics, politics, biology, dramatic and art criticism. It is not merely that Mr. Shaw is wilful; it is also that he lacks the interest in, and capacity for, continuous reasoning.

Mr. Shaw has never cajoled the public; it is no fault of his that he has been taken for a joker, a cleverer Oscar Wilde, when his intention was always austerely serious.[13] It is his seriousness which has made him unpopular, which made Oscar Wilde appear, in comparison, dull enough to be a safe and respectable playwright. But Shaw has perhaps suffered in a more vital way from the public denseness; a more appreciative audience might have prevented him from being satisfied with an epigram instead of a demonstration. On the other hand Mr. Shaw himself has hardly understood his own seriousness, or known where it might lead him: he is somehow amazingly innocent. The explanation is that Mr. Shaw never was really interested in life. Had he been more curious about the actual and abiding human being, he might have been less clever and less surprising.

He was interested in the comparatively transient things, in anything that can or should be changed; but he was not interested in, was rather impatient of, the things which always have been and always will be the same. Now the fact which makes *Methuselah* impressive is that the nature of the subject, the attempt to expose a panorama of human history "as far as thought can reach," almost compels Mr. Shaw to face ultimate questions.[14] His creative evolution proceeds so far that the process ceases to be progress, and progress ceases to have any meaning. Even the author appears to be conscious of the question whether the beginning and the end are not the same, and whether, as Mr. Bradley says, "whatever you know, it is all one."[15] (Certainly the way of life of the younger generation, in his glimpse of life in the remote future, is unpleasantly like a Raymond Duncan or Margaret-Morris school of dancing in the present.)[16]

There is evidence that Mr. Shaw has many thoughts by the way; as a rule he welcomes them and seldom dismisses them as irrelevant. The pessimism of the conclusion of his last book is a thought which he has neither welcomed nor dismissed; and it is pessimism only because he has not realized that at the end he has only approached a beginning, that his end is only the starting point towards the knowledge of life.

The book may for a moment be taken as the last word of a century, perhaps of two centuries. The eighteenth and nineteenth centuries were the ages of logical science: not in the sense that this science actually made more progress than the others, but in the sense that it was biology that influenced the imagination of non-scientific people. Darwin is the representative of those years, as Newton of the seventeenth, and Einstein perhaps of ours. Creative evolution is a phrase that has lost both its stimulant and sedative virtues. It is possible that an exasperated generation may find comfort in admiring, even if without understanding, mathematics, may suspect that precision and profundity are not incompatible, may find maturity as interesting as adolescence, and permanence more interesting than change. It must at all events be either much more demoralized intellectually than the last age, or very much more disciplined.

THE METAPHYSICAL POETS[1]

BY COLLECTING THESE POEMS from the work of a generation more often named than read, and more often read than profitably studied, Professor Grierson has rendered a service of some importance.[2] Certainly the reader will meet with many poems already preserved in other anthologies, at the same time that he discovers poems such as those of Aurelian Townshend or Lord Herbert of Cherbury here included.[3] But the function of such an anthology as this is neither that of Professor Saintsbury's admirable edition of Caroline poets nor that of the *Oxford Book of English Verse*.[4] Mr. Grierson's book is in itself a piece of criticism, and a provocation of criticism; and we think that he was right in including so many poems of Donne, elsewhere (though not in many editions) accessible, as documents in the case of "metaphysical poetry." The phrase has long done duty as a term of abuse, or as the label of a quaint and pleasant taste. The question is to what extent the so-called metaphysicals formed a school (in our own times we should say a "movement"), and how far this so-called school or movement is a digression from the main current.

Not only is it extremely difficult to define metaphysical poetry, but difficult to decide what poets practise it and in which of their verses. The poetry of Donne (to whom Marvell and Bishop King are sometimes nearer than any of the other authors) is late Elizabethan, its feeling often very close to that of Chapman.[5] The "courtly" poetry is derivative from Jonson, who borrowed liberally from the Latin; it expires in the next century with the sentiment and witticism of Prior.[6] There is finally the devotional verse of Herbert, Vaughan, and Crashaw (echoed long after by Christina Rossetti and Francis Thompson);[7] Crashaw, sometimes more profound and less sectarian than the others, has a quality which returns through the Elizabethan period to the early Italians. It is difficult to find any precise use of metaphor, simile, or other conceit, which is common to all the poets and at the same time important enough as an element of style to isolate these poets as a group. Donne, and often Cowley, employ a device which is sometimes considered characteristically "metaphysical": the elaboration (contrasted with the condensation) of a figure of speech to the farthest stage to which ingenuity can carry it.[8] Thus Cowley develops the commonplace comparison of the world to a chess-board through long stanzas ("To Destiny"), and Donne, with more grace, in "A Valediction," the comparison of two lovers to a pair of compasses. But elsewhere we find, instead of the mere explication of the content of a comparison, a development by rapid association of thought which requires considerable agility on the part of the reader.

> On a round ball
> A workeman that hath copies by, can lay
> An Europe, Afrique, and an Asia,
> And quickly make that, which was nothing, *All*,
>> So doth each teare
>> Which thee doth weare,
> A globe, yea world by that impression grow,
> Till thy tears mixt with mine doe overflow
> This world, by waters sent from thee, my heaven dissolved so.[9]

Here we find at least two connexions which are not implicit in the first figure, but are forced upon it by the poet: from the geographer's globe to the tear, and the tear to the deluge. On the other hand, some of Donne's most successful and characteristic effects are secured by brief words and sudden contrasts:

> A bracelet of bright hair about the bone,[10]

where the most powerful effect is produced by the sudden contrast of associations of "bright hair" and of "bone." This telescoping of images and

multiplied association is characteristic of the phrase of some of the dramatists of the period which Donne knew: not to mention Shakespeare, it is
frequent in Middleton, Webster, and Tourneur, and is one of the sources
of the vitality of their language.[11]

Johnson, who employed the term "metaphysical poets," apparently
having Donne, Cleveland, and Cowley chiefly in mind, remarks of them
that "the most heterogeneous ideas are yoked by violence together."[12] The
force of this impeachment lies in the failure of the conjunction, the fact
that often the ideas are yoked but not united; and if we are to judge of
styles of poetry by their abuse, examples may be found in Cleveland to
justify Johnson's condemnation.[13] But a degree of heterogeneity of material compelled into unity by the operation of the poet's mind is omnipresent
in poetry. We need not select for illustration such a line as:

> Notre âme est un trois-mâts cherchant son Icarie;[14]

we may find it in some of the best lines of Johnson himself ("The Vanity
of Human Wishes"):

> His fate was destined to a barren strand,
> A petty fortress, and a dubious hand;
> He left a name at which the world grew pale,
> To point a moral, or adorn a tale,[15]

where the effect is due to a contrast of ideas, different in degree but the
same in principle, as that which Johnson mildly reprehended. And in one
of the finest poems of the age (a poem which could not have been written
in any other age), the "Exequy" of Bishop King, the extended comparison
is used with perfect success; the idea and the simile become one, in the
passage in which the Bishop illustrates his impatience to see his dead
wife, under the figure of a journey;

> Stay for me there; I will not faile
> To meet thee in that hollow Vale.
> And think not much of my delay;
> I am already on the way,
> And follow thee with all the speed
> Desire can make, or sorrows breed.
> Each minute is a short degree,

And ev'ry houre a step towards thee.
At night when I betake to rest,
Next morn I rise nearer my West
Of life, almost by eight houres sail,
Than when sleep breath'd his drowsy gale . . .
But heark! My Pulse, like a soft Drum
Beats my approach, tells *Thee* I come;
And slow howere my marches be,
I shall at last sit down by *Thee*.[16]

(In the last few lines there is that effect of terror which is several times attained by one of Bishop King's admirers, Edgar Poe.)[17] Again, we may justly take these quatrains from Lord Herbert's "Ode," stanzas which would, we think, be immediately pronounced to be of the metaphysical school:

So when from hence we shall be gone,
And be no more, nor you, nor I,
As one another's mystery,
Each shall be both, yet both but one.
This said, in her up-lifted face,
Her eyes, which did that beauty crown,
Were like two starrs, that having faln down,
Look up again to find their place:
While such a moveless silent peace
Did seize on their becalmed sense,
One would have thought some influence
Their ravished spirits did possess.[18]

There is nothing in these lines (with the possible exception of the stars, a simile not at once grasped, but lovely and justified) which fits Johnson's general observations on the metaphysical poets in his essay on Cowley. A good deal resides in the richness of association which is at the same time borrowed from and given to the world "becalmed"; but the meaning is clear, the language simple and elegant. It is to be observed that the language of these poets is as a rule simple and pure; in the verse of George Herbert this simplicity is carried as far as it can go—a simplicity emulated without success by numerous modern poets. The *structure* of the sentences, on the other hand, is sometimes far from simple, but this is not a vice; it is a fidelity to thought and feeling. The effect, at its best, is far less artificial than that of an ode by Gray.[19] And as this fidelity induces variety of thought and feeling, so it induces variety of music. We doubt whether, in the eighteenth century, could be found two poems in nominally the same metre, so dissimilar as Marvell's "Coy Mistress" and Crashaw's "Saint Teresa"; the one producing an effect of great speed by the use of short syllables, and the other an ecclesiastical solemnity by the use of long ones:

> Love, thou art absolute sole lord
> Of life and death.[20]

If so shrewd and sensitive (though so limited) a critic as Johnson failed to define metaphysical poetry by its faults, it is worth while to inquire whether we may not have more success by adopting the opposite method: by assuming that the poets of the seventeenth century (up to the Revolution) were the direct and natural development of the precedent age; and, without prejudicing their case by the adjective "metaphysical," consider whether their virtue was not something permanently valuable, which subsequently disappeared, but ought not to have disappeared. Johnson has hit, perhaps by accident, on one of their peculiarities, when he observes that "their attempts were always analytic"; he would not agree that, after the dissociation, they put the material together again in a new unity.[21]

It is certain that the dramatic verse of the later Elizabethan and early Jacobean poets expresses a degree of development of sensibility which is not found in any of the prose, good as it often is. If we except Marlowe, a man of prodigious intelligence, these dramatists were directly or indirectly (it is at least a tenable theory) affected by Montaigne.[22] Even if we except also Jonson and Chapman, these two were notably erudite, and were notably men who incorporated their erudition into their sensibility; their mode of feeling was directly and freshly altered by their reading and thought. In Chapman especially there is a direct sensuous apprehension of thought, or a re-creation of thought into feeling, which is exactly what we find in Donne:

> In this one thing, all the discipline
> Of manners and of manhood is contained;

A man to join himself with th' Universe
In his main sway, and make in all things fit
One with that All, and go on, round as it;
Not plucking from the whole his wretched part,
And into straits, or into nought revert,
Wishing the complete Universe might be
Subject to such a rag of it as he;
But to consider great Necessity.[23]

We compare this with some modern passage:

No, when the fight begins within himself,
A man's worth something. God stoops o'er his head,
Satan looks up between his feet—both tug—
He's left, himself, i' the middle; the soul wakes
And grows. Prolong that battle through his life![24]

It is perhaps somewhat less fair, though very tempting (as both poets are concerned with the perpetuation of love by offspring), to compare with the stanzas already quoted from Lord Herbert's "Ode" the following from Tennyson:

One walked between his wife and child,
With measured footfall firm and mild,
And now and then he gravely smiled.
    The prudent partner of his blood
    Leaned on him, faithful, gentle, good,
    Wearing the rose of womanhood.
And in their double love secure,
The little maiden walked demure,
Pacing with downward eyelids pure.
    These three made unity so sweet
    My frozen heart began to beat,
    Remembering its ancient heat.[25]

The difference is not a simple difference of degree between poets. It is something which had happened to the mind of England between the time of Donne or Lord Herbert of Cherbury and the time of Tennyson and Browning; it is the difference between the intellectual poet and the reflective poet. Tennyson and Browning are poets, and they think; but they do not feel their thought as immediately as the odour of a rose. A thought to Donne was an experience; it modified his sensibility. When a poet's mind is perfectly equipped for its work, it is constantly amalgamating disparate experience; the ordinary man's experience is chaotic, irregular, fragmentary. The latter falls in love, or reads Spinoza, and these two experiences have nothing to do with each other, or with the noise of the typewriter or the smell of cooking; in the mind of the poet these experiences are always forming new wholes.[26]

We may express the difference by the following theory: The poets of the seventeenth century, the successors of the dramatists of the sixteenth, possessed a mechanism of sensibility which could devour any kind of experience. They are simple, artificial, difficult or fantastic, as their predecessors were; no less or more than Dante, Guido Cavalcanti, Guinizelli, or Cino.[27] In the seventeenth century a dissociation of sensibility set in, from which we have never recovered; and this dissociation, as is natural, was due to the influence of the two most powerful poets of the century, Milton and Dryden. Each of these men performed certain poetic functions so magnificently well that the magnitude of the effect concealed the absence of others. The language went on and in some respects improved; the best verse of Collins, Gray, Johnson, and even Goldsmith satisfies some of our fastidious demands better than that of Donne or Marvell or King.[28] But while the language became more refined, the feeling became more crude. The feeling, the sensibility, expressed in "Country Churchyard" (to say nothing of Tennyson and Browning) is cruder than that in the "Coy Mistress."[29]

The second effect of the influence of Milton and Dryden followed from the first, and was therefore slow in manifestation. The sentimental age began early in the eighteenth century, and continued. The poets revolted against the ratiocinative, the descriptive; they thought and felt by fits, unbalanced; they reflected. In one or two passages of Shelley's "Triumph of Life," in the second "Hyperion," there are traces of a struggle toward unification of sensibility.[30] But Keats and Shelley died, and Tennyson and Browning ruminated.

After this brief exposition of a theory—too brief, perhaps, to carry conviction—we may ask, what would have been the fate of the "metaphysical" had the current of poetry descended in a direct line from them, as it descended in a direct line to them? They would not, certainly, be classified as metaphysical. The possible interests of a poet are unlimited; the more intelligent he is the better; the more intelligent he is the more likely that he will have interests: our only condition is that he turn them into poetry, and not merely meditate on them poetically. A philosophical theory which has entered into poetry is established, for its truth or falsity in one sense ceases to matter, and its truth in another sense is proved. The poets in question have, like other poets, various faults. But they were, at best, engaged in the task of trying to find the verbal equivalent for states of mind and feeling. And this means both that they are more mature, and they wear better, than later poets of certainly not less literary ability.

It is not a permanent necessity that poets should be interested in philosophy, or in any other subject. We can only say that it appears likely that poets in our civilization, as it exists at present, must be *difficult*. Our civilization comprehends great variety and complexity, and this variety and complexity, playing upon a refined sensibility, must produce various and complex results. The poet must become more and more comprehensive, more allusive, more indirect, in order to force, to dislocate if necessary, language into his meaning. (A brilliant and extreme statement of this view, with which it is not requisite to associate oneself, is that of M. Jean Epstein, *La Poésie d'aujourd'hui*.)[31] Hence we get something which looks very much like the conceit—we get, in fact, a method curiously similar to that of the "metaphysical poets," similar also in its use of obscure words and of simple phrasing.

> O géraniums diaphanes, guerroyeurs sortilèges,
> Sacrilèges monomanes!
> Emballages, dévergondages, douches! O pressoirs
> Des vendanges des grands soirs!
> Layettes aux abois,
> Thyrses au fond des bois!
> Transfusions, représailles,
> Relevailles, compresses et l'éternel potion,
> Angélus! n'en pouvoir plus
> De débâcles nuptiales! de débâcles nuptiales![32]

The same poet could also write simply:

> Elle est bien loin, elle pleure,
> Le grand vent se lamente aussi . . .[33]

Jules Laforgue, and Tristan Corbière in many of his poems, are nearer to the "school of Donne" than any modern English poet.[34] But poets more classical than they have the same essential quality of transmuting ideas into sensations, of transforming an observation into a state of mind.

> Pour l'enfant, amoureux de cartes et d'estampes,
> L'univers est égal à son vaste appétit.
> Ah, que le monde est grand à la clarté des lampes!
> Aux yeux du souvenir que le monde est petit![35]

In French literature the great master of the seventeenth century—Racine —and the great master of the nineteenth—Baudelaire—are more like each other than they are like anyone else. The greatest two masters of diction are also the greatest two psychologists, the most curious explorers of the soul. It is interesting to speculate whether it is not a misfortune that two of the greatest masters of diction in our language, Milton and Dryden, triumph with a dazzling disregard of the soul. If we continued to produce Miltons and Drydens it might not so much matter, but as things are it is a pity that English poetry has remained so incomplete. Those who object to the "artificiality" of Milton or Dryden sometimes tell us to "look into our hearts and write." But that is not looking deep enough; Racine or Donne looked into a good deal more than the heart. One must look into the cerebral cortex, the nervous system, and the digestive tracts.

May we not conclude, then, that Donne, Crashaw, Vaughan, Herbert and Lord Herbert, Marvell, King, Cowley at his best, are in the direct current of English poetry, and that their faults should be reprimanded by this standard rather than coddled by antiquarian affection? They have been enough praised in terms which are implicit limitations because they are "metaphysical" or "witty," "quaint" or "obscure," though at their best they have not these attributes more than other serious poets. On the other hand, we must not reject the criticism of Johnson (a dangerous person to disagree with) without having mastered it, without having assimilated the Johnsonian canons of taste. In reading the celebrated passage in his essay on Cowley we must remember that by wit he clearly means something more serious than we usually mean to-day; in his criticism of their versification we must remember in what a narrow discipline he was trained, but also how well trained; we must remember that Johnson tortures chiefly the chief offenders, Cowley and Cleveland. It would be a fruitful work, and one requiring a substantial book, to break up the classification of Johnson (for there has been one since) and exhibit these poets in all their difference of kind and of degree, from the massive music of Donne to the faint, pleasing tinkle of Aurelian Townshend—whose "Dialogue between a Pilgrim and Time" is one of the few regrettable omissions from this excellent anthology.

London Letter, March 1921

1. The essay was published in the *Dial* 70, no. 4 (April 1921): 448–453. "March 1921" was supplied by the editors of the *Dial*, who wanted it to seem up-to-date when it appeared in the April issue. But the essay was actually written over the weekend of 22–23 January, as Eliot informed his mother in a letter dated 22 January 1921: "I have been working this weekend on an overdue article for the *Dial*, the first I have written for many months. It came very hard, and I do not think that it is very good or very well written, but it is a start, and I hope that I shall soon get my hand in again" (*LOTSE*, 432). Confirmation for this date comes from the essay itself, in which Eliot writes: "Next week the admirable Phoenix Society will perform *Volpone or the Fox* . . ." Performances took place on Sunday, 30 January, and on Tuesday, 1 February 1921.

   The *Dial*, published in New York City, was co-owned and co-edited by two men. One was Scofield Thayer, the scion of a wealthy family who manufactured woolens in Worcester, Massachusetts; Thayer had known Eliot both at Milton Academy and at Harvard, and he was the more active and dominant editor. The other was James Sibley Watson, Jr., an heir of a family that had founded the Western Union Telegraph Company. The journal was heavily subsidized by the owners at the rate of nearly $70,000 per year. It had a total circulation of 9,500—6,400 via subscription, the rest via retail sales. The readership was made up entirely of Americans, though Thayer wanted to enter into the English market. This essay was the first "London Letter" that Eliot wrote for the *Dial*.

2. H. L. Mencken and George Jean Nathan, *The American Credo: A Contribution toward the Interpretation of the National Mind* (New York: A. Knopf, 1920).

3. The writer who charged Eliot with "elegant anguish" has not been identified. Eliot may have made up this phrase, just as he assigns the phrase "general reading public" to the publisher of *Some Contemporary Poets: 1920* below in this essay (see n. 6), when in fact the publisher never used those words.

4. The phrase "elegant Jeremiah" was used to describe Matthew Arnold by an anonymous contemporary journalist writing in the *Daily Telegraph*, 8 September 1866. The reviewer has since been identified as James Macdonnell. Arnold had antagonized the staff at the *Daily Telegraph* by referring to them as "young lions" and otherwise attacking them in his essay on "The Function of Criticism at the Present Time." The tag "elegant Jeremiah" stuck and has been repeated countless times in books and essays on Arnold.

5. Harold Monro, *Some Contemporary Poets: 1920* (London: Leonard Parsons, 1920). Monro (1879–1932) ran the Poetry Bookshop at 35, Devonshire Street, Theobold's Road, from its opening in January 1913, until his death. It was the principal bookshop for London poetry readers during this period. Before the First World War he edited the journal *Poetry and Drama*, which came out in eight quarterly numbers between March 1913 and December 1914, and after it the *Chapbook*, which was published monthly between July 1919 and June 1921, quarterly in February and May 1922, monthly again from July 1922 to June 1923, and annually in 1924 and 1925. Eliot's relations with Monro were strained. In 1914, when Conrad Aiken had offered Monro the chance to publish "The Love Song of J. Alfred Prufrock," Monro dismissed it as "absolutely insane." But in both 1920 and 1921 Eliot contributed essays to the *Chapbook*. (See "A Brief Treatise on the Criticism of Poetry," *Chapbook* 2.9 [March 1920]: 1–10 and "Prose and Verse," *Chapbook* 22 [April 1921]: 3–10; reprinted here, 158–165.) When Eliot published *The Waste Land* in 1922, however, Monro expressed serious reservations. (See Harold Monro, "Notes for a Study of 'The Waste Land': An Imaginary Dialogue with T. S. Eliot," *Chapbook* 34 [February 1923]: 20–24.) Notwithstanding this criticism, Eliot contributed three poems to the *Chapbook* in 1924. (See "Doris's Dream Songs," *Chapbook* 39 [November 1924]: 36–37.) Monro was also the publisher of five editions—1911–1912, 1913–1915, 1916–1917, 1918–1919, and 1920–1922—of *Georgian Poetry*, a popular anthology which had large quantities of pastoral poetry and was much criticized by Eliot and Pound. In *Some Contemporary Poets: 1920* Monro reviewed seven established poets (Robert Bridges, William Scawen Blunt, Charles M. Doughty, Thomas Hardy, Rudyard Kipling, Alice Meynell, and W. B. Yeats) and forty-seven younger poets, including Pound, H.D., and Richard Aldington. Eliot was conspicuous by his absence. Monro tried to adopt a moderate, catholic position in the period's debates about poetry, but was criticized for not taking sides.

6. The phrase "general reading public" is Eliot's invention, not that of Monro or his publishers. The text on the dust jacket of the volume reads: "The book

should be of service to students and to foreigners who are in need of introduction to the branch of modern English literature." Matthew Arnold, in
Culture and Anarchy (1869), had applied the term "Philistines" (the name for
warlike people in biblical Palestine who attacked the Israelites many times)
to the newer middle classes who were generally nonconformist in religion
and averse to the cultural activities which they associated with aristocratic
decadence, including poetry, music, or the fine arts. By 1920 the term had
lost its original specificity and come to mean someone commonplace in
ideas and tastes and indifferent toward the arts.

7. Edmund Gosse (1849–1928) was the most influential critic of his day. He
worked in the British Library from 1865 to 1875, lectured on English literature at Trinity College, Cambridge, from 1885 to 1890, and was librarian
to the House of Lords from 1904 to 1915. In 1922 he became editor of the
Sunday Times. He translated three of Ibsen's plays, notably *Hedda Gabler* and,
with William Archer, *The Master Builder.* He wrote many books, including
biographies of Thomas Gray (1884), John Donne (1899), and Ibsen (1907).
Eliot met him at a reading in December 1917, where Gosse publicly reproved
him for arriving a few minutes late from his work at the bank. (See Osbert
Sitwell, *Laughter in the Next Room* [London: Macmillan, 1949], 32–33.)

  Agnes Repplier (1855–1950) was a prolific American essayist and biog-
rapher whose essays, after 1886, appeared in the *Atlantic Monthly, Appleton's
Magazine,* the *New Republic, McClure's, Harper's,* and many others. She also
wrote more than forty books, many of them collections of her essays issued
under such titles as *Essays in Idleness* (1893), *Essays in Miniature* (1892),
or *Books and Men* (1890).

  The Rev. Samuel McChord Crothers (1857–1927) was a Unitarian
minister as well as a prolific essayist and author. He lived in Boston and was
highly esteemed during the period when Eliot was a student at Harvard.
He wrote more than a hundred books, both literary and religious in subject
matter, with such titles as *The Gentle Reader* (1910), *The Wisdom of Experience*
(1911), or *Drawing Near to God* (1920).

8. *Spoon River Anthology,* by Edgar Lee Masters (1869–1950), comprises a series
of poetic epitaphs for residents of a fictional American small town. It appeared at the moment when the small town was fading into history, increasingly viewed through a haze of nostalgia, and the volume enjoyed enormous
critical and popular success. None of Masters's other books did as well, and
in later years he turned to biography, including one of Vachel Lindsay.

  Lindsay (1879–1931) was a mystical and religious poet who achieved
notoriety when his poem "General William Booth Enters into Heaven" was
published in *Poetry* in January 1913, followed by a book of poems of the same
title that autumn. The poem, a tribute to the founder of the Salvation Army,
employs hectic rhythms derived from the hymn "The Blood of the Lamb."
Lindsay continued to give histrionic and very popular readings of his poems
throughout the rest of his life.

9. There were recurrent reports in the British press from 1915 to 1923 that

Turks were massacring Armenians, together with calls for the government to intervene.

10. Vachel Lindsay's poem "The Broncho That Would Not Be Broken" was published in the *Chapbook* 2.11 (May 1920): 38–39. "I was appalled by Lindsay" —i.e., by his poem—Eliot wrote to John Gould Fletcher on 14 September 1920 (*LOTSE*, 410).

11. Eliot is referring to the view that the American president Woodrow Wilson (1856–1924), during the negotiations that led to the Treaty of Versailles in 1919, had been manipulated by the British prime minister Lloyd George (1865–1943; prime minister 1916–1922) and the French premier Georges Clemenceau (1841–1929; premier 1917–1920) into abandoning the idealistic principles which he had earlier said were to govern discussions about the political shape of Europe after the First World War. Instead, the Treaty of Versailles enabled Britain to achieve large territorial gains (under the guise of "mandates") and France to realize its goal of imposing punitive reparations on Germany. Eliot was a firm believer in the thesis articulated by Maynard Keynes, in *The Economic Consequences of the Peace* (1919), that the punitive reparations would have disastrous consequences; he recommended Keynes's book warmly to his brother Henry in early 1920 (see *LOTSE*, 353).

12. Hamilton Wright Mabie (1846–1916) was a prolific essayist and author who wrote more than sixty books, each with a platitudinous didactic note.

13. David Graham Phillips (1867–1911) was a journalist and author of fiction. He worked as an investigative journalist for the *Cincinnati Times-Star*, the *New York Sun*, and the *New York World*. But his first novel, *The Great God Success* (1901), proved so popular that Phillips left journalism to concentrate on fiction. He wrote sixteen novels, many employing journalistic techniques to explore social problems. Eliot may have known his novel *A Grain of Dust* (New York: D. Appleton, 1911), which traces the life of Dorothy Hallowell, a stenographer or typist who becomes an object of obsessive fascination for her boss, Fred Norman, an up-and-coming corporation lawyer. But in this passage Eliot is referring to *Susan Lenox: Her Fall and Rise* (New York: D. Appleton, 1917), a posthumously published novel which recounts the heroine's plunge to prostitution and her rise as a Broadway star.

14. John Drinkwater (1882–1937) grew up in Oxfordshire, left school at fifteen, and became an insurance clerk in Nottingham. When his firm moved to Birmingham in 1901, he followed. He published his first book, *Poems* (Birmingham: C. Cambridge) in 1903, followed by many others. In 1911 he joined an amateur theater company, the Pilgrim Players, which proved so successful that in 1913 it constructed a purpose-built theater, the Birmingham Repertory Theatre, which Drinkwater managed. His first full-length play was *Rebellion* (1914), his first real success *Abraham Lincoln* (1918). Meanwhile he poured out volume after volume of poetry and prose, eventually writing more than 150 books. In *Some Contemporary Poets: 1920*, Monro damns his "derivative and commonplace" poetry (180), condescends to notice his "simple and benevolent mind" (182), yet hopes that *Abraham Lincoln*

marks a new beginning in his work. Drinkwater's work had been published in *New Numbers*, a journal that lasted through four quarterly numbers in 1914, financed in part by Edward Marsh (see next note).

15. "Georgian Anthology" was a familiar term for *Georgian Poetry* (1912), a collection of contemporary poems edited by Edward Marsh, which had proved an unexpected success and sold more than eight thousand copies. Marsh went on to edit four more collections of *Georgian Poetry* (1913–1915, 1916–1917, 1918–1919, and 1920–1922), all published by Harold Monro, but the series increasingly acquired a reputation for tameness and insincerity.

16. John Collings Squire (1884–1958) was a highly influential journalist and essayist, as well as a minor poet. His opportunity came in 1913 when the *New Statesman* was founded, with the blessings of George Bernard Shaw and the Fabian Society, to provide an alternative to the *New Age*, edited by A. R. Orage. Squire, formerly a reviewer and writer for the *New Age*, was literary editor of the *New Statesman* from 1913 to 1919. He then founded and became editor of the *London Mercury* (1919–1939), and was also the chief literary critic of the *Observer*, an influential Sunday newspaper (circulation 200,000). Though Eliot wrote eighteen reviews (1916–1918) for the *New Statesman* when Squire was literary editor, his views of Squire changed as he grew closer to the Bloomsbury group and the Sitwells, who strongly opposed the circle they dismissed as the "Squirearchy," and its hold over contemporary literary opinion. To John Quinn, Eliot wrote in 1920: "*The London Mercury*, which started with a great deal of advertisement, will I hope, fail in a few years' time. It is run by a small clique of bad writers. J. C. Squire, the editor, knows nothing about poetry; but he is the cleverest journalist in London. If he succeeds, it will be impossible to get anything good published. His influence controls or affects the literary contents and criticism of five or six periodicals already" (*LOTSE*, 358). Squire also published poems in two of the *Georgian Poetry* collections published by Harold Monro, 1916–1917 and 1918–1919.

    Mr. Podsnap is a character in *Our Mutual Friend* (1864–1865), a novel by Charles Dickens. He first appears in book one, chapter 11 ("Podsnappery"), introduced with these words: "Mr. Podsnap was well to do, and stood very high in Mr. Podsnap's opinion. Beginning with a good inheritance, he had married a good inheritance, and had thriven exceedingly in the Marine Insurance way, and was quite satisfied. He never could make out why everybody was not quite satisfied, and he felt conscious that he set a brilliant social example in being particularly well satisfied with most things, and, above all other things, with himself." An early working title (May 1921) for *The Waste Land* was *He Do the Police in Different Voices*, a phrase also taken from *Our Mutual Friend*.

17. England entered World War I with the Liberal Party leading the government, headed by H. H. Asquith as prime minister. But by late 1916 the press and public opinion agreed that the war was not being prosecuted with sufficient vigor. Lloyd George, a Liberal member of the cabinet, had earned a repu-

tation for supporting a more vigorous war effort by advocating conscription
and calling for a single, centralized war cabinet. When Asquith resigned in
December 1916, Lloyd George formed a "coalition government" with the
support of the Conservatives and so became prime minister. In 1918, only
one month after the Armistice, he called for general elections, ran on a
promise to continue the coalition, and won a resounding victory. But because
his own Liberal Party won fewer parliamentary seats than it had before, the
coalition became more dependent on Conservative support, and his position
became more precarious. The Conservatives withdrew their support in late
1922, and Lloyd George fell from power. The Liberal Party was now reduced
to third place in Parliament, while the Labour Party had become the viable
alternative to the Tories.

    The years 1919 to 1922 were dominated by talk of a threatened strike
by the Triple Alliance, the trade unions of railwaymen, miners, and dock-
workers. This threat augmented middle-class anxiety already aroused by
the Bolshevik Revolution (1917) and the creation of the Soviet Union. Lloyd
George gave the railwaymen a substantial increase in wages, which effectively separated them from the other two unions, and he persuaded the
miners to delay their strike. But a coal strike began on 1 April 1921 and lasted
for four months.

    The costs of the war and the high rate of public expenditures in its
aftermath required repeated escalations in British income tax rates. Direct
income tax was still a relatively new idea, having been introduced only in
1909 with the "people's Budget" drafted by Lloyd George (then chancellor
of the Exchequer) to help pay for old-age pensions, introduced at the same
time.

18. For "elegant anguish," see n. 4 above. It is not known whether any critic ever
called Eliot a "dusty face." The critic Robert Lynd (see London Letter, May
1921, n. 21), however, in a damning review of *The Sacred Wood*, wrote: "[Eliot]
has undoubtedly gods of his own. But he worships them in the dark spirit
of the sectarian, and his interest in them is theological rather than religious
in kind. He is like the traditional Plymouth Brother whose belief in God is
hardly so strong as his belief that there are 'only a few of us'—perhaps 'only
one of us'—saved. We see the Plymouth-Brother mood in his reference
to 'the few people who talk intelligently about Stendahl and Flaubert and
James.' This expresses an attitude which is intolerable in a critic of literature, and should be left to *précieuses ridicules*" (Robert Lynd, "Buried Alive:
[Review of] *The Sacred Wood*," *Nation* 28, no. 10 [4 December 1920], supplement, 359).

    A "precieux ridicule" is a "laughably precious man" in French. The term
is Eliot's variant of *Les Précieuses ridicules* (1659), the title of a play by Molière
which satirized hyperaesthetic literary ladies of the nobility and their imita-
tors among the bourgeoisie and the countryside. Lynd charges Eliot with
being just such a person.

19. Mrs. Ella Wheeler Wilcox (1850–1919) was a prolific American poet whose

works often appeared in newspapers. She was undoubtedly the most popular American poet of the period between 1890 and her death in 1919.

20. Robert Malise Bowyer Nichols (1893–1944) was a poet and served as professor of English at Imperial University, Tokyo, from 1921 to 1924. He had published three books of verse by 1921, *Invocation* (1915), *Ardours and Endurances* (1917), and *Aurelia* (1920). Harold Monro thought that he had "made certain poems so promising that one may hope that he will outgrow his derivativeness and his megalomaniac poses" (172).

21. Aldous Huxley (1894–1963) became a famous essayist and novelist. By early 1921 he had published three volumes of poetry, *The Burning Wheel* (1916), *The Defeat of Youth* (1918), and *Leda* (1920). Harold Monro thought that "Leda" was "the most finished poem that Huxley has yet written; a sensual and brightly coloured representation of the episode from mythology" (128). In November 1921 Huxley published his witty first novel, *Crome Yellow*, to critical acclaim and success. Jules Laforgue (1860–1887) was the French poet who profoundly influenced Eliot's early poetry; see the Introduction, 4.

22. Edith Sitwell (1887–1964) was a poet who edited an annual anthology of new verse titled *Wheels*. She first met Eliot in 1920 and was rather taken with him. But writing to Wyndham Lewis in April 1921, Eliot said: "Would I think of contributing to Wheels? And so give the S[itwells] a lift and the right to sneer at me?" (*LOTSE*, 446).

23. Herbert Read (1893–1968) became a distinguished literary and art critic. He met Eliot in 1917 and theirs became a lifelong friendship. He had published one book of poems, *Naked Warriors* (1919). Monro wrote that Read "showed promise" (106).

Richard Aldington (1892–1962) became a poet, novelist, critic, and translator. He had been associated with the Imagist poets in prewar London, especially the American poet H.D., whom he married and then divorced. He had published two volumes of poems before 1921, *Images of War* and *Images of Desire*. He was a good friend of Eliot's in 1921, but Eliot ended their friendship in 1931 when Aldington published *Stepping Heavenward: A Record*, which satirized Eliot and his wife Vivien.

24. Robert Bridges (1844–1930) was the poet laureate at the time Eliot was writing in 1921, having been appointed in 1913. His poems were admired for metrical refinement and formal perfection. He was responsible for publishing the work of Gerard Manley Hopkins in 1918, bringing it to public attention for the first time. William Butler Yeats (1865–1939) was the leading elder poet of the day in 1921. He was to receive the Nobel prize for literature in 1924. Ezra Pound (1888–1992), Eliot's controversial contemporary, had left England for good eight months before Eliot wrote this essay. He settled in Paris in April 1920, staying there until late 1924, when he moved to Italy.

25. The journalist who predicted a revival of criticism has not been identified.

26. The Palladium, now the London Palladium, was an opulent, neoclassical music hall designed in 1910 by the architect Frank Matcham (1854–1920),

with seating capacity of 2,300. Matcham designed more than 150 new theaters and music halls and is best known as the architect of the Coliseum, in St. Martin's Lane, London, built in 1904 as the world's largest music hall (seating capacity 4,000), now home to the English National Opera.

Marie Lloyd (1870–1922) was widely considered the greatest of all music hall performers. When she died, nearly a hundred thousand people mourned her funeral cortege, and Max Beerbohm thought it the biggest funeral that London had witnessed since the death of Wellington. Though she was noted for her risqué lyrics and double entendres, by the time that she came to the Palladium in early 1921, she was performing "It's a Bit of a Ruin" (by Harry Beford and Terry Sullivan), for which she portrayed an old woman who has been robbed outside a country pub. The audience at the Palladium is reported to have taken up the chorus "with gusto." Marie, who pronounced her name to rhyme with "starry," collapsed on stage while performing at the Edmonton Empire on 7 October 1922. Eliot promptly wrote an essay lamenting the death of "the greatest music-hall artist of her time." She had exercised a "moral superiority" as "the expressive figure of the lower classes," for there was "no such expressive figure for any other classes" and the middle classes were just "morally corrupt." (See T. S. Eliot, "Marie Lloyd," in *Selected Essays* [New York: Harcourt, Brace, 1950], 404–408.)

"Little Tich" was the stage name of Harry Relph (1867–1928), a minuscule man (barely four feet tall) who created an unforgettable stage character, wearing slap shoes almost as long as himself and doing his Big Boot Dance. He would dance on the tips of the shoe's toes or lean so far forward on the flats of his feet that his nose almost touched the floor; he also sat on the ground, shoes straight up, imitating scissors and demented windshield or windscreen wipers.

George Mozart was the stage name of David John Gillings (1864–1947), a music hall comedian who did character sketches, perhaps best known for "Idle Jack." Between 1930 and 1938 he starred in more than fifteen films.

Ernie Lotinga (1876–1951) was a bawdy music hall comedian who frequently played a fictional character named Private Jimmy Josser. With the decline of music hall in the 1920s, he turned to the stage. Eliot went to see him on tour in a play named *Convicts*, which ran for one week at the Islington Empire, beginning 20 June 1927. To Virginia Woolf, in a contemporary but undated letter, he wrote that he had "just been to see Ernie Lotinga in his new play at the Islington Empire. Magnificent. He is the greatest living British histrionic Artist, in the purest tradition of British Obscenity." In the 1930s Lotinga turned to film, appearing in *Josser Joins the Navy* (1932), *Josser in the Army* (1932), *Josser on the Farm* (1934), and *Love Up the Pole* (1936), among others.

27. Discussions about the possible extinction of the music hall as a cultural form were common in contemporary journalism. The invasion of Hollywood cinema was drawing away audiences. Many halls closed throughout the

1920s and were converted into cinemas, while others limped on till the outbreak of World War II.

Ethel Levey (1881–1955) was a vaudeville singer and dancer who married (1899) and then divorced (1907) the American songwriter George M. Cohan. She continued with her own performing career, which, in a stage act in the early 1920s, featured her rendition of the Grizzly Bear Dance. Beginning 1 September 1920 she had the lead role in *Oh! Julie*, a musical comedy in three acts; it ran at the Shaftesbury Theatre till 25 September, then was transferred to the Prince's Theatre, where it ran till 23 October.

28. The Phoenix Society was founded by Montague Summers (1880–1948) in September 1919. It was dedicated to the revival of Jacobean and Restoration plays, and to having them performed in their entirety. It gave performances of Ben Jonson's *Volpone* on Sunday, 30 January, and on Tuesday, 1 February 1921, at the Lyric Theatre, Hammersmith. Allan Wade was the producer. The cast was: Volpone, Balliol Holloway; Mosca, Ion Swinley; Voltore, D. Lewin Mannering; Corbaccio, Stanley Lathbury; Corvino, George Zucco; Bonario, Murray Kinnell; Peregrine, William Armstrong; Sir Politic, Eugene Leahy; Lady Would-be, Margaret Yard; Celia, Isabel Jeans.

29. On Diaghilev's ballet company and its performances in London, see London Letter, July 1921, n. 14, 241.

30. The exhibition "Works by Pablo Picasso" was held at the Leicester Galleries throughout January 1921. It contained twenty-four oils and forty-eight drawings, and the catalogue preface, "Matisse and Picasso," was written by Clive Bell.

The Romantic Englishman

1. The essay was published in the first issue of the *Tyro*, a journal edited by Wyndham Lewis and produced with financial backing from Sydney Schiff, a writer and occasional patron. Eliot must have written it, or cast it into its final form, over the weekend of 26–27 March, since he refers to a performance of Congreve's *Love for Love* which took place on Sunday, 20 March 1921, while the *Tyro* itself appeared only two weeks later, on 9 April 1921. The *Tyro* was printed in an edition of one thousand copies.

2. Sir Tunbelly Clumsy is a character in *The Relapse; or, Virtue in Danger* (1697), a comedy by Sir John Vanbrugh (1664–1726). Sir Giles Overreach is a character in *A New Way to Pay Old Debts* (1625 or 1626), a play by Philip Massinger (1583–1604). Squire Western is a character in *The Fathers; or, The Good-Natur'd Man* (1778), a comedy by Henry Fielding (1707–1754) which was first performed at Drury Lane more than twenty years after his death. Sir Sampson Legend is a character in *Love for Love* (1695), a comedy by William Congreve (1670–1729). It was revived in a performance sponsored by the Phoenix Society at the Lyric Theatre, Hammersmith, on Sunday, 20 March, and again on Tuesday, 22 March, 1921. Eliot attended it with

Leonard and Virginia Woolf. The part of Sir Sampson Legend was played
by the actor Roy Byford (1873–1939).

3. *Midshipman Easy* (London: Saunders and Otley, 1836) was a novel by Frederick Marryat (1792–1848), the author of boys' adventure stories that were
extraordinarily popular during the period 1850–1920.

Tom Jones is the title character of a 1749 novel by Henry Fielding.
Falstaff is Shakespeare's creation, the legendary companion of Prince Hal
in *Henry IV* (Parts I and II) and *The Merry Wives of Windsor*.

4. "Broad-shouldered genial Englishman" is a phrase used by Tennyson to
describe Sir Walter Vivian, a fictional character in his long poem *The Princess*
(1847). In the Conclusion (lines 84–91), the narrator sees Sir Walter:

No lily-handed Baronet he,
A great broad-shouldered genial Englishman,
A lord of fat prize-oxen and of sheep,
A raiser of huge melons and of pine,
A patron of some thirty charities,
A pamphleteer on guano and on grain,
A quarter-sessions chairman, abler none;
Fair-haired and redder than a windy morn.

G. K. Chesterton (1874–1936) was a prolific journalist and author, an
advocate of a principled, Christian conservatism. On the conservative critic
John Collings Squire, see London Letter, March 1921, n. 16, 206.

5. *The Giaour, a Fragment of a Turkish Tale* was published by Lord Byron in 1813.
"Giaour," which rhymes with "hour," was the Turkish word for any infidel
(i.e., non-Muslim); the poem tells the story of a man who has banished himself to a monastery for causing the death of his lover, Leila, and for slaying
her murderer, the Pasha.

6. *Le vrai honnête homme est celui qui ne se pique de rien* ("The true gentleman is
one who allows nothing to ruffle him," or "who is unpretentious") is maxim
no. 203 in the famous collection of *Réflexions ou Sentences et Maximes morales*
(1678) of Duke François de La Rochefoucauld (1613–1680). "René" refers
to René Descartes (1596–1650), the French philosopher.

"Mythopoeic nihilism" alludes to Dadaism, the anarchic cultural
movement which began life at the Cabaret Voltaire in Zurich in early 1916.
Increasingly under the leadership of Tristan Tzara by 1917, the movement
effectively moved with him in January 1920 to Paris, where he was welcomed and joined by Francis Picabia and the future Surrealists André Breton, Louis Aragon, Philippe Soupault, and Paul Éluard. A flurry of Dada
events, performances, and manifesto readings took place over the next few
months, but Eliot would not have known about these. His knowledge of
Dada would have come primarily from the *Nouvelle Revue*, a journal he sub-
scribed to and read regularly. In April 1920 André Gide, in the *Nouvelle Revue*, assessed Dada's place in the aftermath of the Great War: "It is important

that the mind should not lag behind the material world (which has been destroyed after four years of war): the mind, too, has a right to be in ruins." Four months later, in August, André Breton replied to Gide's essay with "Pour Dada" (For Dada), also published in the *Nouvelle Revue* (August 1920). ("Pour Dada" is now in Breton's *Oeuvres complètes*, vol. 1 [Paris: Bibliothèque de la Pléiade, 1988], 236–241; in English translation, "For Dada" is found in André Breton, *The Lost Steps*, trans. Mark Polizzotti [Lincoln: University of Nebraska Press, 1996], 51–56.) Breton's essay was accompanied by another which immediately followed it in the same issue, "Reconnaissance à Dada," a sympathetic analysis of Dada by Jacques Rivière, editor of the *Nouvelle Revue*. (The essay is reprinted in Jacques Rivière, *Nouvelles Études* [Paris: Gallimard, 1947], 294–310.) Eliot went to France twice in 1920: 14–28 August, though he stayed in Paris for only a few days before pressing on to tour other places with Wyndham Lewis; and 11–18 December. He may also have derived some knowledge of Dada from Fritz Vanderpyl, a Belgian poet and novelist who was art critic for the *Petit Parisien*. The only major Dada publication of early 1921 was the manifesto "Dada Soulève Tout" (Dada Overturns Everything), issued on 12 January 1921; but it is difficult to imagine how it might have come into Eliot's hands.

7. For Podsnap, see London Letter, March 1921, n. 16, 206. Horatio Bottomley (1860–1933) became a court shorthand writer and then a journalist. With the outbreak of World War I, the newspaper he edited, *John Bull,* became stridently patriotic, while Bottomley became a self-appointed recruiting agent for the armed forces, giving speeches at rallies and meetings. He made a fortune through his "patriotic lectures" (more than three hundred during the last three years of war). In December 1918, Bottomley was elected Member of Parliament for South Hackney. *John Bull* had profits of £113,000 in 1918 and a circulation of 1,700,000 by 1920.

In July 1919, with the signing of the Treaty of Versailles, the government issued Victory Bonds to help offset the costs of paying for the war. Priced at £5, they were out of the reach of most ordinary people at a time when an unskilled worker might earn as little as £2.50 a week. Bottomley instituted a scheme whereby poor people (especially unemployed soldiers) might benefit by sending him £1 for a one-fifth share in a Victory Bond. At first the scheme was a roaring success, and soon Bottomley was receiving cash at the rate of £100,000 a day—this was before he had actually bought any bonds, since he was waiting for their price to drop. But some of his poorly supervised staff members were helping themselves to the cash arriving through the post; others were simply unable to issue share statements fast enough to keep up with the influx of subscriptions. Thousands of subscribers soon started to demand the return of their capital, and by the end of 1919 Bottomley had paid out £150,000. Meanwhile, although Bottomley did finally buy around £500,000 worth of bonds at a bargain price, he used the remaining money to buy two newspapers and pay off other debts. It was increasingly rumored that he was a fraud, and whenever he spoke to

meetings, he found himself confronted by aggrieved subscribers demand-
ing their money back. But through 1921 conservative newspapers defended
him under the cloak of patriotism. In May 1922 he was charged with
"fraudulently converting to his own use sums of money entrusted to him
by members of the public." He was sent to prison for seven years but was
discharged in 1927. He became a minor performer in music hall programs.

8. V.C.'s are Victoria Crosses, the highest award for valor in the British armed
forces. "The Spy" and "the Girl who Sank the Submarine" are parodic titles
and types invented by Eliot, the latter imitating such popular wartime songs
as "The Girl Who Wears a Red Cross on Her Sleeve" (1915), words and music
by William Mahoney, or "The Girl Who Helps the Man Behind the Gun"
(1918), words by Arthur Stanley, music by Charles Peter.

9. *Chu Chin Chow* was a musical, with book and lyrics by Oscar Asche (1871–
1936), and music by Gordon Frederic Norton (1869–1946). It opened at
His Majesty's Theatre, London, on 1 August 1916 and ran for 2,238 performances. It was still running at the time when Eliot was writing. It has a complicated plot based on the tale of Ali Baba and the Forty Thieves. The setting
is the magnificent Eastern palace of Kasim Baba, who welcomes the Chinese
merchant Chu Chin Chow, in reality the rascally Abu Hassan, a robber.

10. For Little Tich, Marie Lloyd, and George Mozart see London Letter, March
1921, n. 26, 208–209. George Robey (1869–1954), born George Edward
Wade in London, was the son of an engineer. He was forced to leave Cambridge University due to financial problems and found his way onto the
stage. Known as the Prime Minister of Mirth, Robey made many recordings
of his comic songs and several films in his long career. His character was
a somewhat saucy country parson with big black eyebrows and a red nose.

Nellie Wallace (1870–1948) was born in Glasgow, Scotland. (Eliot was
mistaken, in his London Letter, May 1921, in thinking that she had "a Lancashire accent.") She first appeared on the stage in 1888 in Birmingham as a
clog dancer, then joined a singing group known as the Three Sisters Wallace.
Success arrived when she became a solo turn, famous for her characteriza-
tion of the frustrated spinster, comically dressed, who would bluntly declare:

My mother said always look under the bed,
Before you blow the candle out,
To see if there's a man about.
I always do, but you can make a bet,
It's never been my luck to find a man there yet.

In a strange, rapid account, she told of many romances that went wrong
or never really got started. She made much use of vulgar humor, and in her
later years became a pantomime dame, playing such classic roles as that
of Widow Twankey. She made only one film, in 1939, *Boys Will Be Girls*, in
which she starred alongside Leslie Fuller and Greta Gynt.

Lupino Lane (1892–1959) was an acrobatic music hall performer and
comedian. He starred in the Broadway show *Afgar* from 1920 to 1922, went

on to make several films, and later became a stage and television comedian in England.

George Graves (1876–1949) was a comic actor and music hall and pantomime performer. He first appeared on stage in 1896 in Portsmouth, and in 1903 he had his first London hit as General Marchmont in *The School Girl*, which ran for two years at the Prince of Wales' Theatre. In 1907 he scored another success as Baron Popoff in the operetta *The Merry Widow* (*Die Lustige Witwe*, by Franz Lehár) at Daly's Theatre, effectively transforming the light relief of opéra bouffe into the terms of eccentric low comedy: he adapted his voice to suggest the popping of champagne corks and wore an exaggerated nose and peculiar wig. He became a regular at Daly's and played pantomime at Drury Lane at Christmas, with occasional forays into the music halls. He starred in *Lilac Time* (1922), *Me and My Girl* (1937), and the many revivals of *The Merry Widow*. In his obituary the *Times* noted, "Gravesisms cannot survive print; and some of them indeed were scarcely printable."

Robert Hale (1876–1940) was a comic actor and music hall performer. His first success came in the musical comedy *Floradora* at the Lyric Theatre in 1898, which ran for 455 performances. Thereafter he alternated between musical comedy productions and runs at various music halls. In the 1930s he turned to films, acting in fourteen of them.

11. For *Volpone*, see Eliot's London Letter, March 1921, n. 28, 210.
12. Maida Vale is the name of a road, running northwest from London, which has also been given to the surrounding area. The name has become synonymous with prosperous suburbia, though metropolitan London has long since extended beyond it. *Miles Gloriosus* (Latin for Swaggering Soldier) is the title of a play by the Roman author Plautus.

The Lesson of Baudelaire

1. The essay was presumably composed the weekend of 26–27 March 1921. It was published in the first issue of the *Tyro* (see "The Romantic Englishman," n. 1, 210).
2. [Eliot's note:] Not without qualification. M. Valéry is a mathematician; M. Benda is a mathematician and a musician. These, however, are men of exceptional intelligence. [Editor's note:] Paul Valéry (1871–1945) was perhaps the greatest French poet of the twentieth century. Eliot wrote several essays on him in the years after *The Waste Land*, and Eliot's journal, the *Criterion*, was the first to publish his work in English translation. (See Donald Gallup, *T. S. Eliot: A Bibliography* [New York: Harcourt, Brace, 1969], s.v. "Valéry.") Julien Benda (1867–1956) was a French writer and philosopher, an anti-Romantic thinker who defended reason against the philosophical intuitionism of Henry Bergson. In 1919 he had published, to acclaim and controversy, *Belphégor: Essai sur l'esthétique de la société française dans la première moitié du XXᵉ siècle* (Belphegor: An essay on the esthetics of French

society in the first half of the twentieth century), a probing attack on contemporary intellectual fashions.

3. On Dadaism, see "The Romantic Englishman," n. 6, 211–212.

4. Charles Baudelaire (1821–1867) was a French poet, translator, and literary and art critic. His reputation as a poet rests on *Les Fleurs du mal* (The flowers of evil, 1857), the most influential poetry collection published in Europe in the nineteenth century, and on *Le Spleen de Paris* (1869), a collection of prose poems which virtually created this genre or mode. He translated nearly all of Edgar Allan Poe into French, and his critical essays on art and literature have had an enduring influence.

5. "Il y a du Dante dans l'auteur des *Fleurs du mal*, mais c'est du Dante d'une époque déchue, c'est du Dante athée et moderne, du Dante venu après Voltaire, dans un temps qui n'aura point de saint Thomas." Or in English: "There is something of Dante in the author of *Flowers of Evil*, but it is a Dante of a fallen age, it is of a modern and atheist Dante, a Dante who has come after Voltaire, who lives in an age that has no Saint Thomas Aquinas." The passage comes from an essay titled "Les Fleurs du Mal, par M. Charles Baudelaire," by Jules Barbey d'Aurevilly (1808–1889). The essay was first printed as one of four *Articles justicatifs* (Essays in defense) which Baudelaire published as an independent volume in an edition of one hundred copies in 1857 after he was charged with public immorality over the publication of *Les Fleurs du mal*. The four essays have frequently been reprinted with editions of Baudelaire's poems, and the text I cite from is Charles Baudelaire, *Oeuvres complètes*, ed. Claude Pichois (Paris: Gallimard, Bibliothèque de la Pléiade, 1975), vol. 1, 1191–1196, here 1195.

6. *Vom Haus aus*, a German expression meaning "beginning with the house and going out from there," or idiomatically, "thoroughly."

7. *The Ring and the Book* (1868–1869) was the longest and most important poem of Robert Browning (1812–1889). It recounts a sensational murder and trial which took place in 1698, and to do so it uses in a new way a multi-monologue form of narrative, in which the story is told from a series of personal standpoints, each of which modifies fact and motive with shadings of significance and uncertainty.

Hyperion (1818–1819) is an incomplete poem in three books by John Keats (1795–1821). In it he attempts to recount the legend of the overthrow of the Titans by the Olympian gods. Keats undertook a revised version of the poem later in 1819, now known as *The Fall of Hyperion*, but abandoned it after three months' work.

8. This sentence probably refers to Aldous Huxley, who had studied Laforgue, but whose propensity for light, satirical humor struck Eliot as a concession to popular tastes. See London Letter, March 1921, 139. Bengal lights and the other things listed here are all types of fireworks.

9. "You, hypocrite reader . . ." The last two words are the beginning of the last line in "Au Lecteur" (To the reader); see the annotation to *The Waste Land*, l. 76.

Andrew Marvell

1. "Andrew Marvell" was first published in the *Times Literary Supplement*, no. 1002 (31 March 1921): 201–202. At the time, the *TLS* had a circulation of twenty-four thousand, and its editor was Bruce Richmond (1871–1960), who had filled this role since the journal's inception in 1902 and who had had his attention called to Eliot's writings in the *Athenaeum* by Richard Aldington. It is difficult to state with precision when Eliot wrote "Andrew Marvell." We know, for example, that Eliot finished writing his essay "The Metaphysical Poets" on 16 September 1921, and that it was published in the *TLS* on 20 October, more than a month later. If a similar production schedule was applied to "Andrew Marvell," then we might guess that it was written in late February 1921. Eliot's essay was published anonymously, as were all contributions to the *TLS* at this time.

2. Andrew Marvell (1621–1678) was born at Winestead-in-Holderness, Yorkshire, on 31 March. He moved with his family to Hull in 1624. He took his B.A. from Trinity College, Cambridge, in 1639, moved to London, traveled abroad, and then became a tutor in the house of Sir Thomas Fairfax, the former Lord General of the parliamentary forces in the English Civil War. By early 1653 he was back in London, where he befriended Milton, and later the same year was serving as a private tutor to a protégé of Oliver Cromwell. In 1657 he was appointed Milton's assistant in his office of Latin Secretary for the Commonwealth. Starting in 1659 he was elected a Member of Parliament for his hometown of Hull, which he represented until his death. Virtually all of the sixty or so poems that he wrote were published posthumously in a volume called *Miscellaneous Poems*, issued in 1681. (In all quotations from his poems, I cite from Elizabeth Story Donno, ed., *Andrew Marvell: The Complete Poems* [Harmondsworth: Penguin, 1972].) The tercentenary of his birth in 1921 was marked by having the bishop of Durham conduct a special service in Hull in the presence of the mayor, the corporation, and various civic representatives. Later, Augustine Birrell (1850–1933), who had written a critical study of Marvell in 1905 (*Andrew Marvell* [London: Macmillan]), gave a speech about Marvell at a public meeting. For these events, see "Andrew Marvell: Character and Poetry," *Times*, 1 April 1921, 5, col. 3. For Birrell's speech see William H. Bagguley, ed., *Andrew Marvell, 1621–1678: Tercentenary Tributes by Augustine Birrell, with an Official Record of the Tercentenary Celebrations and Kingston-upon-Hull and in London* (London: Oxford University Press, 1922).

3. Francis Turner Palgrave (1824–1897) edited *The Golden Treasury of the Best Songs and Lyrical Poems in the English Language* (London: Macmillan, 1861), a much cherished and widely reprinted anthology. Arthur Quiller-Couch (1863–1944) edited *The Oxford Book of English Verse* (Oxford: Oxford University Press, 1900). The books shared four poems by Marvell: "Horation Ode, Upon Cromwell's Return from Ireland," "The Picture of Little T.C. in a Prospect of Flowers," "Thoughts in a Garden," and "Bermudas." The *Golden Treasury* was alone in containing "The Girl Describes Her Fawn," the *Oxford*

Book alone in including "A Garden: Written after the Civil Wars" and "To His Coy Mistress."

4. John Donne (1573–1631) is considered the most important lyrical poet of the early seventeenth century. For Baudelaire, see "The Lesson of Baudelaire," n. 4, 215; for Laforgue, see London Letter, March 1921, n. 21, 208, and the Introduction, 4.

5. Christopher Marlowe (1564–1593), an Elizabethan dramatist, wrote *Tamburlaine the Great*, *The Jew of Malta*, and *Doctor Faustus*. Eliot wrote an essay on him in 1919, "Some Notes on the Blank Verse of Christopher Marlowe," *Arts and Letters*, 2.4 (Autumn 1919): 194–199; reprinted in Eliot's *Selected Essays* (New York: Harcourt, 1950), 100–106. Ben Jonson (1572–1637) was a prolific poet and dramatist, best remembered for his great comedies *Volpone* (1606), *Epicoene* (1609), *The Alchemist* (1610), and *Bartholomew Fair* (1614). Eliot saw the first and last of these in 1921. He also wrote an essay, "Ben Jonson," his first publication in the *Times Literary Supplement*, no. 930 (13 November 1919): 637–638, also reprinted in *Selected Essays*, 127–139.

6. Abraham Cowley (1618–1667) is often characterized as the last of the Metaphysical poets, and he is often remembered solely for the damning essay on him which Dr. Johnson wrote for his *Lives of the Poets;* see "The Metaphysical Poets," n. 12, 247.

7. Caroline poets are those who wrote under the reigns of Charles I (1625–1640) or Charles II (1660–1685). For Dryden, see "John Dryden," n. 2, 234–235. Alexander Pope (1688–1744) was the greatest poet of the eighteenth century, known for his complete development of the possibilities of the rhyming couplet. Eliot meditated on him often in the course of 1921, and he wrote a pastiche of Pope's style in the Fresca episode, a passage of some eighty lines which originally stood at the beginning to part III of *The Waste Land*, but was removed at the suggestion of Ezra Pound in January 1922. (See *The Waste Land: A Facsimile Edition*, ed. Valerie Eliot, 22–23, 26–29.)

8. "Cowley's Anacreontics" refers to poems which Abraham Cowley (see above, n. 6) wrote in imitation of the ancient Greek poet Anacreon (see "Prose and Verse," n. 6, 222–223) in a 1656 collection titled *Anacreontiques*.

9. Walter Savage Landor (1775–1864) was a poet, classicist, and essayist. He went to Rugby School then on to Trinity College, Oxford, but was sent down in 1794. The following year he published his first collection, *Poems* (1795). He lived abroad from 1814, not returning to England until 1835. He left again in 1858 and spent the remainder of his life on the Continent, particularly in Florence. He is now remembered for his prose more than for his poetry, his best-known work being *Imaginary Conversations of Literary Men and Statesmen* (1824–1829), a series of dramatic dialogues.

10. Jean de La Fontaine (1621–1695) is famous for his twelve books of *Fables* (1668–1694), often cited as a work typical of French classicism. Théophile Gautier (1811–1872) was a French writer and poet; he combined a taste for the macabre and exotic with carefully chiseled form and severe detachment. *Émaux and camées* (Enamels and cameos, 1852) was his best book of poems;

Ezra Pound encountered it in 1917 and brought it to the attention of Eliot, who used its quatrain form in his poems of the period 1917–1920.

11. Rabbi Zeal-of-the-land Busy is a comic type of the zealous Puritan in Ben Jonson's play *Bartholomew Fair*. The United Grand Junction Ebenezer Temperance Association is a creation of Charles Dickens in *The Pickwick Papers*, chapter 33, which details a comical meeting of its Brick Lane Branch in the East End of London.

12. "It is such a King as no chisel can mend" is line 56 from "The Statue in Stock-Market." The poem is one of three by Marvell (the others are "The Statue at Charing Cross" and "A Dialogue between the Two Horses"), all satirical, which treat statues of Charles I and Charles II that were erected after the Restoration in 1660. In *The Rehearsal Transpros'd* (1672), Marvell looked back on the Civil Wars and commented: "Whether it were a war of Religion, or of Liberty, is not worth the labour to enquire. Which-soever was at the top, the other was at the bottom; but upon considering all, I think the Cause was too good to have been fought for. Men ought to have trusted God; they ought and might have trusted the King with that whole matter. The *Arms of the Church are Prayers and Tears,* the Arms of the Subjects are Patience and Petitions" (*The Rehearsal Transpros'd and the Rehearsal Transpros'd the Second Part,* ed. D. I. B. Smith [Oxford: Oxford University Press, 1971], 135).

13. Eliot is citing poems that are in the tradition of "carpe diem," a Latin phrase meaning "seize the day." In such works the speaker urges a beloved to enjoy sexual pleasure now, while she is still young. "O Mistress mine" is the opening line of the first of two songs sung by the Clown in Shakespeare's play *Twelfth Night, or What You Will* (1601). The two were put together to make a single poem and given the title "Carpe Diem" by Palgrave in his *Golden Treasury*. "Gather ye rosebuds" is the opening phrase of a poem by Robert Herrick (1591–1674), "To the Virgins, to Make Much of Time." "Go lovely rose" is the opening line and the title of a poem by Edmund Waller (1606–1687), another work in the carpe diem tradition.

14. Lucretius (94–55 B.C.), a Roman poet who wrote *De Rerum natura,* a didactic poem in six books which expound the theories of Epicurean philosophy. Catullus (84–54 B.C.), a Roman lyrical poet noted for his learned, intricate, allusive style.

15. The first line of this passage is partly quoted and altered at lines 185 and 196 in *The Waste Land*.

16. Eliot is quoting from the three books of *Odes* left by the Roman poet Horace (65 B.C.–A.D. 8). His satires, epistles, and odes were important models for English poets of the seventeenth and eighteenth centuries. Eliot cites book I, ode IV, lines 13–14: "Pallid Death kicks, with equal strength, at the door / of the poor or the towers of the rich." He also cites from book II, ode XIV, lines 1–2: "Ah, how they glide by, Postumus, Postumus, / The years, the swift years!" And he cites book III, ode I, line 40: "At the horseman's back sits black Worry."

17. Eliot cites from Catullus, poem no. 5, "Viuamus, mea Lesbia, atque amemus" (Let us live and live, my Lesia), lines 5–6, a poem that stands at the head of the carpe diem tradition. The sense of these two lines depends on the preceding line 4: "Suns are able to die and to return; / But once our brief light has been extinguished, / Night is a perpetual sleeping."

18. Cowley, see above, nn. 6, 8; John Cleveland (1613–1658) was a Metaphysical poet who is forgotten by all but specialists in seventeenth-century lyric.

19. "L'Allegro" and "Il Penseroso" are two contrasting lyrics ("The Happy Man" and "The Thoughtful Man") written by John Milton in his youth.

20. Eliot quotes the first two lines of "Buchers et tombeaux" (Wooden pyres and tombs), a poem by Théophile Gautier (see above, n. 10). It was first published in a journal called *L'Artiste* (24 January 1848), then included in his collection *Émaux et camées* (1852). The lines can be translated: "The skeleton was invisible / In the happy ages of pagan art!"

21. Eliot is quoting lines 11–12 and 15–18 from Ben Jonson, "Song: to Celia," another poem in the carpe diem tradition, first published in 1640. He may be quoting from memory, since he substitutes "deceive" for "delude" in line 11, and "sweet sin" for "Sweet theft" in line 16.

22. Propertius (c. 50–2 B.C.) was a Roman lyrical poet noted for his elegance, grace, and wit, one who has often been compared with John Donne. Ovid (43 B.C.–A.D. 17) is the most famous Roman poet after Virgil. His *Metamorphoses,* in fifteen books, collects stories from classical mythology.

23. Thomas Gray (1716–1771) is best known today as the author of "Ode on the Death of a Favorite Cat" and "Elegy Written in a Country Churchyard." William Collins (1721–1759) was a lyric poet who is remembered today for only a handful of poems, chiefly "Ode on the Poetical Character" and "Ode Written in the Beginning of the Year 1746."

24. *Bouvard and Pécuchet* is the last novel that Gustave Flaubert (1821–1880) worked on during his lifetime, but failed to complete. It recounts the story of two clerks who, liberated from an economically dependent existence, make ill-fated sorties into vast areas of experience and knowledge. They found a school for orphans, but their plans go awry partly because of their own obsessions, partly because of the dishonesty and selfishness of leading figures in the town. The novel terminates abruptly at chapter 10, but most editions of it include Flaubert's "Plan" for the end of the book, which would see the mayor seizing all the orphans on the ground that they have not been adopted, so putting an end to the utopian schemes of Bouvard and Pécuchet. Flaubert summarizes: *Ainsi tout leur a craqué dans la main,* or "So everything has come to pieces in their hands" (Gustave Flaubert, *Bouvard and Pécuchet,* trans. A. J. Krailsheimer [Harmondsworth: Penguin, 1976], 288).

25. The distinction between fancy and imagination is drawn by Coleridge in his *Biographia Literaria,* chapter 4.

26. Andrew Marvell, "Upon Appleton House, to my Lord Fairfax," ll. 49–52 and 769–772.

27. Samuel Johnson's "Life of Cowley" is the first chapter in his *Lives of the English Poets*, written between 1778 and 1781 and originally a series of fifty-two short "lives" or prefaces to a collection of works by major poets which a group of booksellers had proposed. The lives were then reassembled as a separate work by Johnson, published in 1781 and 1783.

28. Coleridge's famous definition of the imagination is given at the end of book XIV of *Biographia Literaria:* "This power, first put in action by the will and understanding, and retained under their irremissive, though gentle and un-noticed, control (*laxis effertur habenis* [it is carried onward with loose reins; Virgil, *Georgics* II.364]) reveals itself in the balance or reconciliation of opposite or discordant qualities: of sameness, with difference; of the general, with the concrete; the idea, with the image; the individual, with the repre-sentative; the sense of novelty and freshness, with old and familiar objects; a more than usual state of emotion, with more than usual order; judgement ever awake and steady self-possession, with enthusiasm and feeling pro-found or vehement; and while it blends and harmonizes the natural and the artificial, still subordinates art to nature; the manner to the matter; and our admiration of the poet to our sympathy with the poetry."

29. Eliot is still quoting from Marvell's poem "Upon Appleton House," a long work (776 lines) which belongs to a tradition of poems which celebrate the house of an eminent man. Eliot cites from stanza 49, ll. 385–392, and from stanza 79, ll. 625–632.

30. Eliot is quoting from Marvell's forty-line poem "Bermudas." The "he" in these verses is Providence.

31. Eliot is quoting from Marvell's poem "The Garden," stanza 6, ll. 47–48.

32. Eliot is quoting from Marvell's poem "The Nymph Complaining for the Death of Her Fawn," ll. 91–92; the poem combines pastoral complaint and lament for the death of a pet. The title Eliot gives for the poem in the next sentence, "The Nymph and the Fawn," was invented by Palgrave (see n. 3, 216).

33. Andrew Marvell, "The Nymph Complaining for the Death of Her Fawn," ll. 71–76.

34. Eliot is quoting from William Morris (1834–1896), *The Life and Death of Jason*, book IV, *The Quest Begun: The Loss of Hylas and Hercules*, ll. 577–581, which contains a lament by a nymph over the death of Hylas. The nymph begins by singing these lines.

35. Eliot is quoting from the same poem by Morris, ll. 602–608, the conclusion of the nymph's lament.

36. A further quotation from "The Nymph Complaining for the Death of Her Fawn," ll. 97–100, from a passage near the end where the nymph recalls how her fawn was killed by "wanton troopers riding by," and how the animal wept. The Heliades were the sisters of Phaeton, son of Helios (the sun). He asked his father if he could drive his chariot across the sky, and was killed when he could not control the horses. Disconsolate, the sisters were turned into poplars, their tears into amber.

37. Eliot is quoting from lines 13–16 of Marvell's "Clorinda and Damon," a pastoral poem in which Clorinda, a shepherdess, makes advances to an unresponsive shepherd, Damon. The carpe diem motif is invoked with reversed roles, and the poem modulates into a meditation on the competing claims of hedonism and moralism.

38. Eliot is quoting from "Le Testament," a poem by François Villon (1431–1463), stanza 21, ll. 169–170: "Necessity makes people err / And hunger drives the wolf from the woods."

39. Poe actually gives little attention to "surprise," and the term occurs almost nowhere in his critical writings. The key term for Poe is "effect": "I prefer commencing with the consideration of an *effect*. Keeping originality *always* in view—for he is false to himself who ventures to dispense with so obvious and so easily attainable a source of interest—I say to myself, in the first place 'Of all the innumerable effects, or impressions, of which the heart, the intellect, or (more generally) the soul is susceptible, what one shall I, on the present occasion, select?' Having chose a novel, first, and secondly a vivid effect, I consider whether it can best be wrought by incident or tone —whether by ordinary incidents and peculiar tone, or the converse, or by peculiarity both of incident and tone—afterward looking about me (or rather within) for such combinations of event or tone, as shall best aid me in the construction of the effect" (Edgar Allan Poe, "Philosophy of Composition," *Essays and Reviews*, ed. G. R. Thompson [New York: Library of America, 1984], 13–14).

40. Eliot quotes two passages from Dryden's *Absalom and Achitophel*, the first from part II, ll. 477–478, the second from part I, 529–530.

41. Eliot is quoting from the final chorus of Milton's *Samson Agonistes* (1671), ll. 1749–1754. The pronoun "he" refers back to "highest wisdom," which may seem to turn his face away from the suppliant Israelites, but then returns.

42. Eliot is quoting from Marvell's "Horatian Ode upon Cromwell's Return from Ireland," ll. 29–36 and 105–108. Marvell uses the Latin word "Pict" for Scot as if it were derived from the Latin *picti*, meaning painted or tattooed, in order to play on the words "parti-coloured" and "plaid."

43. Eliot is quoting from the opening stanza of "Ode: Of Wit" by Abraham Cowley (see above, n. 6, 217).

44. "Ode: Of Wit," ll. 57–64.

45. Eliot quotes the entirety of Shelley's poem "To the Moon," which was included in Palgrave's *Golden Treasury* (see n. 3, 216–217).

46. "It was a beautiful soul, such as one no longer finds in London," in French. Perhaps Eliot is adapting the phrasing of the last stanza in the "Complainte du pauvre jeune homme," by Jules Laforgue: "Ils virent qu'c'était un'belle âme, / Comme on n'en fait plus aujourd'hui." Or: "They saw that it was a beautiful soul, / such as one no longer finds today."

Prose and Verse

1. "Prose and Verse" appeared in the *Chapbook* 22 (April 1921): 3–10. This issue had a special title page, *Poetry in Prose,* and contained two other essays which followed Eliot's, by Frederick Manning ("Poetry in Prose," 11–15) and Richard Aldington ("A Note on Poetry in Prose," 16–24). On the *Chapbook* and its editor, Harold Monro, see London Letter, March 1921, n. 5, 203. The *Chapbook* had about one thousand subscribers, all but a handful of them English and resident in London. But even with that circulation the *Chapbook* showed a monthly deficit of £25, a shortage that was met by occasional donations from well-to-do patrons or, more typically, by a monthly contribution from Monro's own (by no means wealthy) purse.

2. Aldington, "A Note on Poetry in Prose," 18.

3. Sir Thomas Browne (1605–1682) was a physician and author who is most noted for *Religio Medici* (The creed of a doctor) (1642) and *Hydriotaphia* (Urn burial, 1658), both admired as examples of an ornate style in English. Sir John Denham (1615–1669) was a poet who is remembered almost entirely for one work, *Cooper's Hill* (1642), a long poem in couplets which have a massive plainness and economy, the opposite of Thomas Browne's style.

4. François-Marie Arouet de Voltaire (1694–1758) was a prolific philosopher, essayist, and occasional writer of fiction. His style has always been noted for its plain lucidity. Edward Gibbon (1737–1794), author of *The Decline and Fall of the Roman Empire,* is also noted for the clarity of his style, though it is considerably more orotund than that of Voltaire. Jacques-Louis-Napoléon Bertrand (1807–1841), who used the pen name Aloysius Bertrand, was the author of *Gaspard de la nuit: Fantaisies à la manière de Rembrandt et de Callot* (Gaspard de la nuit: Fantasies in the manner of Rembrandt and Callot), which was published in 1842, a year after his death. Baudelaire, in his famous preface to the *Spleen de Paris,* called it the "mysterious and brilliant model" for his own prose poems, and it is usually deemed the first prose poem in modern literature. The style is resolutely ornate. Thomas De Quincey (1785–1859) was the author of "Suspiria de profundis" (Sighs from the depths), an incomplete work that was intended to be a sequel to his *Confessions of an English Opium-Eater.* It was classified by him as "prose-phantasy," a work of lyrical prose pieces, much like the prose poem being developed contemporaneously in France. The text is found in *The Collected Writings of Thomas De Quincey,* ed. David Masson (London: A. and C. Black, 1897), vol. 13, *Tales and Prose Phantasies,* 331–369.

5. Edgar Allan Poe (1809–1849) was an American author noted for his exuberant, sensationalist prose style, the antithesis of the sobriety found in the style of John Dryden (see "John Dryden," n. 2, 234–235). For Baudelaire, see "The Lesson of Baudelaire," n. 4, 215. His Romantic style is in contrast to the classical calm of Nicholas Boileau-Dexpréaux (1636–1711), whose *L'Art poétique* codified the precepts of French versification.

6. John Henry Newman (1801–1890) published the *Apologia pro vita sua* (A defense of his life) in 1864. Anacreon (born c. 570 B.C.) was a Greek poet

whose short lyrics, some sixty of them, are chiefly about wine, love, and song
—graceful and charming, but also shallow.

7. "Poe's law," that a poem should not exceed one hundred lines, appears in his
essay "The Philosophy of Composition" (see "Andrew Marvell," n. 39, 221).

8. Logan Pearsall Smith (1865–1946) was an essayist and critic who found his
inspiration in Walter Pater. His work consists typically of epigrams.

9. John Dryden's *Absalom and Achitophel* (1681–1682) is a long (2,100 lines)
satire on the intrigues behind Charles II and his son James, the duke of
York, during the period 1678–1681. Alexander Pope's "Epistle to Dr. Arbuthnot" (1734) is a satirical defense of himself, with rapid alterations of feeling
as the poem moves from anger to indifference, distress to amusement.

10. For Thomas Browne, see n. 3; Jeremy Taylor (1613–1667) was an ecclesiastic
whose ornate style has been highly esteemed. Perhaps his best-known works
are *Holy Living* (1650), *Holy Dying* (1651), and *XXVIII Sermons* (1651).

11. Eliot is paraphrasing any one of several sentences from the concluding
chapter of a book by the French critic Remy de Gourmont (1858–1915), *Le
Problème du style* (The problem of style), in which he takes up the perennial
debate between form and content: "En littérature, le fond des choses a une
importance absolue; aucune des variétés de littérature ne peut se soustraire
à la nécessité de creuser des fondations et de les maçonner solidement. . . .
Décidément, et en tout, c'es le fond qui importe. Un fait nouveau, une idée
nouvelle, cela vaut plus qu'une belle phrase. . . . La forme sans le fond, le
style sans la pensée, quelle misère! . . . Si rien, en littérature, ne vit que par
le style, c'est que les oeuvres bien pensées sont toujour des oeuvres bien
écrites" (Remy de Gourmont, *Le Problème du style*, 17th ed. [Paris: Mercure
de France, 1938; 1st ed. 1902], 151, 153–154). (In literature, the content of
things has an absolute importance; none of the various kinds of literature
can withdraw from the necessity of digging out and building solid foundations. . . . Decisively, and in everything, it is content which counts. A new
fact, a new idea, each is worth more than a beautiful phrase. . . . Form without content, style without thought, what impoverishment! . . . If nothing
in literature lives except by virtue of its style, it is because works that are well
conceived are always works well written.)

12. Thomas Browne, *Hydriotaphia,* the first sentence of chapter 5. The Latin
phrase in the passage means "Might not I prefer to be transformed into such
bones?"

13. Henry King (1592–1669) was an ecclesiastic who became bishop of Chichester. He is known to most readers for a single poem, "Exequy for His Wife,"
which was included in Palgrave's *Golden Treasury* as well as the *Oxford Book
of Verse.*

14. Launcelot Andrewes (1555–1626) was educated at Pembroke Hall, Cambridge, and became bishop of Chichester, of Ely, and of Winchester. His
XCVI Sermons were published after his death, in 1629. The style is often
condensed, jerky, and difficult, matching a severe intellectualism. Critics
typically contrast it with the fiery extravagance of Donne's sermons.

15. See Logan Pearsall Smith, ed., *Donne's Sermons: Selected Passages* (Oxford: Clarendon, 1919).

16. Walter Pater (1839–1894) was educated at Oxford and became a Fellow of Brasenose College, Oxford. His first book, *The Renaissance* (1873), was a collection of essays on various artists and writers of the Italian Renaissance. Its essay on Leonardo da Vinci included a famous description of his painting *La Gioconda* (popularly known as the Mona Lisa), which has been much admired (see Walter Pater, *The Renaissance: Studies in Art and Poetry*, ed. Donald Hill [Berkeley: University of California Press, 1980], 97–99). The volume was also controversial for its advocacy of hedonism. Pater also wrote one novel, *Marius the Epicurean* (1885), and two other books of essays. He was seen as forerunner of the aesthetic or decadent movement of the 1890s. Charles Algernon Swinburne (1837–1909) was a poet and prose writer who published thirty-six books in his lifetime. His is an extremely ornate style in which sound takes precedence over sense.

17. For *La Gioconda*, see the preceding note. Ecclesiastes, chapter 12; Eliot quotes from this chapter in line 23 of *The Waste Land*.

18. *A Sportsman's Sketches* was the first work of the Russian writer Ivan Serge-evich Turgenev (1818–1883), which was translated into English in 1895 by the prolific translator Constance Garnett (1861–1946). It is typically consid-ered a light work which bears the same relationship to Turgenev's mature work as *Sketches by Boz* does to that of Dickens.

19. John Ruskin (1819–1900) was an art critic and a social critic who dominated Victorian letters. He published the first of five volumes on *Modern Painters* in 1843, the *Stones of Venice* (1851, 1853), and his late autobiography *Praeterita* (1888).

20. "Dream Fugue" (1849) is the title given to the third part of Thomas De Quincy's essay "The English Mail-Coach." To admirers of De Quincey this is his best work, an example of ornate prose of a sort that has much in com-mon with the prose poem as it was developing contemporaneously in France under the impress of Aloysius Bertrand and Baudelaire. See *Collected Writ-ings of De Quincey*, vol. 13, *Tales and Prose Phantasies*, 270–330.

21. The conversation is recounted by De Quincey in a late essay entitled "Charles Lamb," first published in the *North British Review* in 1848 and reprinted in *Collected Writings of De Quincey*, vol. 5, *Biographies and Biographic Sketches*, 215–258. De Quincey is explaining how much his tastes differed from Lamb's. While Lamb had an inborn bent toward "the natural, the simple, the genuine," he was also responsive to irritating mannerisms of the sort used by the essayist William Hazlitt. The reason for this defect in his taste, De Quincey goes on, was his inability to appreciate the value of either music or "pomp," the latter a term which could indicate something spurious, but also something genuine. "It is well to love the simple—*we* love it; nor is there any opposition at all between *that* and the very glory of pomp. But, as we once put the case to Lamb, if, as a musician . . . " (235). The point

of the anecdote is that simplicity alone would not be a sufficient criterion
for reaching a decision.

22. Three works by Edgar Allan Poe. "The Murders in the Rue Morgue" (1841) is
the founding story of detective fiction. "Shadow—A Parable" (1835) is a brief
account purportedly by an ancient Greek named Oinos (the word means
"wine"), who, in biblical tones, recounts how he and six companions have
sat beside the enshrouded corpse of one Zoilus, while outside a pestilence
has been raging. A mysterious shadow moves and speaks to them. "The
Assignation" (1834) tells the story of an unidentified stranger in Venice who
poisons his beloved and then, after reciting a few lines from the "Exequy
for His Wife" by the poet Henry King (see n. 13), commits suicide to join her
in the afterlife.

23. Stéphane Mallarmé (1842–1898) was perhaps the most influential French
poet of the nineteenth century after Baudelaire, noted for his grafting of
image on image, and allusion on suggestion—a style in which words take on
new meanings, sentences new shapes, while rhyme and sound contribute
still more suggestiveness.

24. Alexandrianism, a term derived from the ancient city of Alexandria in Egypt,
describes the lifeless formalism that was thought to typify writers and scholars under the Ptolemies, or after the golden age of ancient Greece. Georgianism is Eliot's scathing term to describe poets who published their works
in the *Georgian Poetry* collections; on these, see London Letter, March 1921,
n. 15, 206.

25. James Joyce's *Ulysses* was not published until February 1922; Eliot assumes
that his readers have read it as it was being published serially in the *Little
Review* in New York and the *Egoist* in London (though the latter had a total
circulation of only two hundred). In England, the *Egoist* had gotten only
through the first part of the Wandering Rocks episode (episode 10 of the 18
in *Ulysses*) when the journal was discontinued. In the United States, the *Little
Review* managed to reach the thirteenth episode in its issue of October 1920
but was legally barred from printing further issues after being convicted on
charges of obscenity in February 1921.

26. "The Monna Lisas of prose" refers to Walter Pater's description of the painting; see n. 16. For the "drums and tramplings of three conquests," n. 12.
"The eloquent just and mightie deaths" refers to a frequently anthologized
passage from Sir Walter Raleigh's *Historie of the World* (book V, part I, chapter
VI): "O eloquent, just, and mightie Death! whom none could advise, thou
hast persuaded; what none hath dared, thou hast done; and whom all the
world hath flattered, thou only hast cast out of the world and despised: thou
hast drawn together all the far stretched greatness, all the pride, cruelty
and ambition of man, and covered it all over with these two narrow words,
Hic jacet!" *Hic jacet* is Latin for "Here lies."

London Letter, May 1921

1. The essay was first published in the *Dial* 70, no. 6 (June 1921): 686–691. On the *Dial* generally, see London Letter, March 1921, n. 1. Writing on 21 May to Scofield Thayer, the *Dial's* editor, who was then in Berlin, Eliot noted: "I am glad to hear that my letter was received in time." Given how long it would take for Eliot to send his essay to the *Dial's* office in New York, for the office then to notify Thayer in Berlin, and for Thayer to acknowledge receipt to Eliot, the essay must have been posted by early May. It can be inferred that he wrote it sometime in late April.

2. For this performance of *Volpone,* see London Letter, March 1921, n. 28, 210.

3. "The only connection between The Phoenix and the Stage Society which I could ever discover lay in the fact that we used the same offices, and had the services of the same Secretary, Miss Alice Freedman. It is true that upon our first nineteen programmes appeared the legend 'Under the Auspices of the Incorporated Stage Society,' but so far as I am aware nobody attached the slightest meaning to the phrase, and so far from existing under the auspices, on Friday, 29th June, 1923, The Phoenix gave a matinée of *Volpone* in aid of the funds of the tottering and impoverished Incorporated Stage Society" (Montague Summers, Appendix III: The Phoenix, *The Restoration Theatre* [London: Kegan Paul, 1934], 424–425).

4. The *Daily News* was founded by Charles Dickens as a Liberal rival to the *Morning Chronicle* in 1845, though Dickens retired after seventeen issues and handed over control to John Foster. In 1912 it amalgamated with the *Morning Leader.* From 1912 to 1919 the editor was Alfred George Gardiner (1865–1946), who brought its sales to more than 800,000 a day. He was forced to resign for criticizing Lloyd George (on him see London Letter, March 1921, n. 17, 206–207) and remaining faithful to the Asquith wing of the Liberal Party. The newspaper now shifted its allegiance from the Asquith liberals to Labour, the "Manchester School politics" noted by Eliot. The literary editor of the newspaper was Robert Wilson Lynd (see n. 21, 233). The *Star* was an evening paper launched by T. P. O'Connor in 1888 and edited from 1920 to 1930 by Wilson Pope. In 1912 both the *Star* and the *Daily News* were purchased by the Cadbury family, famous makers of chocolate in England, who retained them until 1960, when both disappeared. On the Ebenezer Temperance Association, see "Andrew Marvell," n. 11, 218.

5. *The Duchess of Malfi* (1614), by John Webster (c. 1580–c. 1634), has often been deemed the greatest tragedy of the English Renaissance after Shakespeare's. It dramatizes the story of the young and widowed duchess, who secretly marries her major-domo, Antonio, a marriage that enrages her brothers, precipitating her disappearance and his murder. The performance Eliot saw, sponsored by the Phoenix Society, was performed at the Lyric Theatre, Hammersmith, on 23 and 24 November 1919. The producer was Allan Wade. The cast: the Duchess of Malfi, Cathleen Nesbitt; Ferdinand, Robert Farquharson; Bosola, William J. Rea; the Cardinal, Ion Swinley; Julia, Edith Evans; Cariola, Florence Huckton; Antonio, Nicholas Hannan. William

Archer (1856–1924) was the most influential drama critic of the New Drama movement in the 1890s and a translator of Ibsen. He considered the period between the Puritans' closing of the theaters in 1642 and the creation of the New Drama to have been the dark ages of drama. His review of *The Duchess of Malfi* appeared in the *Star*, 25 November 1919, 3, col. 5, under the headline: "PHOENIX SOCIETY. / 'The Duchess of Malfy' [*sic*] in an / Elizabethan Setting":

The Phoenix Society, an offshoot of the Stage Society, which proposes to deal in Elizabethan and Restoration plays, opened its activities yesterday at the Lyric Theatre, Hammersmith, with a performance of Webster's "The Duchess of Malfy" [*sic*].

From the time of Charles Lamb onward, critics have vied with each other in lauding this farrago of horrors as a masterpiece only inferior to Shakespeare's greatest work. That it contains some passages of beautiful writing no one would deny; but that is not to say that it is either a great work of imagination or a good piece of dramatic craftsmanship. It is shambling and ill-composed; its horrors, besides being exaggerated beyond all measure, are mechanical and tricky; and its style, even in the most admired passages, is marked by a sort of funereal affectation which places it immeasurably below that Shakespearean level to which fanaticism seeks to raise it.

FINE STAGE SETTING.
For one thing the Phoenix Society deserves great praise. It has commissioned Mr. Norman Wilkinson to design a setting, which is by far the best reproduction of an Elizabethan stage as yet seen in England, or (so far as I know) anywhere else. Certain questions of proportion apart, the middle curtain was the only serious departure from the Elizabethan model; and, as no pretence was made to accuracy, it would be pedantic to object to this concession to modern convenience.

The treatment of the text is a different matter. The producer (Mr. Allan Wade) had the good sense to cut out several pages of the most obviously dead matter, and might well have cut more, for the performance lasted three solid hours, with only one brief intermission. But why did he cut the most famous and beautiful lines in the play:—

Of what is't fools make such vain keeping?
Sin their conception, their birth weeping,
Their life a general mist of error,
Their death a hideous storm of terror.

And why did two of the Duchess's most natural and tragic lines disappear:—

I am acquainted with sad misery
As the tann'd galley-slave is with his oar.

On the other hand, the coarse language of the text was sedulously retained, all except one very gross indecency. Let us be thankful for that small mercy.

ACTING THE MADMAN.

Of the acting it is difficult to speak, for where almost everything is unnatural, there is no sure criterion of merit. Miss Cathleen Nesbit made a beautiful and touching Duchess, without rising to any great tragic height. Mr. Robert Farquharson (rightly, no doubt) presented Ferdinand as a madman from the first, and threw great conviction into his ravings. It seemed to me painful and intolerable stuff; but whether any setting could have rendered it acceptable I am more than doubtful.

Mr. Farquharson enlivened the gloomy proceedings by dying "on his head," with his heels in air—a position which he retained for several minutes, at imminent risk of apoplexy. "C'est magnifique, mais ce n'est pas l'art."

"A LOATHSOME EPISODE."

Mr. William J. Rea—a Bosola with a brogue—gave a very clever and effective performance of that curiously ill-drawn villain. Good work was done by Mr. Ian Swinley as the Cardinal, by Miss Florence Huckton as Cariola, and by Miss Edith Evans as Julia. Surely the loathsome episode of the madmen might have been spared us. It was humiliating to see an audience of educated men and women solemnly affecting to find artistic enjoyment in such barbarous tomfoolery. The company was loudly applauded at the end, as their hard work deserved, but the attempts at applause during the course of the action were very half-hearted.

Another review of *The Duchess of Malfi*, this one by "K. A. N.," appeared in the *Daily News*, 25 November 1919, 7, col. 7, under the headline: "AN ELIZABETHAN / MELODRAMA. / Wholesale Butchery in / 'Duchess of Malfi.' / FUNNIER THAN FARCE":

Did Elizabethan playgoers look on the madness in "The Duchess of Malfi" as comic-relief or were they made cold with fear, as Ferdinand hoped his sister would be? Wholesale butchery on the stage (all the principal characters but one meet with violent deaths) was, we know, considered impressive. To moderns it is funnier than many intentional scenes of fun in musical comedy and farce. As a matter of fact, Webster quite spoiled his play by seeking to be in the fashion.

His characters are of some interest. The Duchess herself, with her courage and independence; her choleric brother, the Duke; her lover, Antonio, an upright, ordinary man; the shameless hussy, Julia; and, above all, Daniel de Bosola, the soldier of fortune who plays the villain in private solely for professional ends and against the grain, a telling satire of the soldier's and politician's trade—all have points of interest

and occasional vitality. They become puppets merely to suit the dramatist's conduct of his plot. The drama is not made by the characters: they
are stretched on the Procrustean bed of theatrical necessity. The conduct of the scenes is arbitrary, and in spite of some fine lines here and
there, generally inspired by Shakespeare, Webster showed himself
yesterday afternoon at the Lyric Theatre, Hammersmith, to have been
a poor tragic poet, but with considerable talent as a writer of comedy.

TEST OF PERFORMANCE
The Phoenix Society is to be thanked for having produced "The Duchess
of Malfi," for its performance will bring home to playgoers the hollow-
ness of the old, uncritical praise of the great Elizabethan dramatists.
Charles Lamb's gentle enthusiasm and Swinburne's boisterous pane-
gyrics have made a legend of Elizabethan drama not founded on fact, as
most critical students have known for a long time. It is time this drama
were put to the test of performance.

Although not perfect, the representation of "The Duchess of Malfi"
was good enough in a general way. Miss Cathleen Nesbitt was, perhaps,
a little lacking in tragic grip, but she made a very sympathetic and handsome figure of the Duchess, and displayed a power for which her work
in the past, good as it has been, had not prepared us. Mr. Nicholas Hannan as the upright Antonio was excellent, but Mr. Robert Farquharson's
Duke hovered too often on the verge of the ludicrous.

THE DUKE
"A most perverse and turbulent nature," the Duke hoped to have gained
an infinite mass of treasure by his sister's death had she continued a
widow. Ferdinand was not a modern decadent gloating over crime and
bloodshed, as Mr. Farquharson attempted to make him. Nor was Bosola
the croaking buffoon that Mr. William J. Rea presented. He would not
have deceived anyone for a moment. Bosola is a cynic and a hater of the
deeds he performs professionally. He is also the author's chorus, and in
person was a soldier with the temperament of Shakespeare's Jacques.

Mr. Norman Wilkinson's setting was effective as a background, only
I thought the brilliant red railings of a balcony made a frieze that upset
the effect of Mr. Tom Heslewood's dresses. Mr. Allan Wade produced
the play with skill, but the incident of the Duchess grasping a dead
hand, thinking it her husband's, was badly managed, and her murder
was not very impressive.

Eliot himself also wrote a review of the performance, and he especially
liked "the incident of the Duchess grasping a dead hand, thinking it her
husband's." It was "extraordinarily fine," he wrote, because "here the actors
were held in check by violent situations which nothing in their previous
repertory could teach them to distort. Here," he summarized, "the play

itself got through, magnificently, unique" ("'The Duchess of Malfi' at the Lyric; and Poetic Drama," *Art and Letters* 3.1 [Winter (1919)/1920]: 36–39, here 37).

6. Sir Leo Money Chiozza Money (1870–1944) was a statistician and politician. Born in Genoa, he moved to London when young and in 1903 adopted his additional surname. From 1898 to 1903 he was the editor of *Commercial Intelligence*. In 1906 he was elected Member of Parliament for North Paddington, and from 1910 to 1918 he sat for East Northhants. He resigned from the Liberal Party in 1918 and contested South Tottenham as a Labour candidate, but was defeated. Already a prolific author of books and pamphlets on economic questions, he turned to journalism in his remaining years, and on occasion published collections of his poetry, such as *The Immortal Purpose and Other Poems* (London: R. Cobden-Sanderson, 1924) and *Sonnets of Life* (London: R. Cobden-Sanderson, 1932). Where he published his review of *The Duchess of Malfi* has not been identified; for Robert Wilson Lynd, whom he cites, see n. 21 to this essay, 233.

7. Sir Johnston Forbes-Robertson (1853–1937), who was sixty-eight at the time Eliot was writing, was a noted Shakespearian actor who played Hamlet many times both in London and New York. Some years he did little else, as in 1913 when he played Hamlet first at the Theatre Royal (Drury Lane, London), then for the opening of the new Shubert Theatre (44th Street, New York), and finally for a film version of *Hamlet*. Sir Henry Irving (1838–1905) was the most famous actor of the late Victorian stage. He played Shylock in *The Merchant of Venice* for the first time in 1879, resolving to play him not as the traditional grotesque common at the time, but as a man of dignity, proud and contemptuous but not evil incarnate. The play was a sensation, running for seven months. Irving repeated the role many times in the years ahead; in one ten-year span, 1893–1902, he revived the play six times. He became the first actor to be knighted, in 1895.

8. Sir Frank Benson (1858–1938) was a Shakespearian actor noted for his performances of Hamlet, Coriolanus, Richard II, Lear, and Petruchio.

9. *Romance* was a play by Edward Brewster Sheldon (1886–1946), which opened in New York in 1913 and became a big hit, so much so that it became virtually synonymous with the notion of a hit play. A young man who is planning to marry receives a cautionary tale from his bishop, based on the sad story of the bishop's own early romance. Its London production, starring Doris Keane, had more than one thousand performances, and in late 1920 the play was made into a Hollywood film, directed by Charles Withey and starring Doris Keane and Basil Sydney. *Peg o' My Heart: A Comedy of Youth* was a romantic comedy by J. Hartly Manners (1870–1928). It opened on Broadway in 1912 and in London in 1914. It dramatizes the story of Peg, a poor, young Irish girl from New York who learns that she has inherited a fortune; she must leave for London, where she will be introduced into society by her aunt, and her life is about to be turned upside down (but in a good way, of course). It proved extremely popular, the longest-running

Broadway play in history when it closed, and it was still being revived in the 1950s.

10. The poet and critic Arthur Symons (1865–1945) and the novelist and essayist Max Beerbohm (1872–1956) were only two of many writers of the 1890s who wrote about music hall. Symons's essay "A Spanish Music Hall" (1892) is reprinted in his *Cities and Sea-Coasts and Islands* (London: W. Collins, 1918), 145–157. Beerbohm wrote several essays: "The Blight on Music Hall" (1899), "Demos's Mirror" (1900), "At the Music Hall" (1901), "The Older and Better Music Hall" (1903), and "Idolum Aularum" (1906), all collected in *Around Theatres*, 2 vols. (London: W. Heinemann, 1924).

11. Marie Lloyd was born in Hoxton, then a working-class area just north of the City (or financial district) in the heart of London, far from Manchester or Lancashire (see London Letter, March 1921, n. 26, 208–209). For Nellie Wallace, see "The Romantic Englishman," n. 10, 213. She had a Scottish, not a Lancashire, accent.

12. For Little Tich, see London Letter, March 1921, n. 26, 208–209; for George Robey, see "The Romantic Englishman," n. 10, 213.

13. For Ethel Levey, see London Letter, March 1921, n. 26, 208–209.

14. For Lane, Hale, and Graves, see "The Romantic Englishman," n. 10, 217.

15. The title of Baudelaire's famous essay is "De l'essence du rire, et générale-ment du comique dans les arts plastiques" (On the essence of laughter, and more generally, on the comic element in the plastic arts). It was published in two separate versions in periodicals in 1855 and 1857, then revised lightly for its appearance within a book, Baudelaire's *Curiosités esthétiques* (Paris: Michel Lévy frères, 1868). It is now contained in his *Oeuvres complètes*, ed. Claude Pichois, vol. 2 (Paris: Bibliothèque de la Pléiade, 1976), 525–543, here 538. The ellipsis is Eliot's, and signals the omission of nine sentences from Bau-delaire's original text. The sentences cited by Eliot can be translated: "To find something of ferocious and very-ferocious comedy, one has to cross the Channel and visit the foggy realms of spleen. . . . The distinctive mark of this kind of comedy is its violence." In his sentence introducing the quotation from Baudelaire, Eliot notes in French that Baudelaire's essay "is much bet-ter than that of Bergson," referring to the French philosopher Henri Bergson (1859–1951), whose book *Le Rire*, or *Laughter*, was published in 1900. Baude-laire, it should also be noted, wrote two essays on caricature, the subject of Eliot's next paragraph: "Quelques caricaturistes français" (Some French caricaturists) and "Quelques caricaturistes étrangers" (Some foreign carica-turists). The second one treats Hogarth and Cruikshank, who are also men-tioned by Eliot. See *Oeuvres complètes*, vol. 2, 544–574.

16. Henry Mayo Bateman (1887–1970) was born in New South Wales, but in 1889 his family returned to England. He studied at the Westminster School of art and the Goldsmith's Institute. His first cartoons appeared in the *Royal Magazine* and the *Tatler*. He began contributing to *Punch* magazine in 1906. He joined the army on the outbreak of the First World War in 1914, but fell ill and was discharged a year later. His cartoons appeared in an ever greater

variety of periodicals, and he published many books. His exhibition at the Leicester Galleries took place 1–28 February 1921, timed to coincide with his publication of a volume entitled *A Book of Drawings*, with a preface by G. K. Chesterton (London: Methuen, 1921), which contains the works shown in the exhibition.

17. Thomas Rowlandson (1756–1827) is one of the most celebrated of all English illustrators. He entered the School of the Royal Academy in London in 1772, visited Paris in 1774, exhibited at the Royal Academy in 1775, and won a silver medal in 1777. Under French influence, he developed a delicate style combined with coarse subject matter. His work was very popular, but Rowlandson was an inveterate gambler and repeatedly had money troubles.

    George Cruikshank (1792–1878) was a British illustrator, by some considered the best that Britain has produced. From 1805 to 1820 he was a maker of satirical prints and caricatures, many of them bawdy. But his career began to change as he became an illustrator for books, his best-known works being his illustrations for Dickens's early novels.

18. Wyndham Lewis's exhibition "Portraits and Tyros" ran 9–30 April at the Leicester Galleries. The tyros were a race of imaginary caricature creatures, and Lewis included five oils of them in the show. William Hogarth (1697–1764) is for many the best English painter and printmaker. His most famous sets of prints are: *A Harlot's Progress, A Rake's Progress, Marriage à la Mode, Beer Street and Gin Lane, The Four Times of Day,* and *Four Prints of an Election.*

19. The *Athenaeum* was an established weekly periodical which had begun publication in 1830. It was read largely by academics and consisted mainly of book reviews. Under the ownership of the Labour politician Arthur Greenwood, it had fallen on hard times, and in 1919 it was bought by Arthur Rowntree, a member of the famous Rowntree candy-making family in York. Rowntree hired John Middleton Murry (1889–1957) to be editor at the princely salary of £800 per year; Murry offered Eliot the job of assistant editor at £500 per year, but he declined, and the position was given first to J. W. N. Sullivan, then to Aldous Huxley. Contributors were generously paid, but Murry was discerning in selecting them. Among those published in the *Athenaeum* were Virginia Woolf, T. S. Eliot, Clive Bell, Leonard Woolf, Bertrand Russell, Walter de la Mare, Julian Huxley, Kathryn Mansfield, E. M. Forster, and Lytton Strachey. The journal opposed the Georgian poets and looked down on J. C. Squire and his publication, the *London Mercury.* Despite Murry's genuine editorial achievement, the journal failed to attract many new subscribers and in early 1921 was sold to the *Nation,* which was rechristened the *Nation and Athenaeum,* under which title it continued until 1931. On the *London Mercury,* see London Letter, March 1921, n. 16, 206; on the *Times Literary Supplement,* see "Andrew Marvell," n. 1, 216.

20. Arthur Clutton-Brock (1868–1924) was a literary critic, reviewer, and author. He advocated a wooly version of Christian socialism. He wrote more than thirty books, with such titles as *The Ultimate Belief* (London: Constable,

1916), *Essays on Art* (London: Methuen, 1919), *Essays on Books* (London: Methuen, 1920), and *Immortality: An Essay in Discovery, Co-ordinating Scientific, Psychical, and Biblical Research* (London: Macmillan, 1922).

21. Robert Wilson Lynd (1879–1949), the son of a Presbyterian minister, was born in Belfast. He became a successful reviewer, critic, and author, and was a lifelong supporter of Irish republicanism. From 1912 on he was literary editor at the *Daily News* (see n. 4 to this essay). From 1918 he wrote a weekly feature for the *New Statesman* under the pseudonym "YY." Eliot reviewed his book *Old and New Masters* (London: F. Unwin, 1919) somewhat harshly (see "Criticism in England," *Athenaeum* 4650 [13 June 1919]: 456–457), and Lynd, in turn, reviewed *The Sacred Wood* very harshly (see London Letter, March 1921, n. 18, 216). Eliot informed his mother about the harsh review: "Robert Lynd's article in the *Nation* has no importance, except that three columns of such violent abuse may be a good advertisement. He is an utter nonentity; his own literary criticism is wholly worthless; I reviewed one of his books in the *Athenaeum* two years ago, none too favourably, and I do not imagine that he has forgotten the fact" (*LOTSE*, 433). Eliot commented adversely on Lynd again in his London Letter, July 1921; see 183. On J. C. Squire and Edmund Gosse see London Letter, March 1921, nn. 16, 206 and 7, 204, respectively. Sir Sidney Colvin (1845–1927) was a prominent critic of art and literature who wrote more than fifty books.

22. On the revival of criticism, see London Letter, March 1921, n. 25, 208.

23. On the activities which marked the tercentenary of Marvell's birth, see "Andrew Marvell," n. 2, 216. The centenary of Keats's death was marked by the announcement of a public subscription to buy the house in Hampstead where he had lived. (See "John Keats: Centenary of His Death," *Times*, 22 February 1921, 13, col. 4.)

24. The City of London is the name for London's financial district (see Fig. 9).

25. Christopher Wren (1632–1723) is often considered the greatest British architect. He is most famous, of course, for St. Paul's in London. But in the aftermath of the Great Fire of 1666, Wren designed and built some fifty churches in the city. Many of these were destroyed in subsequent years, and the question of preserving those that remained was becoming urgent by the early twentieth century. The church of All Hallows on the Wall is located at 83, London Wall, a street that runs east-west and forms a northern boundary to the City; see Fig. 9. (Until 1945 the street's western terminus was at its intersection with Moorgate, a north-south street, but after that it was extended westward.) All Hallows, built between 1765 and 1767, was designed by George Dance the younger (1741–1825). It has a fine plaster ceiling with blue and gold decorations, and parts of the medieval London wall, which gave the street its name, can be seen in its churchyard. St. Michael Paternoster Royal (see Fig. 16) is located on College Street, near the Southwark Bridge (see Fig. 9). The church, first mentioned in 1219, was rebuilt in 1409 at the expense of Dick Whittington, a legendary London mayor. It

burned down in the Great Fire of 1666 and was rebuilt by Christopher Wren between 1689 and 1694, with a tower dating from 1713; it was the last of Wren's City churches.

26. Eliot quotes from Dante, *Inferno* XXXIII, 46, a passage which can be translated as "When I heard the door down below being nailed up." It is spoken by Ugolino di Guelfo di Gherardesca, as he recounts how he was locked up in a tower, together with his two sons and two nephews, whom he cannibalized before dying of starvation himself. The same passage is echoed in *The Waste Land*, 413–414. Lombard Street houses the home office or headquarters of Lloyds Bank, where Eliot worked from 1917 to 1925.

27. Eliot is referring to London County Council, *Proposed Demolition of Nineteen City Churches* (London: London County Council, 1920). The pamphlet consisted of a report, dated 12 October 1920, that was co-written by G. Topham Forrest, the architect to the London County Council, and James Bird, the council's clerk. The report urged the council to reject a proposal first advanced by the Church of England on 14 April 1920 that nineteen churches within the City be demolished, with only the towers of seven to be left standing. "The architect strongly urges that steps should be taken which will secure the retention of most of the churches now threatened with destruction. These constitute, in his opinion, some of the most interesting monuments of the City of London, and their architectural beauty and historical associations render them worthy of preservation." Apart from its general recommendation to preserve the nineteen churches, the thirty-two-page pamphlet chronicled the history and the architectural merits of each church, accompanied by twenty-four photographs of them (for three of these, see Figs. 6, 12, and 16).

John Dryden

1. First published in the *Times Literary Supplement*, no. 1012 (9 June 1921): 361–362. On that journal see "Andrew Marvell," n. 1, 216. It is unclear precisely when the essay was written. But we do know that Eliot finished writing another essay, "The Metaphysical Poets," on 16 September 1921, and that it appeared in the *TLS* on 20 October, more than a month later. If a similar production schedule governed "John Dryden," then it was written by early May 1921.

2. John Dryden (1631–1700) was an English poet, dramatist, and essayist—the leading writer of his age. He received a classical education at Westminster School and Trinity College, Cambridge, then moved to London to commence his career as a professional playwright. His attempts to create heroic tragedy were admired during his lifetime but have fared poorly since, and only his one comedy, *Marriage à-la-Mode* (1672), has lived on. Dryden had a gift for satire, and "Mac Flecknoe," his satire on the contemporary poet Thomas Shadwell, is still highly regarded. *Absalom and Achitophel*, a marvelous poem, is so insistently topical that it attracts few readers today. Dryden's prefaces

are considered the beginning of modern English criticism, but they too are very little read. The change in taste brought about by Romanticism sent Dryden's reputation into a steep decline, and though it was partially rescued by Eliot and his admirers in the mid-twentieth century, it has never really recovered.

3. John Oldham (1653–1683) was the author of *Satires Upon the Jesuits* but is remembered today because of Dryden's elegy "To the Memory of Mr. Oldham." For John Denham, see "Prose and Verse," n. 3, 222; for Edmund Waller, see "Andrew Marvell," n. 13, 218.

4. Edward Phillips (1630–1696) was the nephew and pupil of John Milton; he wrote a *Satyr Against Hypocrites* (1680) but was chiefly engaged in such hackwork compilations as a *Chronicle of the Kings of England* (1674) and *Theatrum poetarum, or A Compleat Collection of the Poets* (1675). Charles Churchill (1731–1764), a clergyman and poet, was noted in the eighteenth century for his rough satires. For Thomas Gray, see "Andrew Marvell," n. 23, 219. William Cowper (1731–1800) was the author of many celebrated lyrics and a long poem, *The Task*. Oliver Goldsmith (1730–1774) was the author of *The Citizen of the World* (1760–1761), a fictional Chinese gentlemen's account of English manners and mores; *The Vicar of Wakefield* (1766), a sentimental novel; *The Deserted Village* (1770), a nostalgic poem about the passing of a simpler, happier, rural past; and *She Stoops to Conquer* (1773), a play. All these authors, according to the book by Mark Van Doren which Eliot is reviewing, attested to Dryden's importance and influence.

5. George Crabbe (1754–1832) was a Romantic poet; Byron defended Pope and the eighteenth-century poets (implicitly Dryden) in his essay *English Bards and Scots Reviewers* (1809). Van Doren argues (265) that the beginning of Poe's poem "Israfel" was influenced by Dryden.

6. From John Dryden, *The Secular Masque* (1700), which treats the transition from one century to another (in Latin, *saeculum* means "century," whence the title). Momus is reviewing the achievements of each of the gods in the last century:

MOMUS: All, all, of a piece throughout;
Pointing to Diana:
Thy Chase had a Beast in View;
to Mars:
Thy Wars brought nothing about;
to Venus:
Thy Lovers were all untrue.
JANUS: 'Tis well an Old Age is out,
CHRONOS: And time to begin a New.

The passage is quoted by Van Doren (*John Dryden*, 189) without speech indications, as if it were an independent poem, and Eliot follows him.

7. From Shelley, *Hellas: A Lyrical Drama*, ll. 1060–1065.

8. *The Oxford Book of English Verse*, ed. Arthur Quiller-Couch (Oxford:

Clarendon, 1900), 700–701. Quiller-Couch excerpts the final chorus from *Hellas* and titles it "Hellas."

9. [Eliot's note:] *John Dryden,* by Mark Van Doren (New York: Harcourt, Brace, and Howe).

10. "Mac Flecknoe" is a short satirical poem (217 lines) which Dryden wrote and published for the first time in 1682. *Absalom and Achitophel,* a longer work (1031 lines), he published a year earlier.

11. Thomas Shadwell (1642?–1692) was an English dramatist and poet. His plays, written in the tradition of Jonson's comedy of humours, are noted for realistic pictures of London life and frank, witty dialogue. They include *The Sullen Lovers* (1668), *Epsom Wells* (1672), and *The Squire of Alsatia* (1688). He succeeded Dryden as poet laureate in 1689. Having attacked Dryden in *The Medal of John Bayes* (1682), he was lampooned as Og in Dryden's *Absalom and Achitophel,* part II, and as "T.S." and "Sh———" in "Mac Flecknoe." Elkanah Settle (1648–1724) is better known to students of music than of literature; he wrote the lyrics for many songs by Henry Purcell. He is satirized as the character Doeg in *Absalom and Achitophel,* part II. Shaftesbury is Anthony Ashley Cooper, first earl of Shaftesbury (1621–1683), an English statesman who was first a supporter and later an opponent of King Charles II. Initially a believer in parliamentary government, he came to oppose the autocratic regime of the English Commonwealth under Oliver Cromwell, and after Cromwell's death in 1658 was influential in restoring Charles II as king of England. He became a key member of the so-called Cabal, an elite advisory group serving King Charles. In 1660 he was made privy councillor, in 1661 chancellor of the exchequer, and in 1672 earl of Shaftesbury. But in 1673, after the king's brother James, duke of York, had publicly acknowledged his conversion to Roman Catholicism, Shaftesbury renounced his earlier religious toleration and supported the anti-Catholic Test Acts. He was dismissed from office and in 1678 supported the anti-Catholic agitation connected with the Popish Plot. As leader of the Whig faction in Parliament, he opposed the duke of York as heir to the throne. In 1681 Shaftesbury was held for treason, but was released and fled to Holland, where he died on 21 January 1683. Dryden, who himself converted to Catholicism, satirizes Shaftesbury in *Absalom and Achitophel.* George Villiers (1628–1687), the second duke of Buckingham, was a member of the Cabal and was made a privy councillor. He wrote a play, *Rehearsal* (1671), which patronizes John Dryden. He was dismissed from office in 1674 on charges of misusing public funds, but continued to intrigue with the duke of York until he retired from politics in 1681. He, too, is satirized by Dryden in *Absalom and Achitophel.*

12. Of the four lines quoted immediately below by Eliot, Dryden quotes the first in his "Author's Apology for Heroic Poetry and Poetic Licences," which prefaced *The State of Innocence* (1677); see John Dryden, *Of Dramatic Poesy and Other Critical Essays,* ed. George Watson (London: J. M. Dent, 1962), vol. 1, 205.

13. Eliot is quoting from *Davideis,* an unfinished epic poem on the life of David

by Abraham Cowley (on him, see "Andrew Marvell," n. 6, 217). Eliot's quotation splices together lines 79–80 and 75–76.

14. John Dryden, "Mac Flecknoe," ll. 72–78.

15. On François Villon, see "Andrew Marvell," n. 38, 221.

16. Matthew Arnold, "Thomas Gray" (1880), in *The Complete Prose Works of Matthew Arnold*, ed. R. H. Super (Ann Arbor: University of Michigan Press, 1960–1977), vol. 9, *English Literature and Irish Politics* (1973), 202. Arnold's passage on Dryden is quoted in Van Doren, *John Dryden*, the book Eliot is ostensibly reviewing, on 322.

17. Walter Pater, "Style," *Appreciations: With an Essay on Style* (London: Macmillan, 1899; rpt. Evanston: Northwestern University Press, 1987), 7. Pater's comment on Dryden is quoted by Van Doren, *John Dryden*, 324. For Eliot's view of Pater, see "Prose and Verse," 162.

18. William Hazlitt, "On Dryden and Pope," lecture IV in *Lectures on the English Poets*, in P. P. Howe (ed.), *The Complete Works of William Hazlitt* (London: J. M. Dent, 1930), vol. 6, 68.

19. For Mallarmé see "Prose and Verse," n. 23, 225.

20. Pope's "portrait of Addison" (the essayist Joseph Addison [1672–1719]) takes up ll. 193–214 of his "Epistle to Dr. Arbuthnot" (1735).

21. Dryden, *Absalom and Achitophel*, part I, ll. 156–158.

22. Dryden, "Cymon and Iphigenia, from Bocacce," *Fables*, ll. 399–408. The same passage is quoted, with the same punctuation that Eliot uses, in Van Doren, *John Dryden*, 213.

23. Eliot is quoting from Dryden's poem "Alexander's Feast, or the Power of Music; an Ode in Honour of St. Cecilia's Day," ll. 66–68 (the entire poem is 180 lines long). The poem, a classic representative of the ode, features a famous flute player named Timotheus. This passage is not quoted by Van Doren.

24. John Milton, *Paradise Lost*, V, 407–413.

25. Nathaniel Lee (c. 1653–1692) is chiefly known for having co-written *Oedipus: A Tragedy* (1696) and a Preface to John Dryden's opera *The State of Innocence, and Fall of Man* (1677), from which Eliot is quoting here.

26. John Dryden, "Author's Apology for Heroic Poetry and Poetic Licences," which served as his preface to *The State of Innocence* (1677); see Dryden, *Of Dramatic Poesy and Other Critical Essays*, vol. 1, 196. Eliot will next quote lines 1–6 from that opera.

27. John Dryden, *Miscellany Poems, in Two Parts: Containing New Translations of Virgil's Eclogues, Ovid's Love-Elegies, several parts of Virgil's Aeneid, Lucretius, Theocritus, Horace etc.* (London: Jacob Tonson, 1685).

28. John Dryden, *All for Love* (1678), ed. N. J. Andrew (New York: Norton, 1975), II.281–291, 295–296. The play is a restaging of the Antony and Cleopatra story, and both passages here are addressed to Cleopatra by Antony. Neither is quoted by Van Doren.

29. "*The Indian Emperor* must have sounded suddenly and loudly like a gong. Dryden broke forth in it with consummate rhetoric, consummate bluff, and consummate rhyme" (Van Doren, *John Dryden*, 110).

30. John Dryden, *Aureng-Zebe* (1675), ed. Frederick M. Link (Lincoln: University of Nebraska Press, 1971), II.257–267 and 272–279. The play dramatizes the virtuous activities of Aurengzebe, a son who defends his aging father, the emperor, against the intrigues of his brother and various high officials.

31. Pierre Corneille (1606–1684) and Jean Racine (1639–1699) are the two great French tragedians of the seventeenth century, more or less contemporaries of Dryden.

32. Charles Baudelaire, ll. 21–22 of "Les Petites Vielles" (Little old women), first published in 1859 and then collected in the second edition of *Fleurs du mal* (1860): "Have you ever noted how some coffins of little old women / Are almost as small as that of a child?"

33. Dryden, *Aureng-Zebe*, V.301–303. Eliot has spliced together speeches spoken by different characters:

> INDAMORA: His love, so sought, he's happy that he's dead.
> O had I courage but to meet my Fate;
> That short dark passage to a future state;
> That melancholy riddle of a breath.
>
> NOURMAHAL: That something, or that nothing, after death:
> Take this, and teach thy self. [*Giving a dagger.*]

The passage is not quoted by Van Doren.

34. John Dryden, "To the Memory of Mr. Oldham" (1684); Eliot quotes the entire poem.

London Letter, July 1921

1. Although dated July 1921 by the editors of the *Dial*, the essay was probably written in mid-June. On the one hand, it refers to two new ballets, *Cuadro Flamenco* and *Chout*, which premiered in London on 29 May and 9 June, respectively; and it refers to a photograph of Einstein which was published in the *Daily News* on 11 June (see n. 3, 239). On the other hand, it contains no reference to *Le Sacre du printemps*, which was first given with new choreography on 27 June. Yet *Le Sacre* is conspicuously mentioned in Eliot's next London Letter, September 1921. It is reasonable to infer that the essay was written before *Le Sacre* had premiered but after the photograph of Einstein was published, or sometime between 11 and 27 June. On the *Dial*, see London Letter, March 1921, n. 1, 202.

2. The *Daily News*, 17 June 1921, 5, col. 4: "The Drought / Lowest Rainfall for / 35 Years / Parched Crops":

There was again no rain yesterday, and the drought has now lasted— with slight showers, which can hardly be taken into account—nearly five months.

In January the fall of rain was very slightly above the average. Of the 136 days which have elapsed since the end of the month, 89 have been

entirely rainless and of the others the total fall recorded amounts to only
3.6 in.

The normal figure for January to June over a long period of years is
rather more than 11 inches. The fall this year has been slightly over six
inches. Since September, the amount of rain which has fallen has been,
except for two months, below the normal average of the past 35 years.

Charles John Darling (1849–1936) was appointed a justice in October
1897 and served until his resignation in November 1923. His reign as a
media favorite began in 1918, when he presided over a sensational libel trial
brought forward when the beautiful American dancer Maud Allen sued the
Conservative MP and journalist Noel Pemberton Billing, who had charged
her with lesbianism (part of his crusade to stop the first London production
of Wilde's *Salomé*). The trial became the most well-publicized since Wilde's
in 1895, and newspapers followed it obsessively. Darling was soon noted for
his double-edged witticisms. "The Law is open to all . . . just like the doors
of the Ritz Hotel" was only one among many. His comment that he could
not distinguish between Albert Einstein and Jacob Epstein the sculptor is
probably an invention of Eliot's.

3. Albert Einstein, returning from the United States to Germany, disembarked
from the steamship *Celtic* in England on 8 June 1921. That same day he gave
the Adamson Lecture at the University of Manchester. On 10 June he went to
London, where he was greeted at the railway station by Lord Richard Burdon
Haldane (1856–1928), the first viscount Cloane, a former politician who also
had lively scientific interests. Einstein gave an address to the Royal Astro-
nomical Society, then was taken to Burlington House to see Newton's portrait, and then to a dinner at Lord Haldane's house with distinguished guests
who included George Bernard Shaw, Arthur Stanley Eddington, Alfred
North Whitehead, and the archbishop of Canterbury. Einstein resumed his
round of appearances on Monday, 13 June: he went to Westminster Abbey,
where he left a gift of flowers at the tomb of Isaac Newton, then to King's
College, where he gave a lecture that was extensively covered in the press.
He appeared in a photograph together with Lord Haldane in the *Daily News*,
11 June 1921, 5, col. 4, under the headline "Some Einstein Perplexities."
The caption read: "Professor Einstein, who is spending the week-end with
Lord Haldane, enjoying a joke with his host outside his chambers in Queen
Anne's Gate, yesterday."

4. The Pons-Winnecke comet was visible from England around 17 June, and
newspapers reported on its appearance. See the *Times*, 1 June 1921, 4, col. 5,
"Stars of the Month." A report on "the sunspots" appeared in the *Daily News*,
10 June 1921, 6, col. 5, under the headline: "SUNSPOTS' NEW TURN. / Electrical
Chases Round a / Discomfited World":

The rotation of the sun on its axis has again brought the great
sunspot area visible, and telescopic observation shows that the titanic
convulsion in the photosphere is still in progress.

Other sunspots may appear at any time while the unrest continues, for the region of the sun involved is little short of 2,000,000,000 square miles. The whole of this region, there is reason to believe, is a huge magnetic field, and it is continually discharging streams of electrified particles into space.

These particles, should they come earthwards, enter the upper strata of the atmosphere and set free its potential electricity, which runs amok, as it were, round the earth, causing aurorae at both poles, upsetting the normal records of the instruments which record the phenomena of terrestrial magnetism, and at times, as last month, rendering temporarily useless the world's telegraphic systems.

If there is a repetition of these happenings this month we may expect it during the next few days.

A discovery which, in the opinion of Dr. Crommelin, of Greenwich Observatory, "seems to make it desirable to rediscuss the dynamics of the stellar system," has just been made by Dr. Pannekoek, a Dutch scientist.

He has demonstrated the existence of a gas or dust cloud to the right of Orion's belt, the area of which, he says, is twenty thousand million times greater than that of the sun.

"The poisonous jellyfish and Octopus at Margate" are probably Eliot's inventions, reports of the sort that typically appear in what is now called "the silly season," the time when Parliament is in recess, theaters have closed, and there is a dearth of news.

5. On Robert Lynd, see London Letter, May 1921, n. 21, 233. It is not known where Lynd made the comment which Eliot attributes to him. For J. C. Squire, see London Letter, March 1921, n. 16, 206.

6. The *Daily News*, 17 June 1921, 5, col. 7, "NEWS IN BRIEF: A New Complaint": "Many people are suffering from a complaint resembling influenza, due, it is stated, to germs being blown about in the air owing to the non-watering of the roads."

7. A strike by miners began on 1 April 1921 and lasted for four months. The complex negotiations between the owners and workers were closely followed by the press. They came back into prominence when the owners and the unions met on Friday, 10 June 1921. See *Daily News*, 10 June 1921, 1, col. 7: "Coal Peace in Sight? / To-Day's Conference of Delegates."

8. Eliot's sentence is a pastiche of two motifs from the Old Testament. One derives from the prophet Jeremiah, who repeatedly laments that the people of Israel "have forgotten the Lord their God" (Jeremiah 3:21), or since God speaks through Jeremiah, that "my people hath forgotten me" (Jeremiah 18:15), or "their fathers have forgotten my name" (Jeremiah 23:27). The other, the invocation "O Sion," or "O Zion," is more typical of the prophet Isaiah (Isaiah 40:9, 52:1).

9. The financial crisis of the theaters was a recurrent subject in newspapers

throughout the first six months of 1921. But the situation was already improving when Eliot was writing. See Anonymous, "The Theatres: The 'Slump' Waning," *Times,* 13 June 1921, 8, col. 3.

10. Norman Macdermott, a Liverpool businessman, purchased a drill hall which he converted into a theater and opened in 1920 as the Everyman. It was dedicated to performing contemporary works that might not be commercially viable. The first season (autumn 1920) included such works as Arnold Bennett's *The Honeymoon* and a children's play, *Through the Crack;* John Galsworthy's *The Foundations* and *The Little Man;* and John Masefield's *The Tragedy of Nan.* The second season (spring 1921) was a retrospective of the works of George Bernard Shaw. See Norman Macdermott, *Everymania: The History of the Everyman Theatre, Hampstead, 1920–1926* (London: Society for Theatre Research, 1975). The Théâtre du Vieux Colombier was established in 1913 by Jacques Copeau (1879–1949), a close friend of André Gide and one of his collaborators in forming *La Nouvelle Revue française* in 1908. The theater was dedicated to reacting "against all the evils of the commercial theater" and to "supporting the reverence for classical masterpieces, French or foreign," and its activities helped to bring about a significant change in French theater of the period between 1913 and 1940. It was inaugurated on 22 October 1913, and continued until 1973. (It was reopened in 1993 under the auspices of the Comédie-Française but is now devoted to a predominantly contemporary repertory.)

11. Sergei Diaghilev (1872–1929) was a ballet impresario who in 1909 brought the Ballet Russe, an independent company which had never performed in Russia, to Paris for the first time, and thereafter made annual visits. It came to London in 1918–1919, 1920, and twice in 1921.

12. Leonide Massine (1895–1979) danced and choreographed for the Ballet Russe from 1914 to 1920, but left in early 1921 when he married. Madame Lydia Lopokova (1891–1981) was the principal female dancer of the company from 1916 through 1921. In 1925 she married the celebrated economist John Maynard Keynes. See the *Daily News,* 13 June 1921, 4, col. 6, "LOPOKOVA," a review by H. Willson Disher, who praises her extravagantly.

13. See n. 1, 238.

14. The Diaghilev Company first came to London for six months at the Coliseum, from 5 September 1918 to 29 March 1919. A second series of performances took place at the Alhambra Theatre from 30 April to 30 July 1920, the one referred to by Eliot ("Two years ago . . ."). That series revived *The Good-Humoured Ladies,* which had already been part of the repertory earlier at the Coliseum, and premiered three entirely new ballets, *La Boutique fantasque, The Three-Cornered Hat,* and *The Gardens of Aranjues.* The Alhambra series also featured four other revivals: *Petrouchka, L'Oiseau de feu* (The firebird), *Narcisse,* and *Daphnis et Chloé.* In addition, it gave the London premiere of *Parade,* the ballet with script by Jean Cocteau and stage decor by Pablo Picasso which had debuted in Paris in 1917. On 13 May 1920, Eliot went with Jack and Mary Hutchinson and Brigit Patmore to see *Le Carnaval,*

which had been added to the program, *Good-Humoured Ladies*, and *The Firebird*. He returned again on 22 July with his wife, Vivien, and the Sitwells to
see the first night of *The Three-Cornered Hat*, with music by Manuel de Falla,
stage decor by Picasso, and choreography by Leonide Massine, who also
danced the role of the Miller. One contemporary wrote of the performance:
"Massine was superb as the Miller and dominated the ballet throughout. In
his hip-tight and ankle-tight black silk trousers and purple waistcoat edged
with white, he danced like one possessed, and received a tremendous ova-
tion. Few of those who saw that first night will have forgotten the colour
and bravura with which he invested his Farruca, the slow snap of the fingers
followed by the pulsating thump of his feet, then the flickering movement
of his hands held horizontally before him, palms facing and almost touching
his breast. All at once this gave place to a new movement in which his feet
chopped the ground faster and faster until he suddenly dropped to the
ground on his hands, and as quickly leapt to his feet and stopped dead, his
efforts greeted with thunderous applause" (Cyril Beaumont, *The Diaghilev
Ballet in London: A Personal Record*, 3d ed. [London: Adam and Charles Black,
1951], 145). The evening's performance also included *Papillons* and *Prince
Igor*, and Eliot returned the next night with the Hutchinsons to see the same
three ballets. During the third series of performances given by the Ballet
Russe, Eliot went on Monday, 27 June, to the first performance of Stravinsky's *Le Sacre de printemps*, which he describes more fully in his London
Letter, September 1921 (see 188–189).

15. Vaslav Nijinsky (1888–1950) was considered the greatest male dancer of his
    age. He toured with the Diaghilev company until 1916 but was fired by Dia-
    ghilev when he married Romola de Pulszky, a Hungarian dancer. After 1916
    he suffered from schizophrenia and spent many years in and out of mental
    hospitals. Anna Pavlova (1881–1931) toured with Diaghilev in 1909 and 1910
    but then formed her own company, which continued to tour for a further
    fifteen years.

16. William Congreve (1670–1729) was the author of many comedies, including
    Love for Love (1695), which Eliot saw together with Virginia and Leonard
    Woolf on 20 March 1921 at the Lyric Theatre, Hammersmith, in a produc-
    tion sponsored by the Phoenix Society.

17. Gordon Craig, "Puppets and Poets," *Chapbook*, no. 20 (February 1921): 3–36.

18. Lytton Strachey's *Queen Victoria* (London: Chatto and Windus, 1921) was
    spectacularly successful. *The Autobiography of Margot Asquith*, vol. 1 (London:
    Thornton Butterworth, 1920), written by the wife of the former prime minis-
    ter Herbert H. Asquith, was a notable book with lively anecdotes and telling
    bons mots. The second volume appeared in 1922.

19. When Strachey published *Eminent Victorians* (London: Chatto and Windus,
    1918), it became an immediate and spectacular success. "Tout entier à sa
    proie attaché" changes to the masculine gender a French phrase "toute en-
    tière à sa proie attachée" which appears in *Phèdre* (1677), by Jean Racine,
    in the concluding speech of act I, scene iii. Phaedra confesses that she is in

love with Hippolytus, driven to it by Venus: "C'est Venus toute entière à sa proie attachée." Or in English: "It is Venus wholly fastened on her prey." Eliot has adapted the phrase so that Lytton Strachey takes the place of Venus, Queen Victoria that of Phaedra.

20. Gladstone and Disraeli are treated by Strachey in chapter 8, "Mr. Gladstone and Lord Beaconsfield," 240–268.

21. On Gibbon, see "Prose and Verse," n. 4, 222. Thomas Babington Macaulay (1800–1859) was a politician and journalist. His oratorical triumphs in the Reform Bill debates of 1831–1832 made him famous. The first two volumes of his *History of England from the Accession of James II* appeared in 1848, the fifth and last after his death, in 1861. He had a nervous, pithy style, quite different from the orotund prose of Gibbon.

22. William Lamb, second Viscount Melbourne (1779–1848), was a Whig prime minister from 1835 to 1841 and became an informal tutor to Queen Victoria after she ascended to the throne in 1837. Strachey writes of him: "Probably, if he had been born a little earlier, he would have been a simpler and a happier man. As it was, he was a child of the eighteenth century whose lot was cast in a new, difficult, unsympathetic age. He was an autumn rose" (63). Thomas Creevey (1768–1838) was a Whig politician who was elected to the House of Commons many times and occupied several prominent positions in various Whig governments. Strachey cites his diary entries for 1837 and 1838 to show the high spirits of Queen Victoria in her first years on the throne: "Mr. Creevey, grown old now, and very near his end, catching a glimpse of her at Brighton, was much amused, in his sharp fashion, by the ingenuous gaiety of 'little Vic'" (66).

23. Henri Bergson (1859–1941) was an influential French philosopher, especially in the period 1900–1914. Eliot at first viewed his work with interest but later dismissed it as merely a late and degraded form of romanticism.

24. Ronald Firbank (1886–1926), a gay writer who by 1921 had published four novels in a style that would now be called camp: *Vainglory* (1915), *Inclinations* (1916), *Caprice* (1917), and *Valmouth* (1919).

25. *Monday or Tuesday* (London: Hogarth, 1921) was a collection of short stories and sketches which signaled a new experimentalism in the work of Virginia Woolf. It was followed the next year by her first major novel, *Jacob's Room*.

26. For Walter Pater, see "Prose and Verse," n. 16, 224, and Eliot's comments on him in the essay itself, 162–163.

London Letter, September 1921

1. The date of September 1921 was furnished by the editors of the *Dial*, an attempt to make the essay seem timely. But in the essay itself, Eliot states that George Bernard Shaw's play *The Shewing Up of Blanco Posnet* is "now running at the Court Theatre." Although *Blanco Posnet* ran not at the Court but at the Queen's Theatre, it began running on 28 July, and its last performance was on Saturday, 13 August. Eliot must have written his essay sometime

before its closing date. On the weekend of 6–7 August, however, he was busy escorting his mother to Garsington, the home of Ottoline Morrell, while the next weekend he took his brother Henry there. ("I have had to devote the last 2 weekends to taking various members of my family to Garsington" [*LOTSE*, 463].) Presumably the essay was composed by about 15 August and typed between 20 and 25 August, since Eliot used the new typewriter that his brother Henry had left him as a present when he returned to America on 20 August. Its date of composition explains why it refers to events which took place chiefly in June and July, the period when Stravinsky was "our two months' lion." On the *Dial*, see London Letter, March 1921, n. 1, 202.

2. On the exhibition by Picasso which took place in January 1921, see the last sentence of London Letter, March 1921, and the accompanying note.

3. Arthur Rubinstein (1887–1983), a Polish-American pianist, studied in Warsaw and Berlin, making his debut in 1900 with the Berlin Symphony Orchestra. He was noted for his lyrical interpretations of Chopin's music and his ardent championship of Spanish works. His enormous popularity spanned many decades. He gave a concert at Queen's Hall on Saturday, 11 June 1921, which included works by Chopin, Albeniz, Saymanovsky, and Liszt. That was his only concert before the season came to an end in mid-July.

4. Eugene Goossens (1893–1962) was an orchestral conductor. Born in England, he received his early musical training in Bruges. In 1907 he was awarded a scholarship to the Royal College of Music. Goossens was always interested in presenting new music, and on Friday, 17 June 1921, he conducted the first English concert program of *Le Sacre du printemps*, at the Prince's Theatre; on Thursday, 23 June, he conducted a second concert program of *Le Sacre*, this time at the Queen's Hall. The program also included "The Eternal Rhythms," a work by Goossens himself, as well as the "Symphony for Wind Instruments" by Stravinsky. These two concerts, in turn, were followed by three further performances of *Le Sacre* as accompaniment to the ballet, all at the Prince's Theatre. The orchestra was led by the Swiss conductor Ernest Ansermet (1886–1969), who toured with Diaghilev's Ballet Russe company from 1915 to 1923. The choreography was the new one which Leonide Massine had fashioned for the revival of *Le Sacre* in Paris in 1920. There were three performances, on Monday, 27 June; Wednesday, 29 June; and Friday, 1 July. Stravinsky attended all three performances. The first featured Madame Lydia Sokolova (1896–1974) as the Chosen Virgin, a role she had danced in the 1920 revival. The other two featured Lydia Lopokova in the lead role (see London Letter, July 1921, n. 12, 241). Eliot's account leaves no doubt that he saw the first night's performance with Sokolova. The anonymous reviewer for the *Times* commented: "Mme. Sokolova, the 'Chosen Virgin,' was given a bank of white roses taller than herself. M. Stravinsky got a laurel wreath of equal size, and the whole house roared itself hoarse while the protagonists held their trophies and each other's hands and bowed themselves to the ground. Thus the London public proves its connoisseurship in contemporary art." The review generally damned

both the music ("and through it all Stravinsky's orchestra tears its way in ever-increasing harshness") and the ballet ("There is no drama, no story only a passionless ritual"). See "The Russian Ballet: 'Le Sacre de Printemps,'" *Times*, 29 June 1921, 8, col. 4. Eliot's sense that Stravinsky had dominated the entire season derived from the fact that Stravinsky had also made a personal appearance earlier, on 13 June, when the first performance of *Petrouchka* was given, and he would make another later, on 4 July, when *Pulcinella* was given. The anonymous *Times* reviewer, on 6 July, commented with scarcely concealed irony: "The whole was received with enthusiasm, and M. Stravinsky was present to bow acknowledgments on behalf of Pergolesi and himself." Finally, to cap off Stravinsky's role as "our two months' lion," the first performance of the season of *The Firebird* was given on 11 July, again at the Prince's Theatre.

5. James Frazer published three editions of *The Golden Bough;* the first consisted of two volumes (London: Macmillan, 1890), the second of three (London: Macmillan, 1900), and the third of twelve (London: Macmillan, 1907–1915). The work is an encyclopedic tour of primitive rituals, and Eliot mentions it in the first of his notes to *The Waste Land;* see 71.

6. George Bernard Shaw, *Back to Methuselah: a Metabiological Pentateuch* (London: Constable, 1921; New York, Brentano's, 1921). The play is introduced by a Preface of thirty thousand words, in which Shaw attempts to articulate a theory of "Creative Evolution," one opposed to the notion of "Natural Selection" advocated by neo-Darwinians, a philosophical outlook which had, in Shaw's view, led to the First World War. The play itself consists of five parts that cover the life and evolution of humanity, beginning with a scene that is set in the garden of Eden and ending with a scene that takes place in the year A.D. 31,290. Shaw (1856–1950) had been a journalist and theater critic during the 1880s and 1890s, and during the decade 1904–1914 he had dominated the London stage with his productions at the Court Theater. After his dramatic output ground to a halt during the years of World War I, *Back to Methuselah* marked his return to the stage.

7. Gilbert Seldes, "Struldbrugs and Supermen" [a review of George Bernard Shaw, *Back to Methuselah*], *Dial* 71.2 (August 1921): 227–231. "The sombre tone and the tragic earnestness with which the ideas are presented suggest that this is Mr. Shaw's last word, a testament more than a pentateuch" (231). The parenthetical remark "(already noticed by Mr. Seldes)" was added in proof. On Norman Macdermott, see London Letter, July 1921, n. 10, 241.

8. On *The Shewing Up of Blanco Posnet* see n. 1 to this essay.

9. Two characters, a He-Ancient and a She-Ancient who have lived eight centuries and embody disillusioned wisdom, are prominent protagonists in part five of Shaw's play *Back to Methuselah*.

10. George Bernard Shaw published *Common Sense about the War* as a supplement to the *New Statesman* for 14 November 1914, and then as an independent pamphlet in 1915 (New Statesman Publishing, [1915]). Shaw argued that the real cause of the war was that mounting wealth throughout Europe had

not been matched by a more equitable distribution of it. While citizens would have to fight, they also had to question their belligerent governments as to what they were fighting about. The work aroused enormous controversy at a time when bellicose jingoism was the norm. The members of the Dramatists Club signified their unwillingness to meet him at their lunches, and Shaw was forced to withdraw from the Society of Authors.

11. Thomas Hardy (1840–1928), English novelist and poet, was eighty-one years old when Eliot was writing in 1921.

12. Denis Diderot (1713–1784) was a philosopher, satirist, dramatist, novelist, and a literary and art critic, perhaps the most versatile thinker of his times.

13. Oscar Wilde (1854–1900), Irish playwright and novelist, was generally thought of as a witty but minor writer at this time.

14. "As Far as Thought Can Reach" is the title of the final part of Shaw's play *Back to Methuselah*.

15. This sentence does not appear in any of F. H. Bradley's published works; instead it is Eliot's cogent summary of Bradley's philosophical outlook.

16. When the curtain opens on part five of Shaw's play *Back to Methuselah*, the audience sees "a dance of youths and maidens . . . in progress." See George Bernard Shaw, *Back to Methuselah* (New York and London: Penguin, 1990), 250. Margaret Morris (1891–1980) founded Margaret Morris Movement, a system of exercise and modern dance which was popular in the 1920s and 1930s. She also wrote many books about it. Raymond Duncan (1874–1966) was the brother of the famed dancer Isadora Duncan. He founded the Akademia Raymond Duncan in Paris, which taught children dance, gymnastics, and systems of physical culture allegedly based on ancient Greek models. The children, dressed in Greek robes, were notorious, the subject of much media interest. Duncan also espoused a philosophy of Actionalism (the idea that actional or physical labor was a necessary complement to intellectual life), wrote poems, and ran a printing establishment within his Akademia, which dutifully published his lectures and poems.

The Metaphysical Poets

1. The essay was first published in the *Times Literary Supplement*, no. 1031 (20 October 1921): 669–670. Eliot wrote to Richard Aldington on 16 September 1921: "I have just finished an article, unsatisfactory to myself, on the metaphysical poets" (*LOTSE*, 469–479). Presumably he worked on it for at least a week during his evening hours, and perhaps the weekend before, or 10–16 September. On the *Times Literary Supplement*, see "Andrew Marvell," n. 1.

2. [Eliot's note:] *Metaphysical Lyrics and Poems of the Seventeenth Century: Donne to Butler*, selected and edited, with an essay, by Herbert J. C. Grierson (Oxford: Clarendon; London: Milsford), 6s. net. [Editor's note:] Sir Herbert J. C. Grierson (1866–1960) was a distinguished scholar who wrote and edited more than fifty books. He was professor of English at Aberdeen Uni-

versity, and in 1915 he took up the chair of English at the University of
Edinburgh.

3. Aurelian Townshend (c. 1583–c. 1651) was a minor Metaphysical poet;
   Grierson included two lyrics by him, "Love's Victory" and "Upon kinde and
   true Love." Lord Herbert of Cherbury (1582–1648) was the oldest brother
   of the religious poet George Herbert; Grierson included two poems by him,
   "Elegy over a Tomb" and "An Ode upon a Question Moved."

4. George Saintsbury, ed., *Minor Poets of the Caroline Period*, 3 vols. (Oxford:
   Clarendon, 1905–1921). For the *Oxford Book of English Verse*, see "Andrew
   Marvell," n. 3, 216.

5. On Donne, see "Andrew Marvell," n. 4, 217; on Marvell, see the same essay,
   n. 2, 216; and on Bishop King, see "Prose and Verse," n. 13, 223. George
   Chapman (c. 1559–1634) translated both the *Iliad* and the *Odyssey* into
   English, for many the greatest poetic translations in the language.

6. For Ben Jonson, see "Andrew Marvell," n. 5, 217. Matthew Prior (1664–1721)
   was a minor poet.

7. George Herbert (1593–1633) was the greatest religious poet of the seventeenth century; Henry Vaughan (1621–1695) wrote religious lyrics deeply
   influenced by George Herbert; and Richard Crashaw (1612–1649) was a
   Catholic devotional poet. Christina Rossetti (1830–1894) was also a religious
   poet who published her first book in 1850 and is best known for "Goblin
   Market" and "Monna Innominata." Francis Thompson (1859–1907) was
   another religious poet, whose "City of Dreadful Night" is often cited as
   a source for *The Waste Land*.

8. For Cowley, see "Andrew Marvell," n. 6, 217.

9. John Donne, "A Valediction: Of Mourning," ll. 10–18.

10. John Donne, "The Relique," l. 6.

11. Thomas Middleton (c. 1580–1627), John Webster (c. 1580–1634), and Cyril
    Tourneur (c. 1580–1626) were dramatists active in the early seventeenth
    century. Lines from Webster are quoted in *The Waste Land* at lines 74–75,
    118, and 408.

12. On Johnson's "Life of Cowley," see "Andrew Marvell," n. 27, 220. The "Life"
    contains Johnson's discussion of the metaphysical poets, on whom he was
    severe. The sentence from which Eliot quotes reads in full: "The most het-
    erogeneous ideas are yoked by violence together; nature and art are ran-
    sacked for illustrations, comparisons and allusions; their learning instructs
    and their subtlety surprises, but the reader commonly thinks his improve-
    ment dearly bought, and though he sometimes admires, is seldom pleased"
    (Samuel Johnson, *Lives of the Poets*, ed. George Birkbeck Hill [Oxford: Claren-
    don, 1905], 20). The metaphysical poets had largely disappeared from the
    canon by the early twentieth century, and Eliot played a key role in restoring
    them to a central place in the history of English poetry.

13. For Cleveland, see "Andrew Marvell," n. 18, 219.

14. From Charles Baudelaire, "Le Voyage," l. 33, the poem which concludes
    Les Fleurs du mal. "Our soul is a three-mast ship searching for its Circeii,"

this last the name of the promontory in Lazio, in Italy, which was identified with the fabulous island of Aeaea, where the goddess Circe lived. Odysseus's adventure with her is recounted in book X of the *Odyssey*.

15. Samuel Johnson, "The Vanity of Human Wishes," ll. 219–221. Eliot misquotes slightly: the first line begins "His fall . . . " and the third "He left the name . . ."

16. On Henry King, bishop of Chichester, see "Prose and Verse," n. 13, 223; Eliot quotes ll. 89–100 and 111–114 of his "Exequy for His Wife."

17. Edgar Allan Poe cites ll. 71–72 from Henry King's "Exequy for His Wife" as an epigraph to his tale "The Assignation."

18. Lord Herbert of Cherbury, "Ode Upon a Question Moved: Whether Love should Continue for ever?" st. 33–35.

19. For Thomas Gray, see "Andrew Marvell," n. 23, 219.

20. Richard Crashaw, "Saint Teresa," ll. 1–2.

21. Johnson, *Lives of the Poets*, ed. George Birkbeck Hill, "Life of Cowley," paragraph 58, 21. "Their attempts were always analytic; they broke every image into fragments: and could no more represent by their slender conceits and laboured particularities the prospects of nature, or the scenes of life, than he, who dissects a sun-beam with a prism, can exhibit the wide effulgence of a summer noon."

22. Michel de Montaigne (1533–1592), the famous French essayist, published the three-volume edition of his essays in 1588.

23. Eliot is citing from the 1641 text of George Chapman's play *The Revenge of Bussy D'Ambois*, IV.i.150–159.

24. Robert Browning, "Bishop Brougham's Apology," ll. 693–697.

25. Alfred Tennyson, "The Two Voices," ll. 412–423. An unnamed speaker is in dialogue with the voice of his own despair, which urges him to suicide. But he sees a family on its way to church (the lines quoted by Eliot) and resolves to "be of better cheer."

26. Benedict (Baruch) Spinoza (1632–1677), the Dutch philosopher.

27. Guido Cavalcanti (c. 1260–1301), Guido Guinizelli (1240–1276), and Cino da Pistoia (c. 1270–1336) were all poets who helped shape the *dolce stil nuovo*, a style of lyrical poetry also adopted by the early Dante, characterized by musicality, sincerity of feeling, and a philosophical and often metaphysical bent.

28. For Collins see "Andrew Marvell," n. 23, 219.

29. "The Country Churchyard" is by Thomas Gray; for him see "Andrew Marvell," n. 23, 219.

30. The "Triumph of Life" is a major philosophical poem that Shelley was at work on when he died, one of few attempts to take up Dante's *terza rima* into English. On Keats and "Hyperion," see "The Lesson of Baudelaire," n. 7, 215.

31. Jean Epstein, *La Poésie d'aujourd'hui, un nouvel état d'intelligence* (Poetry of today: A new state of mind [Paris, Éditions de la sirène, 1921]). Jean Epstein (1897–1953) was an avant-garde intellectual and filmmaker. His first book, *Bonjour cinéma*, appeared in early 1921. His second, the one cited by Eliot, was accompanied by a letter in which the French poet Blaise Cendrars

praised Epstein for being "the first to have said a number of precise and passionate things about today's poetry." Epstein argues that "modern writing, despite schematization and approximation, is in no way characterized by simplicity. Despite their use of schematization, in order to be understood modern writers require an important complementary effort on the part of readers, and will not be pleasing except to a certain category of erudite readers who will be, at the same time, a neuropsychiatric aristocracy" (57). The aesthetics of modern writing are similar to that of film, Epstein urges, and he goes on to specify their similarities. In 1923 Epstein made his first film, *L'Auberge rouge*, and later he made another thirteen films. He also wrote several important books of film criticism and theory, as well as one novel. In France he is still regarded as an important early avant-garde filmmaker.

32. Jules Laforgue, *Derniers Vers* (Last poems) X, ll. 1–10:

Diaphanous geraniums, warlike spells,
Monomaniac sacrileges!
Wrappings, debauchery, showers! Oh! Wine-press
Of parties' harvesting!
Layettes at bay,
Thyrsés deep in the woods!
Transfusions, reprisals,
Churchings, bandages and the eternal potion.
Angelus! Ah! to be exhausted
From these nuptial stampedes! these nuptial stampedes . . .

From *The Last Poems of Jules Laforgue*, ed. and trans. Madleine Bettes (Ilfracombe, Devon: Stockwell, 1973), 35.

33. Jules Laforgue, "Sur une defunte" (On a dead woman), *Derniers Vers*, ll. 57–58: "She is far away, she is crying, / The great wind is also lamenting."

34. On Jules Laforgue, see the Introduction, 4. Tristan Corbière (1845–1875) was a French symbolist poet.

35. Charles Baudelaire, "Le Voyage," ll. 1–4:

For the child, entranced by charts and engravings,
The world is equal to his vast desire.
Ah! How immense the world seems in the brightness of lamps!
To the eyes of memory, the world seems so small!

SELECTED BIBLIOGRAPHY

BIBLIOGRAPHIES

Blalock, Susan E. *Guide to the Secular Poetry of T. S. Eliot.* New York: G. K. Hall, 1996.

Frank, Mechthild, Armin Paul Frank, and J. P. S. Jochum. *T. S. Eliot Criticism in English, 1916–1965: A Supplementary Bibliography.* Edmonton, Alberta: Yeats Eliot Review, 1978.

Gallup, Donald. *T. S. Eliot: A Bibliography.* New York: Harcourt, Brace and World, 1969.

Knowles, Sebastian D. G., and Scott A. Leonard. *An Annotated Bibliography of a Decade of T. S. Eliot Criticism: 1977–1986.* Orono, Maine: National Poetry Foundation, 1992.

Ricks, Beatrice. *T. S. Eliot: A Bibliography of Secondary Works.* Metuchen, N.J.: Scarecrow, 1980.

BIOGRAPHIES

Ackroyd, Peter. *T. S. Eliot: A Life.* New York: Simon and Schuster, 1984.

Behr, Caroline. *T. S. Eliot: A Chronology of His Life and Works.* London: Macmillan, 1983.

Gordon, Lyndall T. *Eliot's Early Years.* New York: Farrar Straus Giroux, 1977.

———. *Eliot's New Life.* New York: Farrar Straus Giroux, 1988.

WORKS AND EDITIONS

Prufrock and Other Observations. London: Egoist, 1917.

Poems. London: Hogarth, 1919.

Ara Vos Prec. London: Ovid, 1920. Also published as *Poems.* New York: Alfred Knopf, 1920. All subsequent titles with both British and American editions were published the same year unless otherwise noted.

The Sacred Wood. London: Methuen, 1920.

The Waste Land. New York: Boni and Liveright, 1922; London: Hogarth, 1923.

Homage to John Dryden. London: Hogarth, 1924.

Poems, 1909–1925. London: Faber and Gwyer, 1925.

For Lancelot Andrewes: Essays on Style and Order. London: Faber and Gwyer, 1928.

Ash-Wednesday. London: Faber and Faber; New York: Putnam's, 1930.

Selected Essays, 1917–1932. London: Faber and Faber; New York: Harcourt, Brace, 1932.

The Use of Poetry and the Use of Criticism. London: Faber and Faber; Cambridge: Harvard University Press, 1933.

After Strange Gods. London: Faber and Faber; New York: Harcourt, Brace, 1934.

Collected Poems, 1909–1935. London: Faber and Faber; New York: Harcourt, Brace, 1935.

Murder in the Cathedral. London: Faber and Faber; New York: Harcourt, Brace, 1935.

Essays Ancient and Modern. London: Faber and Faber; New York: Harcourt, Brace, 1936.

The Family Reunion. London: Faber and Faber; New York: Harcourt, Brace, 1939.

The Idea of a Christian Society. London: Faber and Faber, 1939.

Old Possum's Book of Practical Cats. London: Faber and Faber, 1939; New York: Harcourt, Brace, 1939.

Four Quartets. London: Faber and Faber; New York: Harcourt, Brace, 1943.

Notes towards the Definition of Culture. London: Faber and Faber, 1948.

The Cocktail Party. London: Faber and Faber; New York: Harcourt, Brace, 1950.

The Confidential Clerk. London: Faber and Faber; New York: Harcourt, Brace, 1954.

On Poetry and Poets. London: Faber and Faber; New York: Farrar, Straus, 1957.

The Elder Statesman. London: Faber and Faber; New York: Farrar, Straus, 1959.

Collected Poems, 1909–1962. London: Faber and Faber; New York: Harcourt, Brace, 1962.

Knowledge and Experience in the Philosophy of F. H. Bradley. London: Faber and Faber; New York: Farrar, Straus, 1964.

To Criticise the Critic. London: Faber and Faber; New York: Farrar, Straus, 1965.

Complete Plays. New York: Harcourt, Brace, 1967.

Poems Written in Early Youth. London: Faber and Faber; New York: Farrar, Straus, 1967.

Complete Poems and Plays. London: Faber and Faber, 1969. Also published as *The Complete Poems and Plays, 1909–1950.* New York: Harcourt, Brace, 1971.

The Waste Land: A Facsimile and Transcript of the Original Drafts Including the Annotations of Ezra Pound. Ed. Valerie Eliot. London: Faber and Faber; New York: Harcourt, Brace, 1971.

The Letters of T. S. Eliot, vol. I, *1898–1922.* London: Faber and Faber; New York: Harcourt, Brace, 1988.

The Varieties of Metaphysical Poetry: The Clark Lectures at Trinity College, Cambridge, 1926, and the Turnbull Lectures at the Johns Hopkins University, 1933. Ed. Ronald Schuchard. London: Faber and Faber; New York: Harcourt, Brace, 1993.

Inventions of the March Hare: Poems, 1909–1917. Ed. Christopher Ricks. London: Faber and Faber; New York: Harcourt, Brace, 1996.

CRITICIM

General Studies, 1945–2004

Albright, Daniel. *Quantum Poetics: Yeats, Pound, Eliot, and the Science of Modernism.* Cambridge: Cambridge University Press, 1997.

Armstrong, Tim. *Modernism, Technology, and the Body.* Cambridge: Cambridge University Press, 1998.

Bedient, Calvin. *He Do the Police in Different Voices: "The Waste Land" and Its Protagonist.* Chicago: University of Chicago Press, 1986.

Bergonzi, Bernard. *T. S. Eliot.* London: Macmillan, 1972.

Bishop, Jonathan. "A Handful of Words: The Credibility of Language in *The Waste Land.*" *Texas Studies in Language and Literature* 27, no. 1 (Spring 1985): 154–177.

Brooker, Jewel Spears. *Mastery and Escape: T. S. Eliot and the Dialectic of Modernism.* Amherst: University of Massachusetts Press, 1994.

———. *T. S. Eliot: The Contemporary Reviews.* Cambridge: Cambridge University Press, 2004.

Brooker, Jewel Spears, and Joseph Bentley. *Reading "The Waste Land": Modernism and the Limits of Interpretation.* Amherst: University of Massachusetts Press, 1994.

Bush, Ronald. *T. S. Eliot: A Study in Character and Style.* New York: Oxford University Press, 1983.

———, ed. *T. S. Eliot: The Modernist in History.* Cambridge: Cambridge University Press, 1991.

Calder, Angus. *T. S. Eliot.* Brighton: Harvester, 1987.

Chinitz, David. *T. S. Eliot and the Cultural Divide.* Chicago: University of Chicago Press, 2003.

Clarke, Graham, ed. *T. S. Eliot: Critical Assessments.* London: Christopher Helm, 1990.

Craig, David. "The Defeatism of *The Waste Land.*" *Critical Quarterly* 2 (1960): 214–252.

Crawford, Robert. *The Savage and the City in the Work of T. S. Eliot.* Oxford: Clarendon, 1987.

Cuddy, Lois A., and David Hirsch, eds. *Critical Essays on T. S. Eliot's "The Waste Land."* Boston: G. K. Hall, 1991.

Dana, Margaret E. "Orchestrating *The Waste Land:* Wagner, Leitmotiv, and the Play of Passion." In John-Xiros Cooper, ed. *T. S. Eliot's Orchestra: Critical Essays on Poetry and Music.* New York: Garland, 2000, 267–294.

Davidson, Harriet. *T. S. Eliot and Hermeneutics: Absence and Interpretation in "The Waste Land."* Baton Rouge: Louisiana State University Press, 1985.

Drew, Elizabeth. *T. S. Eliot: The Design of His Poetry.* New York: Scribner's, 1949.

Ellmann, Maud. *The Poetics of Impersonality: T. S. Eliot and Ezra Pound.* Brighton: Harvester, 1987.

Froula, Christine. "Eliot's Grail Quest: Or, the Lover, the Police, and *The Waste Land.*" *Yale Review* 78, no. 1 (Winter 1989): 235–253.

———. "Corpse, Monument, *Hypocrite Lecteur.*" *Text* 9 (1996): 297–314.

Frye, Northrop. *T. S. Eliot.* Chicago: University of Chicago Press, 1963.

Gardner, Helen. *The Art of T. S. Eliot.* New York: Dutton, 1959.

Gilbert, Sandra. "'Rats' Alley': The Great War, Modernism, and the (Anti)Pastoral Elegy." *New Literary History: A Journal of Theory and Interpretation* 30, no. 1 (Winter 1999): 179–201.

Grant, Michael, ed. *T. S. Eliot: The Critical Heritage.* London: Routledge and Kegan Paul, 1982.

Gray, Piers. *T. S. Eliot's Intellectual and Poetic Development.* Brighton: Harvester, 1982.

Hay, Eloise Knapp. *T. S. Eliot's Negative Way.* Cambridge: Harvard University Press, 1982.

Jay, Gregory. *T. S. Eliot and the Poetics of Literary History.* Baton Rouge: Louisiana State University Press, 1983.

Kearns, Cleo McNelly. *T. S. Eliot and Indic Traditions: A Study in Poetry and Belief.* Cambridge: Cambridge University Press.

Kenner, Hugh. *The Invisible Poet: T. S. Eliot.* New York: Harcourt, Brace and World, 1959.

Koestenbaum, Wayne. *Double Talk: The Erotics of Male Literary Collaboration.* New York: Routledge, 1989.

Laity, Cassandra, and Nancy K. Gish, eds. *Gender, Desire, and Sexuality in T. S. Eliot.* Cambridge: Cambridge University Press, 2004.

Langbaum, Robert. *The Mysteries of Identity: A Theme in Modern Literature.* New York: Oxford University Press, 1977.

Lentricchia, Frank. *Modernist Quartet.* Cambridge: Cambridge University Press, 1994.

Levenson, Michael. *A Genealogy of Modernism: A Study of English Literary Doctrine, 1908–1922.* Cambridge: Cambridge University Press, 1987.

———. "Does *The Waste Land* Have a Politics?" *Modernism/Modernity* 6, no. 3 (September 1999): 1–13.

Litz, A. Walton, ed. *Eliot in His Time.* Princeton: Princeton University Press, 1973.

Longenbach, James. *Modernist Poetics of History: Pound, Eliot, and the Sense of the Past.* Princeton: Princeton University Press, 1987.

Manganaro, Marc. "Dissociation in 'Dead Land': The Primitive Mind in the Early Poetry of T. S. Eliot." *Journal of Modern Literature* 13, no. 1 (1986): 97–110.

Martin, Graham, ed. *Eliot in Perspective.* London: Macmillan, 1970.

Menand, Louis. *Discovering Modernism: T. S. Eliot and His Context.* New York: Oxford University Press, 1987.

Moody, A. D., ed. *"The Waste Land" in Different Voices.* London: Edward Arnold, 1974.

————. *Thomas Stearns Eliot: Poet*. Cambridge: Cambridge University Press, 1979.

————, ed. *The Cambridge Companion to T. S. Eliot*. Cambridge: Cambridge University Press, 1979.

Moretti, Franco. *Signs Taken for Wonders: Essays in the Sociology of Literary Forms*. Trans. Susan Fischer, David Forgacs, and David Miler. London: Verso, 1983.

North, Michael. *The Political Aesthetic of Yeats, Eliot, and Pound*. Cambridge: Cambridge University Press, 1991.

————. *The Dialect of Modernism: Race, Language, and Twentieth-Century Literature*. Oxford: Oxford University Press, 1994.

————. *Reading 1922: A Return to the Scene of the Modern*. Oxford: Oxford University Press, 1999.

————. *"The Waste Land": A Norton Critical Edition*. New York: W. W. Norton, 2001.

Pearce, Roy Harvey. *The Continuity of American Poetry*. Princeton: Princeton University Press, 1961.

Perl, Jeffery M. *Skepticism and Modern Enmity: Before and After Eliot*. Baltimore: Johns Hopkins University Press, 1989.

Rainey, Lawrence. *Institutions of Modernism: Literary Elites and Public Culture*. New Haven: Yale University Press, 1998.

————. *Revisiting "The Waste Land."* New Haven: Yale University Press, 2005.

————, ed. *The Annotated "Waste Land" with Eliot's Contemporary Prose*. New Haven: Yale University Press, 2005.

Ricks, Christopher. *T. S. Eliot and Prejudice*. Berkeley: University of California Press, 1988.

Riquelme, John Paul. "'Withered Stumps of Time': Allusion, Reading, and Writing in *The Waste Land*." *Denver Quarterly* 15 (1981): 90–110.

Rosenthal, M. L. *Sailing into the Unknown: Yeats, Pound, and Eliot*. New York: Oxford University Press, 1978.

Ross, Andrew. *The Failure of Modernism: Symptoms of American Poetry*. New York: Columbia University Press, 1986.

Schuchard, Ronald. *Eliot's Dark Angel: Intersections of Life and Art*. Oxford: Oxford University Press, 1999.

Schwartz, Sanford. *The Matrix of Modernism: Pound, Eliot, and Early Twentieth-Century Thought*. Princeton: Princeton University Press, 1985.

Scofield, Martin. *T. S. Eliot: The Poems*. Cambridge: Cambridge University Press, 1988.

Sherry, Vincent. *The Great War and the Language of Modernism*. Oxford: Oxford University Press, 2003.

Shusterman, Richard. *T. S. Eliot and the Philosophy of Criticism*. New York: Columbia University Press, 1988.

Smith, Grover. *T. S. Eliot's Poetry and Plays*. Chicago: University of Chicago Press, 1974.

————. *"The Waste Land."* London: Allen and Unwin, 1983.

Spanos, William. "Repetition in *The Waste Land:* A Phenomenological
De-Struction." *Boundary 2* 7 (1979): 225–285.

Spender, Stephen. *T. S. Eliot.* New York: Viking, 1975.

Spurr, David. *Conflicts in Consciousness: T. S. Eliot's Poetry and Criticism.* Urbana:
University of Illinois Press, 1984.

Stead, C. K. *Pound, Yeats, Eliot, and the Modernist Movement.* Basingstoke:
Macmillan, 1986.

Tate, Allen, ed. *T. S. Eliot: The Man and His Work.* New York: Delacorte, 1966.

Thormählen, Marinanne. *"The Waste Land": A Fragmentary Wholeness.* Lund:
Gleerup, 1978.

Trotter, David. "Modernism and Empire: Reading *The Waste Land.*" *Critical
Quarterly* 28, nos. 1–2 (1986): 143–153.

General Studies, 1924–1940

Blackmur, R. P. "T. S. Eliot." *Hound and Horn* 1 (1928): 187–210.

Brooks, Cleanth. *Modern Poetry and the Tradition.* Chapel Hill: University of North
Carolina Press, 1939.

Leavis, F. R. *New Bearings in English Poetry.* London: Chatto and Windus, 1932.

Matthiessen, F. O. *The Achievement of T. S. Eliot.* Boston: Houghton Mifflin, 1935.

Richards, I. A. *Principles of Literary Criticism.* 2d ed. London: Kegan Paul; New
York: Harcourt, Brace, 1926.

Wilson, Edmund. *Axel's Castle.* New York: Scribner's, 1931.

Contemporary Responses to The Waste Land *(in chronological order)*
British Responses to the *Criterion* Publication

Anonymous. [Review.] *Times Literary Supplement*, no. 1084 (22 October 1922):
690. Rpt. in Grant, *Eliot*, 134–135.

"Affable Hawk" [Desmond McCarthy]. "Current Literature: Books in General."
New Statesman, 4 November 1922, 140. Not reprinted.

Harold Monro. "Notes for a Study of *The Wasteland.*" *Chapbook*, February 1923,
120–124. Rpt. in Grant, *Eliot*, 162–170.

British Responses to the Hogarth Edition

Anonymous [Edgell Rickword]. "A Fragmentary Poem." *Times Literary Supplement*,
no. 1131 (20 September 1923): 616. Rpt. in Grant, *Eliot*, 184–186.

Clive Bell. "T. S. Eliot." *Nation and Athenaeum* 33 (23 September 1923): 772–773.
Rpt. in Grant, *Eliot*, 186–191.

J. C. Squire. "Poetry." *London Mercury* 8, no. 48 (October 1923): 655–657. Rpt. in
Grant, *Eliot*, 191–192.

C[harles]. P[owell]. "The Waste Land." *Manchester Guardian*, 31 October 1923, 7.
Rpt. in Grant, *Eliot*, 195.

F. L. Lucas. "The Waste Land." *New Statesman*, 22 (3 November 1923): 116–118.
Rpt. in Grant, *Eliot*, 195–199.

Humbert Wolfe. "Waste Land and Waste Paper." *Weekly Westminster* n.s. 1
(17 November 1923): 94. Rpt. in Grant, *Eliot*, 200–203.

J. M. H. "Poetry: Old and New." *Freeman* [Dublin], 9 February 1924, 9. Not reprinted.

N[etta]. T[hompson]. "Modern American Poetry." *Aberdeen Press*, 26 May 1924, 3. Not reprinted.

Edwin Muir. "T. S. Eliot." *Nation* 121 (5 August 1925): 162–164. Rpt. in *Nation and Athenaeum*, 29 August 1925, 644–646.

American Responses to the *Dial* and Boni and Liveright Edition

Burton Rascoe. "A Bookman's Day Book," s.v. "Tuesday, October 26." *New York Tribune*, 5 November 1922, sec. V, 8. Not reprinted.

Anonymous. "The Sporting Spirit." *Literary Review Published by the New York Evening Post*, 11 November 1922: 1. Not reprinted.

Edmund Wilson. "The Rag-Bag of the Soul." *Literary Review Published by the New York Evening Post*, 25 November 1922: 237–238. Rpt. in Brooker, *Eliot*, 77–81.

Anonymous. "Books and Authors" [Comment on the *Dial* Award]. *New York Times Book Review*, 26 November 1922: 12. Rpt. in Grant, *Eliot*, 135–136.

Edmund Wilson. "The Poetry of Drouth." *Dial* 73, no. 6 (December 1922): 611–616. Rpt. in Grant, *Eliot*, 138–144.

[Scofield Thayer and Gilbert Seldes]. "Comment." *Dial* 73, no. 6 (December 1922): 685–687. Rpt. in Grant, *Eliot*, 136–138.

A[llen]. T[ate]. "Whose Ox." *Fugitive* 1 (December 1922): 99–100. Excerpted in Brooker, *Eliot*, 90–91.

Burton Rascoe. "A Bookman's Day Book." *New York Tribune*, 3 December 1922, sec. VI, 18. Not reprinted.

Anonymous. "Books and Bookmen." *Christian Science Monitor*, 6 December 1922, 8.

Gilbert Seldes. "T. S. Eliot." *Nation* 115 (6 December 1922): 614–616. Rpt. in Grant, *Eliot*, 144–150.

Gorham B. Munson. "Congratulations and More 'Ill-Mannered References.'" *Secession* 4 (January 1923): 31–32. Not reprinted.

Mary Colum. "Modernists." *Literary Review Published by the New York Evening Post* 3 (6 January 1923): 361–362. Not reprinted.

Burton Rascoe. "A Bookman's Day Book," s.v. "Saturday, December 30." *New York Tribune*, 7 January 1923, sec. VI, 22. Excerpted in Brooker, *Eliot*, 91–93.

Christopher Morley. "The Bowling Green," s.v. "Apollo and Apollinaris." *New York Evening Post*, 9 January 1923, 349. Not reprinted.

Burton Rascoe. "A Bookman's Day Book," *New York Tribune*, 14 January 1923, sec. VI, 23. Rpt. in Burton Rascoe, *A Bookman's Daybook* (New York: Horace Liveright, 1929), 71–72.

Louis Untermeyer. "Disillusion as Dogma." *Freeman* (17 January 1923): 453. Rpt. in Grant, *Eliot*, 151–153.

Elinor Wylie. "Mr. Eliot's Slug Horn." *Literary Review Published by the New York Evening Post* 3 (20 January 1923): 396. Rpt. in Grant, *Eliot*, 153–156.

Burton Rascoe. "A Bookman's Day Book," s.v. "Friday, January 12." *New York Tribune*, 21 January 1923, sec. VI, 27. Excerpted in Brooker, *Eliot*, 97.

Anonymous. "The *Dial's* Prize." *Boston Herald*, 27 January 1923, 6. Not reprinted.

Frederic F. Van de Water. "Books and So Forth." *New York Tribune*, 28 January 1923, sec. VI, 19. Not reprinted.

Fanny Butcher. "Books," s.v. "Help, Help." *Chicago Tribune*, 4 February 1923, pt. 7, 23. Not reprinted.

Conrad Aiken. "An Anatomy of Melancholy." *New Republic* 33 (7 February 1923): 295. Rpt. in Grant, *Eliot*, 156–161.

Anonymous. Title unknown. *Oregonian* [Portland], 11 February 1923, sec. 5, 3. Not reprinted.

John Drury. "World's Greatest Poem." *Chicago Daily News*, 14 February 1923, 15. Not reprinted.

Otto Heller. "T. S. Eliot Awarded $2,000 Prize for *The Waste Land.*" *St. Louis Dispatch*, 24 February 1923, 10. Not reprinted.

Robert L. Duffus. "Genius and the Guffaws of the Crowd." *Globe and Commercial Advertiser* (New York), 28 February 1923, 16. Not reprinted.

N. P. Dawson. "Enjoying Poor Literature." *Forum*, March 1923, 325–330. Not reprinted.

Harriet Monroe. "A Contrast." *Poetry* 31 (March 1923): 325–330. Rpt. in Grant, *Eliot*, 166–170.

J. F. "Shantih, Shantih, Shantih." *Time* 1 (3 March 1923): 12. Rpt. in Brooker, *Eliot*, 77–81.

N. P. Dawson. "Books in Particular." *Globe and Commercial Advertiser* (New York), 6 March 1923, 16. Not reprinted.

Anonymous. "Editorials," s.v. "Hoaxing the American Literati." *Christian Science Monitor*, 23 March 1923, 18. Not reprinted.

H[erbert]. S. Gorman. "The Waste Land of the Younger Generation." *Literary Digest International Book Review* 1, no. 5 (April 1923): 46, 48, 64. Not reprinted.

Henry G. Hart. "New Plays and Poems." *Philadelphia Record*, 1 April 1923, sec. T, 6. Not reprinted.

N. P. Dawson. "Review of the Season's Latest Books," s.v. "Theodoro, the Sage." *Globe and Commercial Advertiser* (New York), 12 April 1923, 17. Not reprinted.

Clement Wood. "If There Were a Pillory for Poets," "*The Waste Land.*" *New York Herald*, 15 April 1923, 3, 6. Not reprinted.

N. P. Dawson. "Books in Particular." *Globe and Commercial Advertiser* (New York), 17 April 1923, 14, 16. Not reprinted.

Burton Rascoe. "A Bookman's Day Book," s.v. "Wednesday, April 18." *New York Tribune*, 22 April 1923. Rpt. in Burton Rascoe, *A Bookman's Daybook* (New York: Horace Liveright, 1929), 96–97.

J. M. [Review.] *Double Dealer* 5 (May 1923): 173–174. Rpt. in Grant, *Eliot*, 170–172.

Anonymous. "Eliot, T. S. *The Waste Land.*" *Open Shelf* (Cleveland Public Library), no. 5 (May 1923): 35. Rpt. in Lawrence Rainey, "[Review of] Jewel Spears Brooker, *T. S. Eliot: The Contemporary Reviews,*" in *Modernism/Modernity* 11, no. 4 (November 2004): 834–837.

Clement Wood. "The Tower of Drivel." *New York Call*, 20 June 1923, 11. Not reprinted.

Elsa Gidlow. "A Waste Land, Indeed." *New Pearson's* 49 (July 1923): 57. Not reprinted.

John Crowe Ransom. "Waste Lands." *Literary Review Published by the New York Evening Post* 3 (14 July 1923): 825–826. Rpt. in Christopher Morley, ed., *Modern Essays: Second Series* (New York: Harcourt, Brace, 1924), 345–359, and in Grant, *Eliot,* 172–179.

Helen McAfee. "The Literature of Disillusion." *Atlantic* 132 (August 1923): 227. Excerpted in Grant, *Eliot,* 182–183.

Allen Tate. "A Reply to Ransom." *Literary Review Published by the New York Evening Post* 3 (4 August 1923): 886. Rpt. in Grant, *Eliot,* 180–182.

Clive Bell. "The Elusive Art of T. S. Eliot: An Enquiry into the Artistic Principles of the Most Disputed of Living American Poets." *Vanity Fair*, September 1923, 53, 110. Same as Bell, "T. S. Eliot," above; rpt. under its English title in Grant, *Eliot,* 186–191.

William Rose Benét. "Among the New Books." *Yale Review*, October 1923, 161–165. Rpt. in Grant, *Eliot,* 192–193.

Edward Shanks. "Books and Authors: New Poets." *Daily News*, 8 October 1923, 9. Not reprinted.

Gorham B. Munson. "The Esotericism of T. S. Eliot." *1924*, no. 1 (1 July 1924): 3–10. Rpt. in Grant, *Eliot,* 203–212.

GENERAL INDEX

When reference is made to notes that are keyed to the line numbers in *The Waste Land,* the page number is immediately followed by the poem's line number(s): e.g., 103 l. 92.

Absalom and Achitophel (John Dryden), 223 n. 9
Aiken, Conrad, 4, 6, 25–26, 35, 118 ll. 377–384
Alain-Fournier, Henri, 4–5
Aldington, Richard, 13, 208 n. 23
Alexandrianism, 225 n. 24
Alighieri, Dante. See Dante Alighieri
All Hallows on the Wall (church, London), 233 n. 25
Anacreon, 222 n. 6
Andrewes, Launcelot, 223 n. 4
Archer, William, 204 n. 7
Arnold, Matthew, 203 n. 4, 204 n. 6
Asquith, Margot, 242 n. 18
Athenaeum (periodical), 14, 15, 230 n. 19
Augustine of Hippo, 113 l. 307, 114 ll. 308–310

Back to Methusaleh (G. B. Shaw), 245 n. 6
Barbey d'Aurevilly, Jules, 215 n. 5

Bateman, Henry Mayo, 231 n. 16
Baudelaire, Charles, 36–37, 81 l. 60, 85 l. 76, 215 n. 4, 231 n. 15, 238 n. 32, 247 n. 15, 249 n. 35
Beach, Sylvia, 28
Beaumont and Fletcher, 78 ll. 28–29
Beerbohm, Max, 231 n. 10
Benda, Julien, 214 n. 2
Bennett, Arnold, 109 l. 222
Benson, Sir Frank, 230 n. 8
Bergson, Henri, 5, 230 n. 15, 243 n. 23
Bertrand, Aloysius, 222 n. 4
Bible
    Job, 79 l. 41
    Psalms, 101 l. 182, 116 l. 324
    Ecclesiastes, 78 l. 23
    Isaiah, 78 l. 26, 121 l. 425
    Ezekiel, 77 l. 20
    Matthew, 116 l. 324
    Luke, 116 l. 324, 116 l. 359
    John, 116 l. 322
    Romans, 115 l. 319
    Philippians, 126 l. 433
Birrell, Augustine, 216 n. 2
Bishop, John Peale, 27, 33–34
Boileau-Dexpréaux, Nicholas, 222 n. 5
Book of Common Prayer, 76 n. to Part I title

Wilcox, Ella Wheeler, 207 n. 19
Wilson, Edmund, 29–30
Wilson, Woodrow, 205 n. 11
Woolf, Virginia, 13, 14, 243 n. 25
Wren, Sir Christopher, 110 l. 264,
    233 n. 25

R

WITHDRAWN